Mary Churchill's War

Mary Churchill's War

The Wartime Diaries of
Churchill's Youngest Daughter

INTRODUCED AND EDITED
BY EMMA SOAMES

In collaboration with
The Churchill Archives Centre, Cambridge

TWO
ROADS

First published in Great Britain in 2021 by Two Roads
An Imprint of John Murray Press
An Hachette UK company

1

Copyright in diaries © The Beneficiaries of the literary estate
of Mary Soames and The Master, Fellows and
Scholars of Churchill College, Cambridge 2021
Selection and editorial contribution © Emma Soames
Editorial contribution © Churchill Archives Centre

A CIP catalogue record for this title is available from the British Library

Hardback ISBN 978-1-529-34150-8
Trade Paperback ISBN 978-1-529-34151-5
eBook ISBN 978-1-529-34153-9

Typeset in Baskerville by Hewer Text UK Ltd, Edinburgh
Printed and bound in Great Britain by Clays Ltd, Elcograf S.p.A.

Two Roads policy is to use papers that are natural, renewable and
recyclable products and made from wood grown in sustainable forests.
The logging and manufacturing processes are expected to conform
to the environmental regulations of the country of origin.

Two Roads
Carmelite House
50 Victoria Embankment
London EC4Y 0DZ

www.johnmurraypress.co.uk

Contents

Introduction

'I am not a great or important personage, but it will be the diary of an ordinary person's life in war time – though I may never live to read it again, yet perhaps it may not prove altogether uninteresting as a record of my life – or rather the life of a girl in her youth, upon whom life has shone very brightly, who has had every opportunity of education, interest, travel and pleasure and excitement, and who at the beginning of this war found herself on the threshold of womanhood.'

With Churchillian prescience for great events, and blessed with the family gene for recording them, Mary Churchill began keeping a diary in earnest in January 1939, recording the thoughts of a rather prim sixteen-year-old obsessed with her pony, the state of her fingernails and with her shortcomings in the sight of the Lord. Eight months later, just before her seventeenth birthday, war was declared and a few days later, on 18 September, she muses on her future – one that turns out to more than fulfil her own, or anyone else's, expectations.

By 1939, the three elder Churchill siblings had all left home, but Mary was living with her parents, moving first from Chartwell to Admiralty House and thence in short order to No. 10 Downing Street. Thanks to her assiduous journalling it is not long before the reader of these diaries is eavesdropping on history and her descriptions of great events as viewed from her father's elbow.

Watching from the Strangers' Gallery, Mary describes the

impact of many of her father's speeches in the House of Commons and – most revealingly perhaps – she records conversations where he was going through the birth pangs of writing them. She tells of travels with her father too, of visiting Bristol and Cardiff as the Blitz raged, and her description of the crowds' reactions to seeing Winston as they crawled out from bomb shelters is better than Pathé footage. Later, in 1943, she went with her parents on a transatlantic journey as her father's aide-de-camp, first to the Quebec Conference and then on to stay with President Roosevelt at the White House. The Americans took her to their hearts.

Mary is also by her father's side the day after VE Day and, in 1944, on another magical, historical journey she goes with her parents to Paris for the celebration of the Liberation of Paris. Mary and Clementine watched from the stands as Winston processed at the side of General de Gaulle down a Champs Élysées packed with cheering Parisians. After many a *vin d'honneur* – one with the cream of the French Resistance – Mary, Winston and de Gaulle board a train for eastern France to inspect – in freezing snow – the reconfigured French forces. There de Gaulle presents Mary with a *Croix de Lorraine*, the symbol of the Free French (which she wore with pride on Remembrance Days for the rest of her life). More soberly she records being with her parents when the results of the 1945 election came in – results that seemed to upset her more than her father, who was a philosophical democrat.

But woven into this narrative of great events, the enormously powerful presiding genius of her father and the long shadow of war, is the story of a teenager who is becoming a woman. The thoughts and feelings of a high-spirited but dutiful daughter, devoted to her parents, but eager to leave home; a young girl turning from an innocent ingénue to an eligible young woman with three years of army experience under her belt, a Captain's stripes on her khaki sleeve and a military MBE. Mary suffers the universal concerns of young women as ever were and will be: she alternately obsesses about food and then the need to lose weight; she compares herself unforgivingly against the society beauties she dines with; she describes dressing up in enthusiastic detail; and her excitement at events like being piped aboard one British Navy vessel and launching another is joyful and infectious. She is beady in her observations and portrayal of the players around her father during these years, canny in her analysis of Pamela 'Spam' Churchill and her descriptions of sitting next to FDR at dinner are charming but not bedazzled. She also falls very out of love with her brother Randolph, who causes so much family unhappiness that she chronicles in detail; it is the first of very few moments where she doesn't support her father who she feels spoils Randolph and forgives him too readily for his boorish behaviours. Sometimes she is very funny.

The most powerful thread that runs right through in the diaries is Mary's admiration of her father. Her feelings for him intensified when she saw up close his conduct of the war, when she came to appreciate the stresses he was under, carrying an often secret and always great burden of the destiny of this country, while the brilliance of his speeches left my mother in awe of his intellect and his personality. After his adept speech to the Commons winding up the censure debate in 1941 she writes, 'I think my love and admiration of Papa is almost a religion to me – I sometimes feel I cannot hold the emotions I have for him.'

Thus the guiding force of her personality became Mary's determination never to let her father down. From her first public speech when she launched Westerham War Weapons Week in February 1941 aged eighteen, 'I could not help feeling mighty proud of Papa – because it was all for him. And it made me determined to do him credit – and so to behave that he would not have to make excuses for his daughter.' This determination coloured her behaviour throughout the war and stayed with her for the rest of her life: she never forgot the responsibilities that went with being her father's daughter. When I sometimes accompanied her on public engagements fifty years later, as the moment came for her to perform, I could see her pulling herself up to her full height to channel her love for her father and her powerful sense of duty to burnish and protect his memory.

In supporting her father, she was doing the same for her sometimes fragile mother, the clever, elegant Clementine who found the hectic life of a wartime PM's consort occasionally frazzling. Mary, who loved her mother deeply, became a frequent understudy for her at dinners and events when Clementine took to her bed. Thus, her parents both came to rely increasingly on their youngest daughter. Mary understood this and, for instance, her decision to join the Auxiliary Territorial Service was made agonising for her as she worried about leaving her parents.

But it wasn't all duty and dinners with Generals. Mary and her best friend, the clever and well-connected Judy Montagu, were longing to do more in the war effort and, in 1941, they signed up for the ATS with the express intention of joining the very first mixed anti-aircraft batteries. They went through the fairly gruelling training together – made particularly excruciating at moments for Mary as the War Office started to use her as a poster girl for the Service while she was hoping to remain private Private Churchill (instructing her mother not to write using envelopes bearing the No. 10 seal). Nonetheless Mary dried her tears and, as ever, did her duty.

Both girls became NCOs and then did Officer training together before going their separate ways – Judy to become eventually a senior instructor in the ATS and Mary to serve in anti-aircraft batteries from Whitby to Newport. But those 'powers that be' close enough to observe the Prime Minister evidently appreciated how beneficial it was to him to have Mary close to hand, and consequently, much of Mary's war service was spent in units close enough to London to allow her to see her family; indeed, her battery in Hyde Park received almost as many official visitors as it did VE bombs. Winston liked to show off his daughter's prowess at dealing with the enemy.

Like that of so many serving soldiers, Mary's leaves were a riot of fun: trips to the theatre, dinners at the Savoy, more champagne and nightclubs than you can imagine and then walks back to Whitehall at dawn. All with a dizzy procession of men, serving soldiers or airmen, some of them childhood friends and others more recent and of the American variety. In camp, barely a night passed that there wasn't a dance. Some remained friends, and a few were killed in action, most notably Tony Coates who Mary had met at Chequers.

Mary's romances were, by current standards, very innocent (she records a kiss only in 1942), but their intensity was dazzling. When she was eighteen she ill-advisedly became engaged to a boy she had met only a couple of months previously. After she had taken Eric Duncannon to Chequers to meet her parents, her mother unleashed an A-Team of the PM's advisors to talk her out of marriage. The team consisted of US Ambassador Averell Harriman, the President's Special Envoy Harry Hopkins and the leading British political figure Max Beaverbrook. After several walks around the lawn at Chequers with the cream of global diplomacy Mary wept, caved in and the wedding was called off.

The Chequers effect became rather a characteristic of her romances which tended to grind to a halt when exposed to the intense oxygen of the place. Men who were fun and flattering in the Mess, and perhaps demons on the dance floor, didn't match up to the high standards of home where the fascinating could suddenly seem dull. Indeed, to this day there is no greater ordeal than taking a boy home.

Mary's narrative opens in January 1939 when she is sixteen and absorbed by school and country life. We have chosen to end her story in 1945 when she decides to leave the Army and return to London from Germany to support her parents after the debacle of the 1945 election. The diaries do not end there, but as marriage and motherhood enter her life Mary spends less and less time on her diary. Other entries are not included for reasons of length, but the entire diaries are available to read digitally at the Churchill Archives Centre, where my co-editors Allen Packwood and Katharine Thomson have provided huge support, invaluable historical background and encyclopaedic expertise.

My mother wrote in the introduction of her life of her mother, Clementine Churchill, 'This is a work of love, but I hope not of blind love'. I echo her words here.

Dramatis personae

The Churchill Family

Mummie, Clementine Churchill, 1885–1977. Mary's mother also referred to in these diaries as 'Mama' or just 'M', was one of the guiding lights in Mary's life. Intelligent and beautiful, Clementine had already had several suitors and broken one engagement before Winston came along (she nearly broke her engagement to him, too, but her brother put his foot down at this point). The couple were married in 1908, just a month after Winston proposed, and enjoyed a long and happy life together, though as Clementine was a woman of strong character and independent opinions, the marriage certainly had its lively moments.

During the war, we see Clementine supporting her husband, and carrying out the social duties of the Prime Minister's wife, besides many other roles such as chairing the phenomenally successful Red Cross Aid to Russia Fund, for which she was awarded the Order of the Red Banner of Labour by Stalin. Clearly all this took its toll, as we see Mary constantly worrying about her mother's health and strength. Due to the demands of Winston's public career, Clementine did not always have time for Mary when she was small, but there is no doubt from these diaries of the closeness between her and her youngest child.

Diana Sandys, née Churchill, 1909–1963. The Churchills' eldest daughter, Diana married the rising Conservative star Duncan Sandys in 1935 (following a short-lived and unsuccessful match with John Bailey), and had three children, Julian, Edwina and Celia Sandys. The marriage eventually failed, ending in divorce in 1960, and after suffering several nervous breakdowns, Diana took her own life in 1963.

Uncle Jack, John Spencer Churchill, 1880 1947. Winston's younger brother served with distinction in both the Boer War and the First World War, before going into the City as a stockbroker. By the later stages of the war he was already suffering from the heart disease that was soon to kill him. He had married **Lady Gwendeline Bertie** ('Aunt Goonie', 1885–1941) in 1908, and two of their three children make occasional appearances in the diaries: 'Pebbin', Jack's younger son Peregrine, 1913–2002, and Clarissa, born in 1920, who would go on to marry Anthony Eden in 1952.

Nana, Maryott Whyte, 1895–1973. Nana, or Cousin Moppet, as she was also known, was, apart from her often absent parents, the most constant and important figure in Mary's childhood. The younger daughter of Clementine's aunt Lady Maude Whyte, Maryott had trained as a Norland nanny, and was the ideal person to call on when her cousin Clementine was looking for someone utterly reliable to look after the infant Mary. Her steady, loving care and strong religious principles (she was also Mary's godmother) were to be a guiding influence on Mary throughout her life. She stayed with the family for 30 years.

Aunt Nellie, Nellie Romilly, née Hozier, 1888–1955. Clementine Churchill's younger sister, and the two women were devoted to each other. Nellie's elder son Giles Romilly

(1916–67) was captured in Norway in 1940, and held at Colditz before escaping in April 1945. His younger brother Esmond, a navigator with the Canadian air force, was lost over the North Sea in 1941.

Pamela Beryl Churchill, née Digby, 1920–1997. Pamela (otherwise Pam, or 'Spam', as Mary occasionally calls her), was the daughter of 11th Lord Digby and great-great niece of the famous Georgian courtesan Jane Digby, to whom she frequently compared herself. She met Randolph Churchill in 1939. Randolph, who had apparently proposed to eight women in the preceding fortnight, proposed to Pamela on the same evening as they met and the couple were married within a few weeks. Their son Winston was born a year later.

Pamela's marriage to Randolph did not last long, and they divorced in 1946. Pamela continued to use the Churchill name, through numerous liaisons with men such as Prince Aly Khan, Gianni Agnelli and Elie de Rothschild. She also married twice more: first to the American stage producer Leland Heyward, from 1960 until his death in 1971; and six months later to Averell Harriman. She took American citizenship on her marriage to Harriman, and became a successful fundraiser and political hostess for the Democratic Party, so much so that Bill Clinton made her American Ambassador to France in 1993.

Randolph Frederick Edward Spencer Churchill, 1911–1968. Mary's elder brother laboured all his life under the disadvantage of being Churchill's only son. Churchill spoiled him and was delighted by his precocious talent as a writer and speaker, but the two soon fell out when Randolph left Oxford without a degree to become – like his father – a journalist. In 1935, without consulting Churchill, he stood as an independent candidate in the Liverpool Wavertree by-election, and succeeded in splitting the Conservative vote so that Labour won the seat. He subsequently made several more attempts to enter Parliament, including in 1936 in Ross and Cromarty against the National Government candidate, which was another embarrassment for Churchill, but finally succeeded in becoming MP for Preston in 1940, though he lost the seat, like so many other Conservatives, in 1945.

During the war Randolph served on the general staff in Intelligence in the Middle East, and was later parachuted into Yugoslavia with the Special Air Service (SAS). Never succeeding in returning to politics, after the war Randolph concentrated on his career as a writer and journalist. He wrote the first two volumes of his father's life before ill health intervened and Martin Gilbert took over. He and Pamela had divorced in 1946, and after another stormy marriage to June Osborne, he finally seemed to achieve some measure of peace with a Suffolk neighbour, artist Natalie Bevan, in the last years of his life. Randolph died in 1968, three years after his father.

Sarah Millicent Hermione Churchill, 1914–1982. Mary adored her glamorous elder sister, the nearest sibling to her in age, but like Diana and Randolph Churchill, Sarah did not have a particularly happy life. Having studied ballet as a girl, she embarked on a career as an actress and dancer in 1935 when she became a member of the chorus line in a revue at the Adelphi and fell in love with the show's Austrian-American star, Vic Oliver. Having already struggled with Sarah's career choice, this liaison was rather too much for the Churchills, not least because Vic was not yet divorced from his first wife. They opposed the marriage, and Sarah ran away to America in a blaze of publicity, marrying Vic on Christmas Eve 1936.

She and her husband returned to England in the following year, to pursue their stage careers, and Vic was received into the family. Unfortunately the marriage did not last, and though Vic remained in England once war broke out, he and Sarah grew further apart, Sarah becoming involved with the American ambassador Gil Winant. They were divorced in 1945.

During the war, Sarah joined the Women's Auxiliary Air Force, serving in the highly secret Photographic Interpretation Unit at RAF Medmenham. She accompanied her father as his aide at the Tehran and Yalta Conferences in 1943 and 1945 (she and Mary shared this duty between them, Mary taking over at Quebec and Potsdam). After the war she resumed her acting career, but never achieved great success: she is probably best known now for appearing in the 1951 film 'Royal Wedding', where she danced with Fred Astaire. In her personal life, Sarah eloped for a second time in 1949, this time with the society photographer Antony Beauchamp, and went to live in the United States for several years. That marriage too failed, and a third marriage to Lord Audley in 1962 ended in tragedy with his death just fifteen months after their wedding. Though she achieved some success in writing and painting in her later years, the latter stages of Sarah's life were overshadowed by problems with money, and increasingly with alcohol.

Papa, Sir Winston Leonard Spencer Churchill, 1874–1965. Born the elder son of Lord Randolph Churchill, himself a leading politician and younger son of the Duke of Marlborough, and Jennie Jerome, the beautiful daughter of an American tycoon, Winston had a privileged, but not especially happy childhood. Sent to boarding school at an early age, he was a troublesome boy, and clashed repeatedly with his father, who was deeply disappointed by his son's apparent lack of intelligence and application. However, once he left school, Winston began to find his feet. As a young cavalry officer, he served in India and the Sudan, but quickly realised that his determination to make a name for himself would be better served outside the army. He used his flair for words to become a successful war reporter, and published his first book, an account of the campaign on the North-West Frontier, in 1898. Thanks to his mother's social contacts, he secured a highly paid job with the *Morning Post*, reporting on the Boer War, but was taken prisoner while defending an armoured train derailed in an ambush. He quickly escaped, and made use of this as a springboard to launch his political career, becoming an MP in 1900, aged just 25.

Churchill continued his meteoric ascent, first as a Conservative, then a Liberal, and reached Cabinet rank by 1908. His first serious check came in the First World War, when as First Lord of the Admiralty he presided over the disastrous Dardanelles Campaign in 1915. Obliged to resign, Churchill then greatly enjoyed himself commanding the 6th Royal Scots Fusiliers on the Western Front. However, his phenomenal energy and drive made him too valuable to leave in obscurity for long, and in 1917 he was brought back into the Government.

Having rejoined the Conservatives a few years after the war, Churchill was appointed Chancellor of the Exchequer in 1924, but this appeared to be the high-water mark of his career. After the Conservatives were defeated in the 1929 election, Churchill fell out with his colleagues following several unpopular moves, opposing self-government for India and supporting Edward VIII during the Abdication Crisis. The 'wilderness years' of the 1930s saw him increasingly isolated, and he turned his energies to writing once more, producing a steady stream of articles and books from the family home at Chartwell. His warnings about the growing power of a resurgent Germany fell largely on deaf ears, but as events began to prove him right, Neville Chamberlain had little choice in 1939 but to bring Churchill back as First Lord of the Admiralty, and in May 1940 Churchill succeeded him as Prime Minister.

After his stunning defeat in the 1945 election, Churchill remained leader of the Conservatives, and was duly returned to office in 1951. By this time he was 76 and his health was beginning to fail: he suffered several strokes while Prime Minister (though these were kept secret, even from most of the Cabinet) and he eventually stepped down in 1955.

The Churchills' circle

Max, William Maxwell Aitken, 1st Lord Beaverbrook, 1879–1964. The Canadian newspaper magnate Max Aitken, owner of the *Daily Express* and *Evening Standard*, had been a strong supporter of appeasement, but gave his backing to Churchill and the war effort in 1940. Churchill made him Minister for Aircraft Production, 1940–41, then Minister of Supply, 1941–42 and finally Lord Privy Seal, 1943–45.

Brendan Rendall Bracken, 1901–1958, later 1st Lord Bracken. At various times a press-man, politician and publisher, Bracken met Winston Churchill in the 1920s, working as one of his election aides, and the two men formed a lifelong friendship. Elected as an MP himself in 1929, Bracken was one of Churchill's most ardent supporters, and became his parliamentary private secretary in 1939 and then, in July 1941, Minister of Information.

CIGS, Field Marshal Sir Alan Francis Brooke, 1883–1963, later 1st Lord Alanbrooke. When Mary refers to Churchill's 'CIGS', or Chief of Imperial General Staff, it is Brooke that she means. Brooke served in the role from December 1941 to June 1946. One of the few men tough enough to stand up to Churchill, he formed an extremely successful (and extremely abrasive) partnership with him, while acting as the chief military adviser to the War Cabinet as well as the head of the army.

Jock, Sir John Rupert Colville, 1915–1987. Jock Colville had been one of Neville Chamberlain's Private Secretaries on the outbreak of war and continued on to serve Churchill and later Attlee. His diaries, *Fringes of Power*, are an important eyewitness account of 10 Downing Street during the war.

Duff, Alfred Duff Cooper, 1890–1954, later 1st Viscount Norwich. Duff Cooper had been one of the few Conservative ministers who agreed wholeheartedly with Churchill in the 1930s about the threat from Nazi Germany, and resigned as First Lord of the Admiralty in 1938 over the Munich Pact. Churchill brought him back into the Government as Minister of Information in 1940, then as Chancellor of the Duchy of Lancaster, 1941–43, but Cooper's most significant contribution to the war was as British representative to the Free French in Algiers, 1943–44. He had the unenviable job of keeping the peace between Churchill and Charles de Gaulle, and continued to do so once he became Ambassador to France in 1944.

Diana, Lady Diana Cooper (née Manners), 1892–1986, later Viscountess Norwich. A legendary political hostess, a successful writer and considered one of the most beautiful women of the age, Lady Diana was one of the leaders of a society group known as 'the Coterie' before the First World War. She married Duff Cooper, one of the few surviving members of the Coterie, in 1919 and began a limited, but lucrative, theatrical career as the Madonna in Max Reinhardt's play 'The Miracle' in 1923. Lady Diana toured with 'The Miracle' off and on for the next 12 years, in Britain, Europe and the United States, the money from which enabled Duff Cooper to embark on his political career.

Diana Cooper had a great deal to do with her husband's later success as Ambassador to France as well, queen of a brilliant group of actors, artists and writers, called 'La Bande', not unlike the Coterie of 30 years before. It was while staying with the Coopers, that Mary met her future husband Christopher Soames, then serving as one of Duff Cooper's military attachés.

Ally, Alastair Cameron Forbes, 1918–2005. The journalist, inveterate gossip and general man about town Ally (or Ali) Forbes was a childhood friend of Mary's and a frequent guest at Chequers.

Jean-Louis Sebastien Hubert de Ganay, 1922–2013, later Marquis de Ganay. One of Mary's more serious relationships during the war, de Ganay had served with the French Resistance, helping Allied airmen who had been shot down to escape from France. In 1943 he fled to Britain but continued to serve with the Resistance, initially in Indo-China, but returned to France before D-Day to blow up a railway line and canal lock vital to the transport of supplies to the German forces. He and Mary remained lifelong friends.

Judy Venetia Montagu, 1923–1972. Mary's closest friend at this time, Judy was the only daughter of Clementine

Churchill's cousin Venetia Stanley ('Cousin V') and the Liberal politician Edwin Montagu. The Montagus lived at Breccles Hall in Norfolk where Mary spent two happy summers at the beginning of the war, greatly enhanced by the nearby presence of the RAF at Watton aerodrome. Judy and Mary joined the ATS and trained together. Judy went on to become a senior instructor, travelling around the country to conduct teaching courses for ATS recruits. Always wildly popular as well as clever, after the war Judy became a close friend of Princess Margaret. In 1962 she married the American photographer Milton Gendel and went to live in Rome.

Charles McMoran Wilson, 1882–1977, 1st Lord Moran (1943). Dean of St Mary's Hospital Medical School, 1920–45, President of the Royal College of Physicians, 1941–50, and Churchill's doctor, 1940–65. Wrote a highly controversial memoir, *Winston Churchill: the Struggle for Survival* in 1966, shortly after his patient's death and Mary never spoke to him again.

Victor, Nathaniel Mayer Victor Rothschild, 1910–1990, 3rd Lord Rothschild. A member of the Rothschild banking dynasty, Victor Rothschild had largely turned his back on the family business, becoming a noted zoologist at Cambridge. During the war Rothschild headed the counter-sabotage section of MI5, where one of his duties was to check the many anonymous gifts of cigars, food and wine sent to Churchill for poison (much to the Prime Minister's indignation). Though some years older than Mary, he was one of her circle of friends through Clementine's cousin Venetia Montagu.

Archie, Archibald Sinclair, 1890–1970, later 1st Lord Thurso. Archie Sinclair was an old friend of Churchill's; they had served together during the First World War and Sinclair had later spent several years as Churchill's private secretary. He became Liberal leader in 1935 and served as Secretary of State for Air from 1940 to 1945, but lost his seat in the 1945 election. Married to Marigold Forbes; their son Robin Sinclair was one of Mary's close friends.

Political figures

Clement Attlee, 1883–1967, later 1st Earl Attlee. The Labour Party leader Clement Attlee went on to serve in Churchill's National Government in various Cabinet posts, including Deputy Prime Minister from 1942–45. He then defeated Churchill in the 1945 election, with Labour winning a landslide victory.

Neville Chamberlain, 1869–1940. The Conservative politician Neville Chamberlain served as Prime Minister from 1937 until May 1940, when he was replaced by Churchill. Anxious to avoid war, he pursued a policy of appeasement, and is probably best known for signing the Munich Pact with Germany in 1938, declaring that he had secured 'peace in our time', but when Germany invaded Poland a year later, he had no choice but to declare war. He continued to serve in Churchill's War Cabinet until shortly before his death from bowel cancer in late 1940.

General de Gaulle, Charles André Joseph Marie de Gaulle, 1890–1970. The French officer General Charles de Gaulle led the 4th Armoured Division against the German invasion of France in May 1940, and then served briefly as Under-Secretary for War. Following the Vichy government's armistice with the Nazis in June, de Gaulle fled to Britain to join the Allies and continue the fight, as leader of the Free French. However, de Gaulle was never easy to deal with, being famously prickly and defensive of French interests: in his view, "the Anglo-Saxons" never treated the Free French as real allies, but used them for their own purposes. Churchill and Roosevelt were both infuriated by him, but Churchill could not help admiring his intransigence; as he later said in his war memoirs, 'He had to be rude to the British to prove to French eyes that he was not a British puppet. He certainly carried out this policy with perseverance.'

Following the Liberation of France in 1944, de Gaulle then headed the interim Provisional Government until 1946. In later years he came out of retirement to serve first as Prime Minister, then President of France from 1958 until his final resignation in 1969.

Anthony, Robert Anthony Eden, 1897–1977, later 1st Earl Avon. Anthony Eden had already been Foreign Secretary once in the 1930s – resigning in 1938 following a disagreement with Chamberlain about attempts to appease both Hitler and Mussolini – when he was brought back into the Government on the outbreak of war as Dominions Secretary. Despite not being one of Churchill's natural allies, he became first his Secretary of State for War, then Foreign Secretary once again, from December 1940 until the end of the war. Eden frequently disagreed with Churchill on policy, but remained loyal to him. Though he was groomed to be his successor from as early as 1940, Eden finally succeeded Churchill in 1955.

Averell Harriman, 1891–1986. A successful American businessman and Democrat, Harriman was President Roosevelt's Special Representative to Britain in March 1941. He was made Ambassador first to the Soviets in 1943, and then to Britain in 1946. While in London in 1941 he had an affair with Pamela Churchill; many years later she became his third wife. Harriman's daughter Kathleen, who served as his unofficial aide during the war, much as Mary did with Churchill, also appears in the diaries.

Harry Hopkins, 1890–1946. Few stood closer to Franklin Roosevelt than Harry Hopkins. He had been a key figure in the President's administration since Roosevelt's election in 1932, taking on several important administrative roles, as well as that of Secretary of Commerce, 1938–40. Though already a sick man, due to the stomach cancer that was soon to kill him, Hopkins was instrumental in running the Lend-Lease aid programme to the Allies, and was Roosevelt's Special Envoy to both Churchill and the Soviets throughout the war, also serving as Roosevelt's adviser at all of the main Allied conferences.

Pug, General Sir Hastings Lionel Ismay, 1887–1965, later 1st Lord Ismay. Chief of Staff to Churchill, 1940–45, and also Deputy Secretary (Military) to the War Cabinet, 1940–45 and Additional Secretary (Military) of the Cabinet, 1945.

Prof, Frederick Alexander Lindemann, 1886–1957, later 1st Lord Cherwell. The physicist F A Lindemann had been an early advocate of the need to improve Britain's air defences in the 1930s. On the outbreak of war Churchill made him his personal assistant, and also head of his statistical section. He advised the Prime Minister on scientific topics, particularly experimental weapons development, but also on the statistics of vital areas such as munitions production, shipping totals and food imports.

Franklin Delano Roosevelt, or **FDR**, 1882–1945. Franklin Roosevelt entered politics in 1910, when he was first elected as a senator. He was appointed Assistant Secretary of the Navy in 1913, then became Governor of the State of New York, 1929–33, and was the Democratic nominee for the Presidency in 1932. He was duly elected for the first of his four terms of office.

At the start of the war, Roosevelt tried to keep the United States neutral, while supporting the Allies financially. When France fell and Britain was threatened with invasion in 1940, he began to send Britain all possible aid short of actual military involvement. However, when Japan attacked the American fleet at Pearl Harbor in December 1941, Roosevelt finally had to bring America into the war.

Roosevelt's success as a politician and war leader came despite the crippling polio that he had suffered from since 1921. Though he fought to retain use of his legs, he was gradually confined to a wheelchair. His health worsened in the latter stages of the war, and he died in April 1945, shortly before the German surrender. Throughout his life, he was ably supported by his wife and cousin Eleanor Roosevelt, who makes several appearances in Mary's diaries, as does their eldest son Elliott Roosevelt, who much like Mary, served as his father's aide on various occasions.

Sandys, Edwin Duncan Sandys, 1908–1987, Baron Duncan-Sandys. After an early foray into a diplomatic career, Sandys became an MP in 1935, the same year as he married Churchill's eldest daughter Diana. During the war he fought first in Norway in 1940, then commanded an anti-aircraft regiment, but a car crash in 1941 left him with serious injuries to his feet and he was invalided out of the army. Churchill appointed him as financial secretary to the War Office, and despite murmurs of nepotism he proved a success, rising steadily through the ministerial ranks and also encouraging his father-in-law in the cause of post-war European unity. His marriage to Diana was less successful and they divorced in 1960.

Frank Sawyers, d. 1972. Churchill's valet until 1947.

Tommy, Commander Charles Ralfe Thompson, 1894–1966. Flag Lieutenant to Churchill as First Lord of the Admiralty, 1939–40, then his Personal Assistant once Churchill became Prime Minister.

Gil Winant, John Gilbert Winant, 1889–1947, was American Ambassador to Britain from 1941–46, and a staunch supporter of Churchill's government. He was also very much in love with Sarah Churchill and the end of their relationship is likely to have contributed to his suicide in 1947.

A Note on the Diaries

When we began this project back in 2019, I initially had some doubts: Mary had published a memoir of her wartime experiences, *A Daughter's Tale*, back in 2011, and drew on her diaries then. When they arrived at the Archives Centre a few years later, they were bristling with her post-it notes (which made an interesting challenge for our conservation team). Would she not have cherry-picked the best bits already?

But when we came to look at the diaries in detail, there was so much more in there – over the 15 volumes which cover the war years – that the problem became instead having too much material to try and squeeze into one book.

Mary is never boring (she clearly inherited her father's skill with words), but we have had to cut out some things: a few of the many parties she crams in, especially before she joins up; some of her longer teenage glooms about what a terrible person she is; and, inevitably, a lot of day-to-day entries where nothing very much happens. By and large, though, we have been able to keep most of what she writes, which, as the war went on, tended to be scribbled down in old exercise books, or anything else that came to hand.

Much of the fun of Mary's writing comes from her invincibly bubbly style (pretty much unchanged fifty years later when she was writing her diary as Chairman of the National Theatre). We have kept that as far as possible – with her clusters of exclamation marks and frequent 'woofs' and 'wows'

– but have just smoothed out some of her more idiosyncratic spellings and many, many dashes. Significant cuts are marked with ellipses, and where there are gaps in the diaries, we have added in some additional material, mostly letters between Mary and her parents, which tend to be rather more sober in tone.

Digitised copies of the diaries are available for consultation by appointment at Churchill Archives Centre.

Katharine Thomson, Archivist

Mary Churchill's War

1939

Last Days of Childhood

*'If I may never know happiness or joy again I shall
always have the memory of my first seventeen years.'*

18 TUESDAY (199-166)

When I consider what an eventful
existence I lead and what
exciting times I live in, I am
ashamed that I do not take more
trouble to write my diary (a) Regularly
(b) Legibly (c) Coherently.
     The past weeks have been
full of events, some pleasanter
than others, but none boring.
I must try to keep a more faithful
and consistent record of my life.

Mary was just sixteen years old when she resolved to keep a diary at the beginning of 1939. The early entries capture the innocence of the last days of her childhood, spent in comparative isolation in the beautiful countryside around Chartwell, the family home in Kent. Her religious faith and her love of riding are evident, while episodes of teenage angst are interspersed with occasional forays into a more glamorous adult world. She is unquestioningly loyal to her 'Papa' but initially at least the political news and deteriorating international situation only occasionally intrude into her cosy domestic narrative.

This all begins to change in the second half of the year, which is dominated by the descent into war. Mary accompanies her parents to France in August, though the worsening political situation means that her father both goes out first and comes back early. Suddenly 'war seems so horribly near, so inevitable'. On 1 September, Germany moves against Poland, after having first secured a non-aggression pact with the Soviet Union. Prime Minister Chamberlain recalls Churchill to the war cabinet as First Lord of the Admiralty. Two days later, the British ultimatum to Berlin expires, and war with Germany is declared. Mary's country life is now over as she moves to London and into Admiralty House, from where her father is conducting the war at sea. She is not yet seventeen but already at the heart of events and starting to enjoy a new-found independence.

She throws herself into voluntary work, learns to drive, explores the big city, and enjoys the high-profile wedding of her older brother Randolph to Pamela Digby. But she has to give up her horse and beloved country home. The storm clouds are starting to gather.

Sunday 1 January

Saw 1939 out & 1939 in with Punch at Breccles [...] Went for longish walk in a.m. with Nana. Walked again in p.m. Great fun & most energetic. Read mainly after tea.

My resolutions are

(1) to say prayers much more carefully
(2) to be much more regular re letters, accounts etc & especially my zoo is to be attended to
(3) to have greater strength of purpose
(4) to keep a diary
(5) to read lots of good books

I am really going to try to keep these. May God bless my year & be with all those I love!

Friday 6 January

Read and finished *Bleak House* during day. I enjoyed it very much but the ending was not altogether satisfactory, what with Richard dying and Caddy's baby being a deaf mute, and anyway I don't believe I ever got over Esther being pock-marked!!

Rode in pm, fears re hunting [because of] frost. After tea rang up SM* – NO HUNTING –

Boo-hoo. But 2hrs later SM rang me – weather for[e]casts & thaw made prospect of hunting probable <u>Whoopeeeeee</u> Oh dear, God <u>is</u> so <u>wonderful</u>, I do appreciate everything he does.

---

* Sam Marsh, who ran the local riding school and kept Mary's mare Patsy at livery

Saturday 7 January

Patsy refused & I funked a Sussex gate & it had to be opened for me – complete shame & ignominy . . . I am determined to pluck up more courage & be braver. I <u>do try</u> but my courage just oozes away at the last minute.

Saturday 18 March

The crisis seems to be becoming more serious.[*]

Papa said, 'Before God Almighty I swear I do not wish for war.' I write this as a witness.

Friday 24 March

Miss Gribble[†] said on Wednesday that it was more important for me to keep a diary than Algebra, Latin & History all put together. When I think of the gloriously happy, interesting & full life I lead I feel she is right & I feel I should keep it so that later I may look back on this my testament of youth!

Rumania has signed a trade agreement with Germany. Things look very, <u>very</u> grave. Yet people do not seem so worried as at last crisis.

Memel[‡] goes, Rumania next – then what?

Wednesday 5 April

I can now see where the temptation to let personal appearance go comes. It begins by tending to slide round all day in

---

[*] German invasion of Czechoslovakia, 15 March
[†] Katharine Gribble, Mary's headmistress
[‡] Part of Lithuania, which Germany demanded back on 20 March

jodhpurs & then gradually hands are allowed to get coarse & rough, negligence to complexion following soon after – my hands were a disgrace – & still are. I must be <u>very</u> careful not to get slack about my personal freshness & neatness.

Friday 7 April

[Good Friday, after a picnic] The afternoon was lovely – sunshiny & the primroses were exquisite – the whole wood was gay – lush & fragrant, on returning home after such a peaceful beautiful day – after such carefree joy – we hear Italy has attacked Albania. Is all the world as I know it breaking up. Must the world go mad again – must Christ hang in vain – O God <u>lighten</u> our darkness!

Thursday 27 April

In afternoon went to London with Mummie & from the Speakers Gallery in HoC watched & heard part of the debate on conscription. The PM was indistinct & v slow, but made quite good speech. I think it may be true that he is now pushing something in which he has little real faith. Attlee made a narrow bitter but none the less 'holding' speech. Archie declaimed sonorously to a more than ½ empty house. I think he is missing a chance over this – he is allowing narrow prejudices to prevent him supporting so necessary a measure. Papa made a just & sensible speech – the House filled up the minute he began.[*]

---

[*] This was the debate on six months' compulsory military training for men aged twenty and twenty-one, the first step towards wider conscription. Churchill supported the measure

Friday 5 May

Went to London. Had hair done – dentist. Went to lunch with Aunt Goonie with Mummie & Papa to meet Dr & Mrs Julian Huxley. Also there were Mr 'Bluey' Baker, Uncle Jack, Pebbin.* After lunch Sarah joined us & we all went to Zoo for private audience with Ming the BABY GIANT PANDA who has stolen the limelight from Greta Garbo and sent Chamberlain & the Dictators onto the second page!! She is DIVINE – so charming, so easy going & amiable, as Papa said 'The Baby Giant Panda satisfies the much felt sense of world <u>cuddlability</u>!!

Monday 8 May

I have come to the frightful conclusion that (a) I am insincere (b) a coquette (c) I bite my nails (d) I think too much about myself. Reform is needed & I am <u>determined</u> to try to be more natural & nice.

Friday 26 May

Miss Loweson-Browne† talked to me very sweetly today about whether I would consider going to the University on classics, i.e. Greek, Latin, History. I feel it is a compliment she has paid me and I am taken aback & overwhelmed. I don't somehow fancy the University, & I also feel very deeply that I want to be near Mummie & especially Papa, to help if I can & also I am enthralled by the magnitude of Papa's brain & personality. I fear I have not appreciated him sufficiently or loved him till just lately – but now

---

* Jack's younger son Henry Peregrine Churchill, 1913–2002
† Likely to be a teacher

my heart has been awakened & thrilled & I am torn between pride & a deepening & ever increasing love for him.

Saturday 3 June

Submarine tragedy casts a shadow over every face today. 75 men are still trapped in the *Thetis* & hope for their recovery is v slight. It is v very terrible & I can only hope that those who wait & hope may be comforted by Him who understands everything – for indeed they will go through the Valley of the Shadow of Death with their men . . . Papa v unhappy because of submarine & also Philip Sassoon's death.[*] Art & culture have lost a great patron.[†]

Tuesday 18 July

When I consider what an eventful existence I lead and what exciting times I live in, I am ashamed that I do not take more trouble to write my diary (a) Regularly (b) Legibly (c) Coherently. The past weeks have been full of events, some pleasanter than others, but none boring. I must try to keep a more faithful and consistent record of my life.

Tuesday 8 August

I must go to sleep now until 12.30 when I shall be called to hear Papa's American broadcast. The great air battle has begun & the noise of the planes is continuous.

---

[*] Sir Philip Sassoon MP 1888–1939, Trustee of the Wallace Collection, Tate Gallery and British School at Rome

[†] The Royal Navy submarine HMS *Thetis* sinks during sea trials. 99 men suffocate and only 4 escape. Sir Philip Sassoon's death is unrelated and from influenza

2.20 am. Papa's broadcast was excellent. His phraseology is <u>so</u> wonderful. I thought of those hundreds of thousands of American people listening. Papa has never, never ceased to work for 'life, liberty and the pursuit of happiness'. God spare him to us for many a year.

'BUT TO COME BACK TO THE HUSH I SAID WAS HANGING OVER EUROPE. WHAT KIND OF A HUSH IS IT? ALAS! IT IS THE HUSH OF SUSPENSE, AND IN MANY LANDS IT IS THE HUSH OF FEAR. LISTEN!'

Broadcast to the United States from London, 8 August

Thursday 17 August

Arrived in Paris – city of my dreams! And rushed straight [to] the [Hotel] Prince de Galles and had bed, baths & breakfast. A diversion being caused by Minnie* leaving Mummie's sponge bag in the train!! XXX†! We went and shopped in the Trois Quartiers where Mummie bought the prettiest little evening dress with CHERRY COLOURED velvet bows, like Mrs Strong in *David Copperfield*. Had lunch & rested until Papa joined us after his tour of the Maginot Line.‡ Papa says the spirit among the French soldiers is wonderful.

Papa took me to see le Tombeau de Napoléon. There he sleeps, guarded by his calm, wide[e]yed victories – '*au bord de la Seine au milieu de ce people français que j'ai tant aimé*'.§ Motored to

---

* The Churchills' maid
† Mary adds 'XXX' here to indicate swearing
‡ An elaborate line of fortifications in north-eastern France supposed to protect France from German invasion
§ 'By the Seine in the middle of the French people who I love so much'

St Georges Motel* which is lovely. Was seized by violent indigestion & shivering at dinner & retired to bed immediately after.

Tuesday 22 August

As I write this, war seems so horribly near, so inevitable. If it comes – then millions of young men will march to their bloody death and millions of hearts will be torn. O God, O God, let not this plague descend upon us – in thy great and almighty wisdom protect us from this ghastly peril from which can come no good. I can write no more tonight, I can only pray & wait. Waiting in suspense.

Wednesday 23 August

Today has been one of suspense. Papa left early this morning for London.

If war comes I hope that we all will face it bravely & courageously. I hope that I will have sufficient 'guts' to put my back unselfishly & laboriously to whatever task I feel it my duty to perform. Our plans are uncertain – we may return tomorrow evening. 'For we are all like swimmers in the sea.'†

Thursday 24 August

After certain amount of flap & indecision we determined to return at once to England – farewell Dinard!!

. . . Paris seems calm but prepared & very busy. We lunched at the Prince de Galles and after resting walked into a cinema

---

* Home of Jacques Balsan and Consuelo Balsan, formerly Consuelo Vanderbilt and Duchess of Marlborough, in Normandy
† Line from 'Sohrab and Rustum' by Matthew Arnold, 1853

to pass the time. Saw Papa returning from Maginot Line on the news reel! On arriving at station felt miserable that there was no one to wave me off, so much I must say to my discredit I held three officers in play & as the train moved out I was waved off by 3 French officers!!

Goodbye dear France, I don't know when I shall ever see you again. God bless & keep you & preserve you from all danger.

The ferry was nearly 2 hours late because of fog and the Nancy connection being late. Diana met us at the barrier & told us that the babies have been sent to Chartwell and that Duncan has been called up. All the people I have talked to seem to say – 'Oh, there won't be any war, what does the loss of Russia really matter, it's all fluff' – Well all I can say is – I hope you're <u>absolutely</u> & <u>entirely</u> right.*

Saturday 26 August, Chartwell

. . . I had a really heavenly ride with Mr Marsh alone, which was very peaceful, and we jumped and schooled. Well, if there *is* a war Patsy will have to go. It seems silly to fuss about a horse, when millions of men are going to face death, but there, I can't help it. I love my Patsy so dearly, but she will of course go. I consider it a privilege that I can send her.

General Ironside† arrived to spend the weekend. What a giant! I am so much impressed by him. He seems so

---

* The Molotov–Ribbentrop non-aggression pact between Soviet Russia and Nazi Germany is signed on 23 August 1939. Unbeknownst to Mary at the time, it contains a secret protocol regarding the partition of Poland, making her response extremely prescient

† General Sir William Ironside 1880–1959, Chief of the Imperial General Staff

thoroughly sensible and calm, v intelligent too (he speaks 20 languages). He gives a very bad report of our govmt.

Sunday 27 August

Throughout the earlier part of the day a fear and dread that another 'Munich' was afoot possessed us, encouraging reports however reached us later. Let us at LEAST hope that we will have 'war with honour'. A telegram from Mr Parsons, editor of the *New York Herald Tribune*, at dinner reports that the Germans still think we shall capitulate & that a bold action is needed to convince them, such as forming a wartime cabinet. Duncan, Diana, Major Morton,* General Ironside to dinner. Noel Coward & Bob Boothby† came afterwards. NC was charming, & sang & played many of his songs – 'Stately Homes of England', 'Mrs Worthington', 'Mad Dogs and Englishmen', 'Bitter Sweet Waltz'.

Friday I September

Up early moving furniture making beds & generally turning everything upside down in order to be ready for the evacuated children.

Rumour confirmed by the Polish ambass came through at about 9 a.m. that Germany has marched on Poland & that bombing is proceeding. May God bless & strengthen the Poles & prosper their cause against tyranny. Went down on bicycle to Crockham Hill schools‡ to act as messenger. Message came through to say 'children arriving at 3.45'. I was helped up the hill by John & Elizabeth in their car . . . Returned to schools

---

* Desmond Morton 1891–1971, personal assistant to Churchill
† Robert Boothby 1900–1986, Parliamentary Secretary, Ministry of Food
‡ The local evacuation centre

to learn that children not arriving till tomorrow. Ha! Ha! I had to sweat up that hill again . . . Blackout begins from tonight. Papa left for London [before] lunch, having been summoned by the PM, & this evening he told us he has been asked to join a War Cabinet of 7 – over the entire cabinet of 22. God guide him in this great work.

Saturday 2 September

Down to schools in morning – no children. Returned to Little Mariners & sewed [blackout] curtains for Elizabeth . . . Sewed again after lunch and at 3.45 went down to schools again. This time at last the children arrived, BUT they were not school-children as had been expected but mothers & babies!! We gave them (158!) tea in the canteen and then proceeded to allot them to various places. At about 5.45 I collected my party of 2 mothers and 7 children varying between 3 mths–7 yrs & John drove us all to Chartwell . . . Nana was out buying mackintosh sheeting (!) and Mummie was in London so I had to organise the lot of them. They seem v nice, however. Papa is in the War Cabinet. I retired to bed somewhat flattened!!!*

Sunday 3 September

DECLARATION OF WAR.

At 10.am came news of our ultimatum to Germany expiring at 11.am . . . 11.15 am announcement by the PM of a state of war between Great Britain & Germany. O God, I thought, I hoped, I prayed that our generation would never see a war and that those who fought last time would never have to face the ordeal a second time.

---

* Later note stapled to page says the evacuees 'Drifted back abt 3 weeks later'

Standing in the sitting room at Scamperdale and looking out at the blue sunny sky, just as blue and gay as ever, with great white clouds floating slowly by, I found it impossible to believe, that war has come. <u>WAR HAS COME</u>. <u>Still</u> I cannot believe it.

Monday 4 September

Worked hectically at curtains & at breakfast discussed plans with Mummie. At the moment it is planned that Mummie, Papa & myself will live in a flat in Admiralty House. Chartwell will be turned into a maternity home under Nana's direction and we will come down to the cottage at weekends.

I hate London, and London in wartime will be even worse than London in peacetime, but it is my own choice to live there. I would rather be with Mummie & Papa & try to help & comfort them both in these days of darkness & anxiety. Papa has given me the lovely scarlet-bound testament on which he took his oath to the King yesterday. I shall keep it & treasure it as one of my most sacred possessions.

Signed on for duty as a telephonist at the ambulance HQ at Westerham of the WVS . . . Did telephonist duty from 4–8. V interesting but not as yet v arduous.

Tuesday 5 September

Sewed curtains in morning. I think the whole sinking of the *Athenia* is a ghastly affair. My God, what a thing to do – without warning, relentlessly.* I hope that when Julian

---

* The passenger liner the SS *Athenia* was the first ship to be sunk by a German U-boat in the war, on 3 September, with the loss of 117 civilian passengers and crew

and Edwina[*] and their contemporaries grow up a better order of things will have been born of our struggles and sufferings.

. . . Mummie rushed unexpectedly to London to say good-bye to Randolph. May God be with him and keep him safe. Oh please, please, keep him safe!

Thursday 14 September

The last day of my 17th year. Tomorrow I shall be SEVENTEEN. I can scarcely believe it! The years have flown – 7 and then 17 – the years between seem like fleeting shadows that passed quickly, happily. I may never live to see another year – I shall <u>never</u> see the world again as I knew it before this bloody war. But if I were never to know another happy day in my life – (and I know that I shall probably do that, because in the human soul there is that 'spirit of gallantry and courage, that makes strange heaven out of unbelievable hell'[†]) but if I may never know happiness or joy again I shall always have the memory of my first 17 years – a golden, glowing memory of pleasures, loves, friendships and heavenly rapture of living at peace in the beautiful place that is my home.

. . . Lunch at Sarah's. The table looked simply too 'story book' & lovely for words – white cloth, pink birthday cake. Mummie, Papa, Randolph, Diana, Sarah, Vic,[‡] Nana & self.

---

[*] Julian and Edwina Sandys, Mary's nephew and niece

[†] Mary is quoting Noel Coward

[‡] The actor and comedian Vic Oliver 1898–1964, married to Sarah Churchill 1936–45

Monday 18 September

So far I have never been able to write my diary very regularly, being impeded by my natural laziness and irresoluteness. But I am determined that the following pages shall contain a true and consecutive record of my life.

I am not a great or important personage, but it will be the diary of an ordinary person's life in wartime – though I may never live to read it again, yet perhaps it may not prove altogether uninteresting as a record of my life – or rather the life of a girl in her youth, upon whom life has shone very brightly, who has had every opportunity of education, interest, travel and pleasure and excitement, and who at the beginning of this war found herself on the threshold of womanhood. What will these pages tell of? How will this fortunate being adjust herself to days altogether unlike those she has hitherto seen? How will she live her new life – let us hope and pray that she may never repine.

Sunday 24 September

Talked to Pamela this morning in her room. As far as I can gather I think she is quite aware of the serious side of marriage, and I think she is wildly in love. She is v independent and has a strong will of her own but I think, and Oh God I pray, that it will be a great success.

Went to church and then to duty for the last time, as it has been decided that I shall go up to London to help Mummie with the wedding because owing to Lady Digby having no house in London – we are giving the party. I explained to Mrs Papillon who quite understood. When they all said goodbye I felt choky – I don't know quite why – I suppose I may never see any of them again . . .

Monday 25 September

Packed hectically and left in a loaded car for London. Mummie's driving is really too extraordinary for words – we crossed some red lights once and nearly got sandwiched between 2 trams! To add to all this – she would look for street names – I was in terror! All the afternoon I arranged the vast expanse of my room. I have a telephone – <u>such</u> a thrill. It really is going to be very nice when it's quite arranged.

Rested and went to Savoy for dinner with cousin Venetia*, Judy, Rosemary Scott-Ellis, Arthur Serocold, Peter Hanbury, Mr Thursby and Captain Montagu. It was great fun – oh what heaven to dance again after such a long time. Alas it was over <u>all</u> too soon.

Tuesday 26 September

Walked in the Park. I have got a latchkey, which is the height of grandeur! . . . Pamela came to lunch, and I am glad to say they are going to be married in St John's Smith Square.

In the afternoon I went down to the HoC. Chamberlain spoke calmly, clearly and comprehensively, Papa arose amidst good applause, and made a wonderful speech. He has such a gift of language and declamation, he pulled us all together – he cheered us up, he strengthened our courage & resolution.†

---

* Venetia Montagu, née Stanley
† This was a speech by Churchill about the war at sea against the U-boats

Thursday 28 September

Shopped by myself in morning. Great fun learning about London. When in doubt I look helpless & ask a p'liceman! ... Lunched with Sarah & Miss Philipps – HAMBURGERS!! Had my hair set in new page-boy at Erlande. Had EYEBROWS TIDIED Oh wow!! Actually I was TERRIFIED but they look heaven & just tidy!!

Saturday 30 September

Drove car to Oxted! . . . I do enjoy driving so, but I still 'have kittens' going round corners . . . Had a glorious ride all by myself on that sweetest of horses – Patsy, alas, no longer mine. Up on the hills and commons one could scarcely believe that there was a world where men fought & killed each other . . .

Wednesday 4 October

A grey, dry, breezy day. Visited Pamela in the morning. Dressed for wedding – my new hat (although I says it as shouldn't!) is a wow!! Mummie looked lovely. Just before we started off a parcel arrived addressed clearly to Miss Churchill – I opened it hastily and inside lay the most lovely diamond & sapphire brooch – 'with best wishes from Mr Seymour Berry'. I was flabbergasted and the only conclusion that we all came to was that I received this gift as a potential bridesmaid. I wore it on my dress. I can never forget the wonderful ovation Papa received when he arrived at the church. Wave on wave of cheering, from about 250–300 people. It was touching & made me feel quite choky. The church was packed & as I slipped into my pew I had the opportunity of thanking

Mr Berry for his present. In the light of subsequent events I realised the look he gave me was one of shock & bewilderment!!!*

Thursday 5 October

Went to Cadogan Sq & volunteered [for the Red Cross]. I am to begin by making bandages and then I am to do secretarial work afterwards. Lunched with Diana in Kingsway where she is working v hard as a WREN.† I would like to be a WREN.

Friday 6 October

Went to work for the first time. I have bought myself a white overall and a very natty little cap in which I look like a naughty Quaker. I struggled all morning with herringbone stitch. I am the youngest in the room by about 40 years I think. After lunch went down to Chartwell . . . Installed myself at Horatia's where I am staying because Chartwell's virtually shut up & the cottage isn't ready.

Friday 13 October

Hectic preparations all pm for 'Les J'aimberlins' . . . dinner went off quite satisfactorily. I think Mrs Chamberlain is lovely & v sweet but she asks 'cuckoo' questions – she is v good & gracious to workers when being shown round everywhere. Mr Chamberlain seems v nice – but rather vacant.

---

* Perhaps the brooch was meant for Pamela
† Women's Royal Naval Service

Sunday 31 December

So this is the end of 1939 – what a year! After Munich the tension hardly slackened for a moment, I think although we reasoned that a war must & would come – yet we never really believed or imagined that it could – at least I didn't. It seemed fantastic that such a thing should come about – one was lulled into a momentary confidence – and then some shattering event would take place – and all one's fears and instincts were once more brought into the foreground.

And yet although this calamity was fast and undeniably approaching yet our lives moved pleasurably and swiftly. Parties – friends – activities – but always over the brightest event the shadow hung – enhancing rather, by its very frightfulness the gaieties & pleasures

1940

Plunged into Adulthood

'I have learnt more about human suffering
& anxiety than ever before.'

When you think of Winston Churchill, you tend to think of 1940. This year will change everything for him and his family; their darkest but also finest hour. Yet for Mary it begins relatively inauspiciously. It certainly starts cold, with frequent frosts and heavy snowfalls that ultimately culminate in one of the most severe ice storms ever to hit the United Kingdom. And while there is no thaw in international relations, the full reality and horror of war is yet to register.

As the year opens Mary is shooting with her new sister-in-law's family in Dorset. Thereafter she shops in London, skates at Chartwell, visits the theatre and listens to the wireless. But duty is already starting to call, and she accompanies her father on an official visit to the navy at Portsmouth. At this point, such occasions are still glamorous and novel, and the reader cannot help but be swept along by her youthful delight at being piped aboard a battleship.

The entries for 23 and 29 February provide an unintentionally powerful juxtaposition between reality and romance, describing two events in London that each, in their own way, mark the beginning of a coming of age. Mary attends the royal inspection of the victorious crews of the Royal Naval cruisers HMS *Ajax* and HMS *Exeter*, just returned from South American waters where they have fought successfully in the battle of the River Plate against the German pocket battleship *Graf Spee*. While she cannot hide her excitement at the occasion, she is clearly uneasy about coming face to face with those widowed and orphaned by the action. Nevertheless, she does not let this dampen her enthusiasm for her 'debut' a few days later. This is a formal occasion at which daughters of the aristocracy are presented to high society. Given the constraints of wartime, there is no ceremony at Buckingham Palace but there is a dinner dance, Queen Charlotte's Ball, at the Grosvenor House Hotel.

Everything changes again in May when her father becomes prime minister. A crucial debate in the House of Commons is triggered by defeat in the Norwegian campaign, where the British have failed to forestall a German invasion. It quickly widens into a confidence debate about Neville Chamberlain's leadership. On 9 May, Mary is in the gallery of the House of Commons to watch her father wind up for the government, a most difficult speech in which he has to walk a tightrope between defending Chamberlain, justifying his own role and maintaining his credibility as a likely prime minister in waiting.

The following morning she dances the night away in London, blissfully unaware that momentous events are unfolding. Hitler has unleashed his blitzkrieg invasion of the Low Countries and Chamberlain has agreed to resign. Jock Colville, already in Downing Street as one of Chamberlain's private secretaries, records in his diary, how he: 'Dined with Mrs Henley and went on afterwards to dance at the Savoy. Sat between Mrs H and Mary Churchill (Winston's youngest progeny) . . . I thought the Churchill girl rather supercilious: she has Sarah's emphatic way of talking, and is better looking, but she seemed to me to have a much less sympathetic personality.' Colville was also rather critical of her father at this time, writing of his assumption of office that it was: 'a terrible risk, it involves the danger of rash and spectacular exploits, and I cannot help fearing that this country may be manoeuvred into the most dangerous position it has ever been in.' He was soon to revise both opinions, serving as one of Churchill's private secretaries and becoming a key confidant of the family and friend to Mary.

With Churchill now prime minister, Mary is truly at the heart of events and expected to play a role. In July, she performs her first solo engagement, the launching of the naval destroyer HMS *Gurkha* at Birkenhead. She does not record a trip to the theatre to see her sister Sarah in Ivor Novello's play *Murder in Mayfair*, of which Colville writes that: 'The Churchills en famille were delightful and very amusing. They made a certain amount of fun of the Chamberlains and Mary described how Mrs Chamberlain had taken her for the wife of one of the officers on the *Exeter* . . . I devoured cherries, gossiped with Diana, and aroused Mary's indignation to a high pitch by telling her that when Chamberlain was PM I had refused to wake him up to see the papers which Winston sent over sporadically from the Admiralty at 2.00 am. "You dared to do that to Papa!" she said.'

As the year progresses, the Battle of Britain, in which the Luftwaffe tries to break the air superiority of the Royal Air Force, gives way to the large-scale bombing of the Blitz. At her parents' insistence, Mary spends much of the summer in the comparative safety of her cousin Judy Montagu's home in the Norfolk countryside at Breccles. Here she is exposed to a more typical and lively teenage social life than she had hitherto experienced at Chartwell.

From September, and her eighteenth birthday, Mary is living in the prime minister's country residence, Chequers, a sixteenth-century manor house in Buckinghamshire, and working for the Women's Voluntary Services. Her diaries show her following the military campaigns on which her father's premiership now depends. She is part of his inner circle and feels the reverses and successes very keenly. The failed attempt by a British and Free French expedition to take control of the strategic port of Dakar in Senegal, from forces loyal to the Vichy French regime, is damaging to both Churchill and de Gaulle. Yet the year ends on a high note with a small taste of victory against the Italians in North Africa and the family united in celebration.

Monday 1 January

New Year's Day at Minterne.* Went out with the guns – in the morning we shot rabbits – and saw plenty of roebuck, they are so pretty and elegant. After lunch we went out to shoot the snipe bog – v cold, ice, wind. About 5 flew out – killed one. Then we beat an adjacent wood – woodcock, pigeons. A glorious afternoon – I do so love the vast immensities of open country.

Played about in the evening. Had continual struggle for 'the last word' at dinner and afterwards with Duke and Duchess of Norfolk – both of whom I think are the greatest fun. Lovely time playing records – then, prompted by her – the Earl Marshal [the Duke of Norfolk] allowed himself to do his 'strong man act' & hurl me about the room – he must be pretty strong. V gay mouvementée evening!!

Thursday 4 January

Work – very little to do. Driving lesson in pm – then went on the 'bargain hunt' to Marshalls stocking sale. Had to walk miles because I took wrong bus! Outside St George's a pavement artist had extraordinarily good caricatures of public personalities – among them a v good one of Papa – so I gave him 6d, which I thought a bit stingy afterwards, & I told him who I was – the man looked absolutely flabbergasted – & raised his hat on recovering! When I have a torch & plenty of time I like London in the blackout – it's rather thrilling & different.

---

* Minterne House, Dorset, home of the Digbys, Pamela Churchill's family

Saturday 13 January

I began life at 2am by the Admiralty wanting Papa & ringing my number by mistake!! We left Waterloo by the 7.45 & had breakfast on the train. Mr Seal,[*] the Naval Sec Admiral Syfret, Mummie, Papa, myself – a secretary and Inspector Thomson[†] completed the party. We were met at Portsmouth by the C-in-C – Sir William James of Bubbles fame![‡] We went straight to Mount Vernon – torpedo school – then looked at some mines – <u>queer things</u>!! Then Mummie & myself went to the officers' mess & had coffee – while something terrifically hush-hush was shown to the others. Then we all went in a battleship – Papa just looked at a couple of cruisers & I was simply longing to go in one – & Adm Syfret was perfectly sweet & divining my wish took me onto one whose captain he knew. All the others went off to look at something else & oh – proud moment of my life – I was PIPED OVER THE SIDE – both going on & coming off – I nearly fainted when I realised what was happening. I suppose it's because I have a big sense of the spectacular and romantic – because the uniforms – the gold – the saluting – the trumpeting – & the piping.

Monday 12 February

I develop German Measles. We are definitely NOT amused.

---

[*] Eric Seal 1898–1972, Principal Private Secretary to Churchill, 1938–41

[†] Detective Inspector Walter Thompson 1890–1978, Churchill's police guard

[‡] Admiral Sir William James 1881–1973, who had been the model as a child for the painting *Bubbles* by his grandfather, John Everett Millais

Friday 23 February

THE INSPECTION OF THE OFFICERS AND MEN OF THE AJAX & EXETER BY THE KING.* Quite early crowds began collecting along the streets & especially on the Horse Guards parade. Tremendous bustlings & hustlings not only on the parade, where commanders & marines rushed about, but also indoors – where secretaries & myself flew about in a great state. A tragic group of widows & orphans collected underneath the windows of Admiralty House, where chairs were arranged for them. They looked cold & miserable, and Mummie had the wonderful idea of providing coffee & biscuits for them – so Lyons after some persuasion arranged it, & I flew across to the shop to guide the nippies over [waitresses in Lyons teashops]. I was so hot by this time, as I was all in my best & tidied up!! Mummie & I went down & I helped give them the coffee. It was terrible their grief & courage, & I crept away. I felt too much moved & I felt I had no right to intrude on their sorrows. People began arriving – personal friends upstairs & official friends down . . . Mummie, self, Mrs Fitzroy, Lady Pound & Mrs Chamberlain (who was late) all were in Papa's room, where little platforms had been put in the windows. Lady Harewood, Lady Woodhouse & Mrs Bell, Adm Syfret & Mr Seal came in to be presented to the Queen, I was v much excited & stood behind Mummie.

Thursday 29 February

MY DEBUT. I couldn't believe when I woke up this morning that today was the day I have been longing for for such ages. I began dressing at about 5.30 & managed to be 10 mins late!

---

* The crews from the Battle of the River Plate

Well I must say it was lovely to wear such a really beautiful white taffeta hooped dress (slightly off the shoulders!) I wore tiny camellias in my hair – my pearl necklace – my aquamarine & pearl drop earrings, long white gloves – & a sweet little diamond naval crown which Vic sent me as a present – the angel! Mummie looked stunningly beautiful in a lovely pale pink gown with sequins embroidered on it.

The Party

I can only say that the evening was a dream of glamour & happiness. Everyone was so sweet to me – But the evening was made for me by Papa, in spite of all work & everything, coming in & sitting with us for a little while.

Wednesday 8 May

The debate on the Norwegian campaign continued throughout today. Attacks, queries, suspicions & suggestions came from all sides of the House. In the evening at 10 after Mr A.V. Alexander (Labour)* had sat down after a minute questioning of the Norwegian campaign (the unrest in the House was aggravated by Papa arriving rather late for Mr A's questions – however this point was entirely submerged by later events). Papa rose to wind up the debate. It was the first time in 11 years that he had wound up for the govt. The House was in a most uncertain, unpleasant & sensitive & restless mood. There were frequent interruptions – also quite a lot of cheering. Papa's handling of the actual matter and of the House was nothing short of SUPERB. I listened breathless with pride, apprehension & desire. A storm of

---

* Albert Victor Alexander 1885–1965, later 1st Lord Alexander of Hillsborough, succeeded Churchill as First Lord of the Admiralty, 1940–45

interruptions arose making Papa sit down & the speech ended amid catcalls from both sides of the House. There was a spirit of criticism & ferocity to be felt most strongly. Bitter opposition to Chamberlain & many members of the Cabinet even within the ranks of the Tory party.

Thursday 9 May

The papers full of the debate yesterday evening. Rumours in nearly all of them that Papa might form a govt: & a general feeling that a coalition govt on the broadest base should be formed.

In the efforts to beat off a cold I think I took an overdose of quinine & cinnamon, anyway I felt mighty sick from about 4.30 until 8.13 when all my troubles ended by my being VERY VERY sick – all dressed up in my best too – however all was well & I went to a lovely dinner party given by Cousin Sylvia* for Judy and myself. Mark† was there & made himself v agreeable to me. We went to the Savoy & then (despite a few conscience pricks which I firmly banished) on to the 400 [Club]‡. Danced almost exclusively with Mark. V nice! Home & bed 4am – tut-tut! Jock Colville, secretary to PM told me that on leaving the House of Commons last night one French journalist was said to remark to the other: '*Dieu! Que les femmes députés sont laides'*§!! V charming I think!

---

* Sylvia Henley, Clementine Churchill's cousin
† Major Mark Howard, of Castle Howard, in Yorkshire, who was to be killed fighting with the Coldstream Guards in Normandy in 1944
‡ The 400 Club was a night club at 28A Leicester Square, London. For two decades the 400 Club catered to 'the upper classes at night time' and during the Second World War it was much frequented by the armed forces, and by young men trying their luck
§ 'God! These women MPs are ugly!'

Friday 10 May

While Mark & I were dancing gaily & so unheedingly this morning – in the cold grey dawn Germany swooped on 2 more innocent countries – Holland & Belgium. The bestiality of the attack is inconceivable.

Went to college. A cloud of uncertainty & doubt hung over us all day. What would happen to the govt? What is the news from abroad? French towns – open towns – were raided. The rumours of Chamberlain's resignation increased . . .

Just before the 9 o'clock news Mr Chamberlain spoke to us & told us that he had resigned & that Papa was forming a new govt. It was the speech of a patriot.

Saturday 11 May

At Chartwell. The Cabinet is announced.

Sunday 12 May

At Chartwell. Church – we prayed for Papa.

'I SPEAK TO YOU FOR THE FIRST TIME AS PRIME MINISTER IN A SOLEMN HOUR FOR THE LIFE OF OUR COUNTRY, OF OUR EMPIRE, OF OUR ALLIES, AND, ABOVE ALL, OF THE CAUSE OF FREEDOM. A TREMENDOUS BATTLE IS RAGING IN FRANCE AND FLANDERS. THE GERMANS, BY A REMARKABLE COMBINATION OF AIR BOMBING AND HEAVILY ARMOURED TANKS, HAVE BROKEN THROUGH THE FRENCH DEFENCES NORTH OF THE MAGINOT LINE.'

Radio broadcast, 19 May

Sunday 19 May

Rode in the morning. Heavenly hot weather. Home in the evening & a very hysterical journey up in the train. We succeeded in entirely monopolising a carriage & we had a lovely supper in the train. We made a disgraceful amount of noise & giggled ceaselessly – what fun! On arriving home we all of us got stuck in that antediluvian lift & only just got up in time for Papa's speech. Papa's speech was absolutely magnificent. He will lead us to victory if anyone can.

Wednesday 22 May

College. Uncle Jack for lunch. Papa had left early by aeroplane for Paris. It was terrible flying weather & I was so anxious. The news is unbelievably bad – one can only hang on by praying it will come all right.

Friday 24 May

I was so silly in the French lecture & made insulting remarks about French politicians chiefly Bonnet & was severely snubbed. Quite rightly too – I must try to curb my tongue.

Friday 31 May

The evacuation of Dunkirk continues – the epic of the 'little ships' that rescued the British army from either a shameful surrender or a bloody destruction. Stories of such incredible gallantry & courage.

Tuesday 4 June

Papa's speech in HoC truly magnificent – to my mind one of the greatest I have ever heard him make. 335,000 men evacuated.

> **'WE SHALL FIGHT ON THE BEACHES, WE SHALL FIGHT ON THE LANDING GROUNDS, WE SHALL FIGHT IN THE FIELDS AND IN THE STREETS, WE SHALL FIGHT IN THE HILLS; WE SHALL NEVER SURRENDER.'**
>
> Address given to the House of Commons, 4 June

Thursday 13 June

Papa went to France. I do <u>hate</u> it when he goes. We all have a ghastly premonition that the French are going to give in. O God France can't do it! She must go on she must go on.

Friday 14 June

Paris is declared an open town. Paris is taken. That dream city is sullied by the contaminating presence of the German army.

Out with Ally, Jean & Charles. Not a very gay party.

Saturday 15 June

We are staying at the Carlton while the move into Downing Street is going. The Chamberlains have left the place very dirty. Mummie has left Admiralty H[ou]se like a new pin.

Sunday 16 June

Mummie, Sarah, Nana and I went to Southwark Cathedral, where there was really a most beautiful choral communion. The sermon was the best I think I have _ever_ heard preached. The text was 'Why do ye fear? How is it that ye have no faith?' It was so comforting and filled me with courage and faith. I was so glad Sarah was there, because I think she has suffered so much from mental fear these last few months about what she should do if Vic decided to go to America. She is so gallant and so idealistic & I think she has worried terribly.

Monday 17 June

We are in – just – to No. 10.

Mummie had terrible row with David Margesson* whom Papa brought to lunch. I was most ashamed & horrified. Mummie & I had to go & have lunch at Carlton. Good food wrecked by gloom. Today came the announcement that following Reynaud's resignation and Pétain's assumption of leadership France asks for peace terms.

Oh _chère_ France – I can never love you one jot the less – but why have you failed in this. We have been expecting this – & yet now it _has_ come – we all feel shocked – bereaved of a great & brilliant ally. Now we are alone. May God be with us and grant that we shall not fail.

---

* The Chief Whip

Tuesday 18 June

We are more or less installed in Downing Street. Mummie has given me a lovely bedroom, sitting room & most spacious clothes closet (this latter most <u>Hollywood</u>).

Papa spoke in the House.* He was quite wonderful. I can't ever express my admiration and love for him, because they are unexpressable.

Had great fun being photographed by Antony Beauchamp†
– a friend of Jean's. I felt and looked a mass of affectation but HOW I enjoyed it.

Saturday 22 June

Lounged very late in bed, having read *The Constant Nymph* till nearly 2 o'clock. Then walked round garden & house most of morning with General Alexander. I think he is so charming & the morning passed very agreeably. General Ismay to lunch. Duncan & Diana, Brendan, Major Morton & Roger Lyttelton arrived after tea (both generals had departed). Papa however was woken out of his rest by very urgent & distressing news & rushed immediately back to London with Max B who had just arrived.

Bed & read. News bloody awful.

Sunday 23 June

A wrathful & gloomy breakfast downstairs. Church. French peace terms announced in evening. They are SHAMEFUL & cruel. Papa returned for lunch. Randolph & Pam, Stuffy

---

* 'Their Finest Hour' speech given in House of Commons
† Antony Beauchamp 1918–1957, society photographer, became second husband of Sarah Churchill in 1949

Dowding* & charming v good-looking young S African airman who in the raids of last week in one night [word missing] himself 2 German planes, he's got the DFC.

Tuesday 25 June

At about 1.10am the sirens went in London. I was awakened by Mummie putting the lights on & saying 'Quickly get up – there is a raid warning.' Well I didn't really feel frightened – just rather breathless & excited. We all bundled down into the shelter – except of course Papa & some of the staff who stayed & worked. In the shelter were Sir John Anderson†, Mr Greenwood & Mr Attlee. I did not feel very much in the mood for scintillating conversation & my dressing gown would keep bursting open – most tiresome. We all had tea – & finally got so sleepy that we all went to bed at about 3.15. 'All Clear' sounded at 4. I didn't hear it.

Wednesday 3 July

Great anxiety about future of French fleet. Chief of Air Staff, Sir Cyril Newall came to lunch & promised to send me a miniature of the scimitar which the Gurkhas use for next Monday!! . . . During dinner news kept on coming in of the action against the French fleet at Oran. It is so terrible that we should be forced to fire on our own erstwhile allies. Papa is shocked & deeply grieved that such action has been necessary.

---

* Air Chief Marshal Sir Hugh Dowding, 1882–1970, Air Officer Commanding-in-Chief Fighter Command
† Sir John Anderson 1882–1958, later 1st Lord Waverley, Home Secretary and Minister of Home Security, plus Arthur Greenwood 1880–1954, Minister without Portfolio

Thursday 4 July

This morning at the lecture M. Thierry told me – with grief written mostly plainly on his face – that he was entirely for the course the Gov. had taken over the fleet – & that it was the only thing that could be done. I am sure thousands of Frenchmen all over the world must feel the same.

This afternoon Mummie & Pam & I went to the House. It was a very sad day for Papa – he who has always loved & admired the French so much & worked so much for the entente cordiale. His statement was sombre – sorrowful, but resolved & encouraging. He explained the situation & the Government's action to a gloomy, crowded attentive house. When, after nearly an hour he sat down – the House began to cheer – the cheering grew & grew – until the House was on its feet.

Friday 5 July

Lunched with the Vansittarts* & Colly, who I find v agreeable. Found a simply hootsy-tootsy hat at Selfridges – 3 gns reduced to 30/- !! BARGAIN. Mummie says I may have it – Whoops! I am feeling a bit frightened about the weekend.

Saturday 6 July

[Launch of HMS *Gurkha*] Poured with rain all morning. Went to a music lesson & then left for Liverpool. I felt a little lonely starting out all by myself, but it all seemed rather like a very exciting adventure – going all alone to be with people I have never met & then – <u>the</u> moment, the first really big official occasion of my life.

---

* Sir Robert Vansittart 1881–1957, Chief Diplomatic Adviser to the Foreign Secretary, and his wife Sarita

The train was rather crowded & v stuffy. However we arrived eventually & Mr Johnson, the Managing Director of Cammell Laird, was there to meet me. He is very delightful. We then drove to his house across the river at Birkenhead, & we went through the Mersey Tunnel which is perfectly amazing & most exciting. Their house is <u>not</u> pretty – but <u>very</u> comfortable. '*Très cossue*'. Mrs Johnson is charming. After dinner Robbie their son (tall & good-looking & 28) arrived. I went to bed sleepy & happy.

Sunday 7 July

Slept late & after breakfast Mr J, Robbie & I went down to Cammell Laird's shipyards. We spent the whole morning walking round, & it was really thrilling & interesting. What a wonderful & romantic career a shipbuilder's is! How wonderful to feel that so much of one's country's life & greatness depends on the skill & craftsmanship of one's firm.

We saw many ships, both of war & merchantmen, & among them the *Thetis*, being reconditioned & renamed the *Thunderbolt*. It was very sad & it sent a chill through as I watched her lying there so quietly in the basin. And I thought of the grey seas running high in Liverpool Bay, & the tugs & destroyers standing round & 99 men sweating & gasping their life away in 40 foot of water.

I was shown my *Gurkha*. She looked such a beauty, such strong graceful lines. I'm sure no destroyer has ever looked <u>quite</u> so beautiful before!!

Monday 8 July

THE LAUNCH OF HMS *GURKHA*
I felt excited but quite calm this morning until about 11 when a fit of nerves overcame me. I couldn't have felt more nervous if it

had been my wedding day!! At about 11.45 I went & got dressed & felt better. I wore my tailored blue & white spotted dress with a white taffeta petticoat, white shoes, white gloves, white bag & my blue & white pill box hat. My gold & blue earrings & the little Gurkha badge given to me by Sir Cyril Newall.

We arrived at the shipyard at 12.45, & for ¾ hr people kept on arriving. The room was hot & I must say I felt pretty awful – but it was just emotion & excitement. The Controller [of the Navy] arrived & a <u>very</u>, <u>very</u> old Gurkha general with drooping white moustaches.

Tuesday 9 July

Long, hot dirty journey home. Mummie & Papa knocked endways by my diamonds!*

Monday 22 July

It is in the papers today about poor Commander Bickford[†]. It is practically certain that he & his crew & their *Salmon* are lost. God rest their souls in peace. I feel so sorry for his poor newly-wed wife. Poor girl. I must say he was one of the best-looking men I have ever seen – & such vitality & charm. I find it difficult to realise that he no longer exists – & that somewhere his dead body is being dashed &

---

* Mary was given a Victorian diamond necklace by the Cammell Laird shipbuilders

† Lieutenant-Commander Edward Bickford DSO, commanding officer of the submarine HMS *Salmon*, was quite well known to Churchill, and had visited the family several times. Concerned about his obvious fatigue, Churchill had urged him in February 1940 to take a post at the Admiralty for a time, but Bickford had preferred to return to active duty. He and his crew were lost off Norway, probably after the *Salmon* struck a mine

mouldered by the cold sea waves. It must be terrible knowing that you will never, never see or hear someone one
loves dearly again.

I don't think I have at all comprehended the unhappiness
this war is causing & is going to cause – it just shows how self-
centred I am & unintelligent too & yet I do firmly believe that
however great the suffering we must go through with it.

Thursday 25 July

General de Gaulle came to lunch with Madame de Gaulle.
Also Ivor*. The general is a stern, direct giant. We all thought
him very fine. He told us that Pétain combined: (1) Great age
(2) Ambition (3) (I <u>think</u>) Anti-British feeling. *La France n'existe
maintenant que dans les âmes des ses fils fidèles, et dans les coeurs de ceux
qui dans un pays étranger luttent toujours contre la tyrannie.*†

Sunday 28 July, Chartwell

Lunched with Horatia at Lady Oppenheimer's – such a nice
house & a heavenly garden . . . Went to bed early & wrote
v long letter to Mark [Howard]. At 9.50 two fairly loud explo-
sions took place, Nana & I both thought they were the AA
guns & descended hastily to find a sky lit with searchlight
beams & the constant drone of aeroplanes.

11.15 Violent explosion lasting about 2 or 3 seconds. House
trembled. Thought I heard enemy plane overhead – felt
frightened but excited & robust.

---

* Lord Ivor Spencer-Churchill or Ivor Guest (2nd Lord Wimborne)
† 'France now only exists in the souls of her faithful sons and in the
hearts of those in a foreign land who still fight against tyranny'

Monday 29 July

Learnt this morning that bombs fell at Edenbridge! No one hurt – my my my my.

Tuesday 30 July

Interview with Lady Reading.* She was absolutely charming to me – and talked to me in a most motherly fashion. She said I had to uphold so much 'precedent' – that I was the big girl of the future – that I should do a really good & useful job. I am to work for 3 months in the registry at the WVS . . . Left for Breccles. Good journey down, the last ½ hr of which was lightened by conversation with a charming soldier & airman. So glad to get to Breccles. Judy most welcoming.

Thursday 1 August

Searched out an evacuated hairdresser in the morning & in the afternoon we had our heads all toozled up in preparation for the evening.

Party given by officers of Watton aerodrome. Great fun & very crowded. Judy obstinately assured us all that it was sure to be evening dress & so we arrived all teed up to find about one other person in a long dress! Practically everyone was very tight† but so charming that it didn't matter at all.

---

* Stella, Lady Reading 1894–1971, chairman and founder of the Women's Royal Voluntary Service (WVS)
† Tipsy

Friday 2 August

Morning after the night before.

Monday 5 August

. . . Watton came and gave us the most superb aerial beating up that anyone could possibly conceive. A flight of Blenheims appeared & one after another swooped down to within 25 or 30 feet of the ground. We all nearly passed out with excitement. It lasted about 10 or 15 minutes! Only fly in the ointment was the escape of the horses! Rung up Robin – he had a wild & charming idea that he will be able to come tomorrow – it didn't materialise.

Tuesday 6 August

Horses retrieved from Wretham Hall by Judy & Kathryn. Rosemary & I & Cousin Venetia & evacuees helped to stook corn. 'Each stook stooked is a kick-in-the-pants for Hitler,' I said to myself encouragingly. Lovely picnic at the Mere. Donald & Ben Newlands came – we were joined later by Cecil Beaton,* who took photographs of us at tea in most unaesthetic attitudes, such as when we were cramming our mouths with drop scones (made there, yum yum!) & golden syrup.

Saturday 10 August, Chequers

Gossiped to Jock & wrote quantities of letters . . . Lunch – Mummie & Papa, Jock & me. I like Jock – he is very pleasant

---

* Cecil Beaton 1904–80, photographer, during the war worked for the Ministry of Information

– but I think he is very 'wet'. Mummie & Jock & I all climbed Coombe Hill in afternoon. Pug Ismay returned for tea & General de Gaulle also came for a while . . . Long talk with Mummie till midnight.

Sunday 11 August

AIR BATTLES. The conclave of generals dispersed soon after breakfast . . . An intensive air battle raged all day. The Huns are now coming in hundreds. May God be with us now.

Walked to Beacon Hill with Jock – discussed marriage – much the same views with regard to this knotty problem – on politics however we differ violently!*

Monday 12 August, London

Shopped & did jobs all morning. Mr Whitelaw Reid and Sir Sergison Brooke came to lunch. The former is Mrs Ogden Reid's son. She is the owner of the *New York Herald Tribune* – which in Papa's words has been running 'the most majestic campaign in the history of journalism' by directing American public opinion towards active participation in the war against Nazism. General Sergison Brooke is in charge of all the London area Home Guard – numbering about 50,000.

After lunch the General took us onto the parade where there is an army pigeon loft with about 50 carrier pigeons

---

* Jock Colville's diary records that: 'After lunch I was soundly beaten by Mrs C[hurchill] at croquet and then walked to the top of Beacon Hill with Mary. We sat on the top in the sunshine and prattled gaily, looking at the magnificent view of the plain below. Even though she takes herself a little seriously – as she confesses – she is a charming girl and very pleasant to look upon.'

which are being carefully trained, in case all communications should be severed. The man in charge is a corporal – and is a lion in the racing pigeon world! He won the *News of the World* contest in 1938!

Wednesday 14 August

Mummie paid a visit to the French at the White City. I went too, also little Ivor [Churchill] and Mrs Crawshay. It was terrible to see how lost they all look. Here we saw all the worst qualities of the French. Here we saw men who have lost their country – their faith – their '*amour propre*'. Miserable, disaffected! It made a most profound impression upon me. I felt I wanted to fling my arms round them and tell them how much we sympathise – how much we love them. I was quite overcome with the misery of it all.

Mlle de Gaulle came to lunch & spent afternoon with us. She is sweet, sixteen & beautifully mannered & hard work. I took her to see *Les 9 Célibataires* which made me laugh no end . . . Felt crushed and miserable in evening, also rather exhausted. Papa told us that a Blenheim squadron had been very badly knocked about.

Thursday 15 August

. . . It appears that 11 out of 12 from Watton didn't return. Hugh Painter, Ben Newlands, Donald Wellings are all safe. It is horrid to think that most of the boys at that lovely party aren't there any longer. Poor mothers & sisters & girl friends, I feel so much for you.

. . . On the midnight news we heard that over 88 Nazi raiders have met their doom. Thank God for the RAF.

Friday 16 August

Shopped in morning. Caught by sirens in Harrods at about 12.30. I wish Hitler could have seen the complete calm of the great crowd assembled on the ground floor. All Clear at 1.20 . . . Shopped again in pm. Went to Sarah's to pick up earrings – sirens again. Vic & I had tea & he drove me home. All Clear went about ½ hr later. I must say life is quite exciting. Yesterday's figures are now 169 with our own losses 34. The knights of King Arthur's Table assume a prosaic air in comparison with our pilots.

Saturday 17 August

Travelled to Minterne. Journey from Waterloo to Sherborne scheduled to take 3 hours, in fact took 5 hours. Owing to line being blown up between Andover & Basingstoke, the train was diverted & it went to Salisbury & Sherborne via SOUTHAMPTON!! We had a raid warning & had to pull blinds down – but it was a false alarm. Saw wreckage of 2 planes. Also got entangled in political discussion with acidulated old woman – who cast aspersions on the French – the old bitch! Also said we must remember the Germans are children of God. Also she was nauseatingly smug about the British. Ugh. Only Pam & Lady Digby at Minterne, which is very peaceful.

Sunday 18 August

A rather fascinating Brigadier Lumley & his wife came to lunch, also an old Blimp called General Ramsay, who nearly made Pam & myself sick by saying that 'the country had begun to go downhill ever since the working classes & the trades unions got power'. He however did tell a very amusing story about Papa. It was on a ship going to the South African war (I think) & a friend of Papa's was rather unpopular with the rest of the officers of the regiment; & so one night to pass the time the officers determined to try this fellow by Court Martial for 'being a cad & not being able to conceal it'. He was found guilty, & sentenced to have half his moustache shaved off. Papa had sat through his friend's trial in silence, but at the end remarked that the accused 'had one great advantage – he was tried by his peers'. Very Churchillian.

'NEVER IN THE FIELD OF HUMAN CONFLICT WAS SO MUCH OWED BY SO MANY TO SO FEW.'

Speech to the House of Commons, 20 August

Tuesday 20 August

. . . Mummie told me raid round Westerham had been quite bad & very alarming. Poor Mrs Beville was killed instantaneously by a bomb. Altogether about 131 bombs dropped near Westerham. One in belt at Chartwell. Felt very depressed. Hate the war.

Tuesday 27 August, Breccles

. . . After supper Papa rang Mummie & said that in Ramsgate 700 houses had been blown up by shelling & bombardment. Down here – despite air activity & especially during this lovely day one had almost forgotten the war.

Wednesday 28 August

. . . Mummie & Cousin Venetia left for London. We – that is – 'les girls' – spent most of the morning 'pansying up' for the luncheon at Watton officers' mess. The Wing Commander was perfectly charming & a lovely lunch had been arranged for us. After lunch – tennis – then tea – then highlight of the whole afternoon – we were shown over a Blenheim. It was thrilling – it made me feel very useless; there can never be a true measure of my love for England, because I am a woman – I feel passionately that I would like to pilot a plane – or risk everything for something that I believe in so entirely & love so very deeply. I may not be heroic for my country – I must lick down envelopes & work in an office & live a comfortable, happy life.

Friday 6 September

. . . Lovely day again. Papers full of Papa's speech – which seemed cheerful & confident. It is a long time, poor darling, since he has had anything as cheerful as the Anglo–American Pact to tell the House about.

Saturday 7 September

[Later note]: Beginning of Blitz (London bombed nightly until Nov 2). Invasion thought to be imminent.

Worked in the kitchen. Lunched at the Mere & bathed with some of the evacuees. It was so lovely – joie de vivre overcame vanity & I bathed minus a cap after Judy ducked me.

Tuesday 10 September

Kitchen work all morning. Then general pansying up for nothing in particular till lunch. A rainy, gloomy afternoon – News from London very bad – Judy and I unanimously decide that Hitler is bloody.

Saturday 14 September

The last day that I shall be 'sweet seventeen'! What a wonderful year it has been! I think it will always stand out in my memory. It has been very happy for me too – despite the misery & unhappiness in the world. I hope that does not mean that I am unfeeling – I really don't think I am, but somehow I just haven't been able to help being happy. On the other hand, I have felt things more acutely & impersonally – I think I have felt fear & anxiety & sorrow in small doses for the first time in my life. I do so love being young & I don't very much want to be 18. Although I often behave in a completely idiotic & 'haywire' fashion – yet I feel I have grown up quite a lot in the last year.

Sunday 15 September

[Later note] My 18th birthday. Climax of Battle of Britain.

Nana & I walked to Holy Communion. I prayed especially for courage & endurance, I feel I shall need both.

Mummie & Papa both gave me cheques for £10! What a <u>lovely</u> present. Sarah came down, bringing with her a lovely leather writing portfolio from her & Vic – chocolates & silk stockings from Phyllis . . . how sweet everyone is in these terrible times to remember me being 18! I do appreciate it terribly . . . Mummie had ordered a lovely cake for me despite raids! How sweet she is. It was <u>so</u> lovely having Nana with me for my birthday – it seemed almost like old times. I went to bed eighteen & <u>very</u> happy.

Saturday 21 September

All this week I have been working with WVS to help refugees. This is the twentieth century – Look on London – look at the crowds of homeless, destitute & weary people in Aylesbury alone. I have seen more suffering & poverty this week than ever before.

I cannot find words to describe my feelings about it. I only know I am moved to a greater & wider realisation of the suffering war brings. I only know that I have learnt more about human suffering & anxiety than ever before. O God be with the homeless & anxious. I have seen so many worried & sad & lost expressions – & a great deal of courage & optimism & good sense.

Monday 23 September

Today the papers are full of the torpedoing of the liner carrying children to Canada.* 89 children killed. May God rest their souls, and help us to wipe the curse of Hitler & the vilest burden mankind has ever borne from the world.

Thursday 26 September

A land mine having landed in Walton Grange garden – the WVS are refugees. Only 19 hurt. The withdrawal from

* SS *City of Benares*, torpedoed by a German submarine with heavy loss of life, including 77 evacuated children

Dakar is made known.* I don't see how in the course of having to make endless decisions one can avoid some mistakes. But <u>was</u> it a mistake – or was it a muddle *sur le champ* – between Gen de Gaulle & our people? O God – somehow this minor reversal has cast a shadow over everything. I do hope the government will pull through – All my feelings are so mixed. Of course I want Papa to pull it off but not <u>only</u> for personal reasons – but <u>also</u> if he went WHO is to come??

Friday 27 September

. . . <u>133</u> Nazis shot down. All today seemed overcast with the gloom of the Dakar affair. It certainly does seem that there was misjudgement somewhere. Oh I am so anxious for Papa. He loves the French so much, & I know longs for them to do something grand & spectacular – but I fear he will take rather a bump over this. The papers exhibit varying degrees of rage & disapproval. The *Mirror* – hysterical & fierce queries & judgements. 'The Gallipoli Touch?' Oh – how unkind. The *Mail & Express*: More moderate – but demanding explanation. The *Sketch* – 'whose responsibility?'. *Telegraph* – calm – considered – awaiting full statement.

Saturday 28 September

. . . Dakar 'horoosh' seems to have quieted down today.

---

* Unsuccessful Allied attack on the port of Dakar (then part of French West Africa), which attempted to replace the Vichy French administration with the Free French under de Gaulle

Tuesday 1 October

Am invited to dinner with officers for tomorrow. Yippeeee.

Hospital in the morning. Mrs Dixon helped me. Felt very young, inefficient & miserable. Saw quite clearly that library is full time job* – quandary & dismay, because I grieve to relinquish useful work in Aylesbury . . . Am to remain with WVS but work whole time at library . . . wish <u>passionately</u> I could do both. Oh please why aren't there 10 days in the week & 2 of me? Feel faintly pathetic – I want to help so much – & yet I really think I have done best thing. Oh dear how bloody life is.

Thursday 3 October

<u>Cabinet</u> changes. CHAMBERLAIN resigns. He is very ill – I am sorry for that but I am glad he has gone at last.† I am an inveterate – unforgiving – unforgetting contre-Munichoise‡. Even more delighted that that bloody old fool Lord Caldecote (known to some irreverents as Caligula's Horse) has been booted out.

---

* Red Cross library for patients at Stoke Mandeville hospital

† Neville Chamberlain has remained a member of Churchill's war cabinet and is still leader of the Conservative Party. He is suffering from the bowel cancer that will kill him a little more than a month later. His resignation from the government allows Churchill to carry through a reconstruction that strengthens his position. Lord Caldecote is sacked as Lord Chancellor, but it was his previous appointment by Chamberlain in 1936 as Minister for the Co-ordination of Defence (a job coveted at that time by Churchill), and for which he was felt by many to be so patently unsuitable, that Churchill's circle often described as the most remarkable appointment since the Roman Emperor Caligula had made his horse a consul.

‡ i.e. against the Munich Pact of 1938

Tuesday 8 October

. . . Very agreeable dinner party in the officers' mess brought to an abrupt close by the swishing, crescendoing clatter of a bomb uncomfortably near. Everyone ducked ineffectually – & waited – it seemed an age – before a comparatively small bump – found us rather breathless but intact & morale on all sides good. They were all sweet to me – and I was feeling terribly excited & rather breathless – but thank God – not all white & trembly as I so often have imagined & feared I would be. We all went to the slits [trenches] – very muddy & spoilt my suède shoes. No more excitements SO FAR – but I was escorted home soon after. Damn those Bloody Huns for breaking up an enjoyable party.

Wednesday 9 October

First thing that greeted my eyes this morning was LARGE crater about 100 yds from the Mess tent where I dined last night! I am not feeling so ignored by the war.

Thursday 10 October

4.40 am WINSTON CHURCHILL junior arrived! Hooray. Pam weak but happy. Baby not at all weak & only partially happy!

Monday 21 October

. . . Tonight Papa spoke to France.* So frankly – so encouragingly – so nobly & tenderly. I hope his voice reached many of

---

* Broadcast 'Dieu protège la France'

55

them, and that its power & richness will have brought them new hope & faith.

'*Aux armes citoyens! Formez vos bataillons, Marchons, marchons, Qu'un sang impur Abreuve nos sillons.*'* Dear France – so great & glorious, be worthy of your noblest sons & of that high cause you twice bled for – Liberty.

Thursday 31 October

Papa said the other day – 'It is a very remarkable thing that the young should be so much braver than the old – for they have so much more to lose – but it is so.'

Wednesday 6 November

President Roosevelt elected for third term. Glory Hallelujah!! A delicious poke in the snoot for Hitler.

Monday 11 November

. . . There was no armistice service this year – no 2 minutes silence. But poppies were sold everywhere & I think everyone was thinking of the millions whose great struggle came to an end 22 years ago.

Sunday 24 November

Papa said: 'Of all wars, this is the most unnecessary. In 1933 or 1934 a dispatch would have stopped the German rearmament.

---

* Line from 'La Marseillaise', the French national anthem, 'To arms citizens! Form your batallions, March, march, Let impure blood water our furrows'

In 1935 an ultimatum – in 1936 general mobilisation of France & England.' After the war – Papa said he had considered very seriously the formation of training colleges for those who embarked on a political career – for he considers that the quality of the personnel of the House has deteriorated.

Sunday 1 December

Drove home very early for little Winston's christening . . . Have rather sore throat.

Monday 9 December

The others went up early – leaving myself, Mr Seal & Papa to lunch. Papa was very worried and preoccupied and told me that at dawn this morning an attack was launched by the British troops in Libya. 'Pray,' he said 'for the victory of British arms.' I prayed most fervently. Very anxious waiting.

Wednesday 11 December

. . . Wrote out Christmas cards – I took more trouble than I ever have before with them – somehow there's more point now that I am separated from most of my friends & acquaintances.

Mummie rang up at about 7.45 and told me that our army has had a victory – Sidi Barrani is taken & many prisoners.[*] Thank God – thank God – it is too wonderful – after this dreary winter with so many blows – I could weep with excitement.

---

[*] Port on the Mediterranean coast of Egypt, recaptured from the Italian 10th Army

Mummie tells me that Papa conceived this campaign last July – and has been planning and developing it ever since. I am glad that it is a success so far anyway – of course for England's sake, but a little bit for my darling father as well. There have been so many buffets and burdens to bear – so much to discourage and dismay – so many heart-blows – but now this – ah dear God – it is wonderful.

How <u>passionately</u> I long for the day of Victory.

Thursday 12 December

Work. Papers full of the <u>victory</u> at Sidi Barrani. Nana returned to London. Mummie and Papa came – also Jock. Papa tells us that approximately <u>30,000</u> prisoners have been taken!!

Our joy and elation is however a little darkened by the sudden sad death of Lord Lothian.* He will be a great loss. At dinner (Mummie went to bed with sore throat) Papa was pondering who to send to Washington – names mentioned were – Lloyd George, Lord Camborne, Mr Robert Hudson, Archie Sinclair, Vansittarts –

Papa in very bad mood over food and of course I couldn't control him & he was very naughty & rushed out & complained to the cook about the soup, which he (truthfully) said was tasteless. I fear the domestic apple-cart may have been upset! Oh dear!

---

* Lord Lothian had been the British Ambassador to Washington DC. He was ultimately replaced by Lord Halifax, the former foreign secretary and Churchill's main rival for the premiership in May 1940

Tuesday 24 December

Day off. Drove with Mummie to Hitchin. Lunched with Pam, took babies their presents. Party arrived in evening. Diana – Duncan – Sarah – Pamela – Papa – Mr Martin*. Everyone in good spirits. No reports of any air land or sea activity. <u>So</u> wonderful to have a family party. I have never had the family feeling so strongly.

Wednesday 25 December

This was one of the happiest Christmases I can remember. Despite all the terrible events going on around us. It was not happy in a <u>flamboyant</u> way. But I've never before seen the family look so happy – so united – so sweet. We were complete, Randolph & Vic having arrived this morning. I have never felt the 'Christmas feeling' so strongly. Everyone was kind – lovely – gay. I wonder if we will all be together next Christmas? I pray we may. I pray also next year may be happier for more people.

---

* Sir John Miller Martin, 1904–1991. Private Secretary to Churchill, 1940–45 (Principal Private Secretary from 1941)

1941

Gunner Girl

'When I am old I shall remember all this wonderful life.'

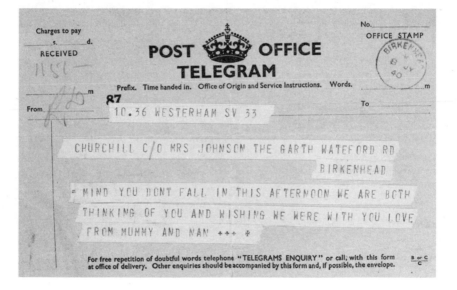

POST OFFICE TELEGRAM

Prefix. Time handed in. Office of Origin and Service Instructions. Words.

Charges to pay
s. d.
RECEIVED

87

From

10.36 WESTERHAM SV 33

To

OFFICE STAMP

CHURCHILL C/O MRS JOHNSON THE GARTH WATEFORD RD
BIRKENHEAD

= MIND YOU DONT FALL IN THIS AFTERNOON WE ARE BOTH
THINKING OF YOU AND WISHING WE WERE WITH YOU LOVE
FROM MUMMY AND NAN +++ +

For free repetition of doubtful words telephone " TELEGRAMS ENQUIRY " or call, with this form at office of delivery. Other enquiries should be accompanied by this form and, if possible, the envelope.

B or C
C

C hequers in 1941 is where Churchill likes to hold court at weekends and Mary becomes a willing participant in his international intrigues. His focus is on securing greater American involvement in the conflict. Mary is a witness to her father's verbal courting of President Roosevelt through his speeches and an assistant in his dinner diplomacy with the president's emissaries – Harry Hopkins, Averell Harriman and Gilbert Winant.

But there are also more personal intrigues. The diary for the second quarter of 1941 is dominated by Mary's lightning courtship, betrothal and break-up with Viscount Duncannon, eldest son of the 9th Earl of Bessborough. The relationship develops and then founders as Clementine and Pamela force Mary to confront and rethink her emotions with the somewhat unlikely aid of Lord Beaverbrook and Averell Harriman. Such concerns of the heart occur against the backdrop of bad news in the Balkans and Greece and do not stop her accompanying her father on a moving trip to Swansea and Bristol.

There is a palpable sense in her summer entries of trying to hold on to the luxuries and entertainments of pre-war life. And yet, as the moving account of a visit to her beloved but neglected Chartwell makes clear, Mary is also increasingly aware that life has changed, possibly forever. She admits to feeling 'numb' 'soulless' and 'unreal'.

Her day-to-day life alternates between mundane war work and a presence at great events. She is at Chequers on Sunday 22 June when her father broadcasts his response to the German invasion of the Soviet Union.

Then comes a defining moment. Torn between her duty to her parents and her desire to do something herself, Mary's decision to join up marks a major turning point in her life. Quoting from her diary entry for 6 October 1941, she will later reflect, 'I firmly averred that "as long as I live I shall never never regret joining the ATS" – and I never did.' The Auxilary Territorial Service had been formed in 1938 with the aim of allowing women to perform a variety of roles that freed up men for front line service, including working on anti-aircraft batteries. By the summer of 1941 it has been granted full military status but is still manned by volunteers.

Mary and her cousin Judy undertake their basic training for the ATS at a camp in Aldermaston, just outside Reading in rural Berkshire. Mary has a clear wish to remain anonymous, which is frustrated when her presence is seen as a potential recruitment tool. She struggles with the press interest once it is revealed that the daughter of the prime minister has enlisted. A month later, the two new recruits are transferred to Park Hall Camp outside Oswestry in Shropshire for anti-aircraft training.

No diary survives between October and December 1941. During this period Mary and Judy successfully complete a course at Park Hall Camp to become non-commissioned officers with supervisory roles (initially lance corporals with the potential to become corporals and sergeants). They endure a period of isolation during an outbreak of cerebral spinal meningitis in their hut but survive unscathed and are posted to 469 Heavy (Mixed) Anti-Aircraft Battery in Enfield on the outskirts of London.

Thursday 2 January

Work. Jean and Ally [Forbes] came for the night. Jean was suffering slightly from 'bomb blast' – as far as I could make out had been rushing round with unexploded fire bomb in her bicycle basket. Ally was charming & at his best – gay – witty – he can be most captivating.

In retrospect I think I was in a trying & tiresome mood. I must try to be a little less coarse – a little less noisy. It is this awful shy-making (to myself & to other people) show off – centre of attention complex. I sometimes dislike myself quite intensely.

Friday 3 January

Work. Ally & Jean left after lunch, Nana left early in the morning. Snow lying lightly on the ground. Roads rather bad. Mummie & Papa came in evening.

Fiona [Forbes] & I had a long gossip in the bath. She was feeling 'mis'* & I did try to encourage her. I so long for her to be a terrific success and I know she will be. She has so much to make her one.

Sunday 5 January

<u>CAPTURE OF BARDIA</u>†
Long sleep. Breakfast in bed. Fetched Aunt Nellie from Long Crendon. Norwegian PM to lunch & interpreter. After lunch we were in the long gallery. Papa came in & said 'News from the battlefront.' This telegram said northern section of Bardia

---

* Family slang for miserable
† Capture of the Italian fortress of Bardia in Libya by Australian forces

defences pierced by Australians. Large numbers of prisoners. Only perimeter defences were holding out.

. . . At dinner came news – Bardia village taken – further advanced. After dinner came the final <u>triumphant</u> communiqué. All resistance in Bardia has ceased – 25,000 prisoners – including 2 corps commanders – & it is rumoured one bishop accompanied by 3 nuns!!!!!! This is WONDERFUL. Thank God. After so many blows & disappointments it is glorious to have a victory . . . I shall never forget this evening – <u>January 5th 1941, The Capture of Bardia</u>.

Wednesday 8 January

Fiona left. It was such fun having her. Work. Hospital dance in the evening. Wore my new cherry red dress with silver embroidered belt. Danced a <u>great</u> deal. Enjoyed myself tremendously. Oh I do <u>love</u> dancing.

Saturday 11 January

Dark cold morning. Ann forgot to call me – slept late – left in awful rush at 8.10. Despite icy roads – late start & diversion 'cos of bombs caught train. Sukie* was with me.

Arrived for first time in London since August – feeling strange – country-cousinish & very flustered. And as I drove through the well remembered streets – and saw the scars & wounds I felt I loved London very deeply. Shorn of her smartness – in wartime attire – I suddenly loved her very much. I have had that feeling once or twice before – once when I bicycled on a hot brilliant summer afternoon into Hyde Park – and I leant on the bridge & watched the people in the boats

---

* Mary's poodle

– & then when I stopped under the trees & there was a band playing. And once again I can remember when I turned on the bridge in St James's Park & saw the Whitehall roofs rising above the trees in the evening sun like distant domes of a magic city – And once again when I was sitting on the window-sill of my room in Admiralty House reading & I suddenly longed for the country – & looking up over St James's Park I suddenly saw the perfect beauty of the tree at the water's edge – all these times I have suddenly loved London. Otherwise I have rather wearied of her – the misery of a rainy cold day in London – the wearisomeness of heat in London. And the NOISE. But all the same despite myself I have to love her.

Not feeling <u>very</u> well. Shopped with Nana. Caught train. Arrived early in afternoon at Petworth – to find an enormous house party . . . Violette* was in excellent form dressed in a pale blue v necked jumper – loaded with jewellery & wearing scarlet corduroy slacks!! . . . Everyone went to a movie – but I was rather cold & tired so I went & meditated in my room which was ancestral & <u>bloody</u> cold. Had tea in lovely teashop in Petworth. Dressed for ball! I wore my new cherry red with the silver-embroidered belt & diamond (paste!) earrings. Feeling better – slight cold – cold & icy outside. Large dinner party – in the middle of which **WHO** should appear but **ANDY!**† Hooray!! Well the dance was nothing short of heaven. Positively pre-war. Oh the GLAMOUR of not having tickets – & its not being in a hotel. My III private dance! I felt <u>incredibly</u> gay – I waltzed with Jean-Pierre [Montaigne] incorrectly wildly & very fast – great fun. I missed very few dances – I had mad fun & enjoyment. Knew quite a lot of people.

---

* Lady Leconfield, Mary's hostess
† Lieutenant Andrew Drummond-Hay of the Coldstream Guards, 1910–1942

Friday 31 January

London with Nana. Heard guns!! (First time for me). Judy came to lunch. Alert sounded – also roof spotter's signal. Quite heavy barrage. Awfully exciting.

Saturday 1 February

Had moments of panic – but not as bad as I had feared.* Notes or not? Manuscript or not? . . . Eventually <u>no</u> notes were decided upon – only a card with the technical data re savings on it. I wore – my summer ermine coat & Olga Polowski hat. Blue dress with pale blue collar. <u>Elegant</u> silk stockings & <u>very</u> elegant gloves & blue shoes & my blue bag with the naval crest on it. Gold flower brooch & blue & gold earrings. Signet ring – and oh – just – a – mere – soupçon – of Amberdew scent. MOST sophisticated.

Quite a crowd on the green. And 2 terrifying rows of soldiers drawn up. It was so lovely seeing old familiar faces I almost forgot my fright – & then suddenly it was time. Mr Streatfeild† led me out – there was very subdued applause. Then the soldiers were brought to attention – terrific yellings & shoutings – and suddenly I didn't feel nervous – just a queer feeling of tenseness & excitement – and I could not help feeling mighty proud of Papa – because it was all for him. And it made me determined to do <u>him</u> credit – and so to behave that he would not have to make excuses for his daughter. Then 2 RASC & Royal Fusiliers officers saluted me & called me 'Madam'. And I had to inspect their men which was <u>most</u> impressive & I hope I did it right. Then I climbed onto the

---

* Mary was opening Westerham War Weapons Week
† Presumably a local official

platform – & a little Brownie with a heavenly aspect presented me with a bouquet. Then we sang 4 verses of O God our help. Only unfortunately Mr Streatfeild had told the band to play 3, so he and I sang a duet of the last verse!

Then Mr Streatfeild & Mr Fox made speeches. And then it was me. And strangely I didn't feel nervous – just elated & determined. My voice sounded far away. It was so quiet & peaceful there – & so familiar – my home town & all my friends. And I really & truly meant & felt every word I said. Then it was over – & I signed my defence bond – Nana had given me a wonderful 'nest-egg' which I duly put into defence bonds. Then there were three cheers & quite loud too. And then it was over. Everyone was so sweet – all my friends – people I have known always – but the words I shall <u>never</u> forget – not so long as I live – were said to me by Sir Percy Mackinnon. I write them here in all humility. He said: 'It was worthy of your father.' What higher praise could I wish? And so after all my aim for today was accomplished.

'GIVE US THE TOOLS, AND WE WILL FINISH THE JOB.'

Radio broadcast, 9 February

Sunday 9 February

Drove home – Lucia* to lunch. Also the de Gaulles (v late) & Mr Justice Oliver. Archie [Sinclair] & Marigold staying. Papa was preoccupied & 'with' speech.

Papa's speech this evening was <u>magnificent</u>.

---

* Lucia Lawson, a friend of Mary

Monday 10 February, Liverpool

Newspapers say Papa's speech was his best since he became PM. They are full of just & jubilant praise. Left for London early. On arrival in 10 Downing St found Lucy had packed shockingly – MOST vexatious . . . Received <u>poisonous</u> letter from some idiotic man – burnt it.

Set out with Pamela as my duenna for Liverpool. Good but long journey. Went to Knowsley. Lord Derby gay & charming. Lady Derby <u>very</u> deaf, but very kind & much less frightening (so far!) than I had imagined.

Am in bed covered with fascinatingly elegant bed spread of white taffeta with pale blue garlands on it which have run slightly – giving a lovely misty effect. Must go to sleep to gather strength for tomorrow!!!

Tuesday 11 February

Set out at 11 – after careful titivating. Pamela & I were shown round the C of E cathedral by Dean Dwelly. Sir George Scott* was asked what he had in mind when he designed the cathedral. He answered 'The majesty of God.' And that is what I felt when I entered this most beautiful building – the sense of the majesty of God. This is one of the most beautiful & impressive sights I have ever seen. We climbed right to the top – and I helped to lay a stone. Then – scurrying down ladders precariously placed over the edge of an abyss – Pamela & I rushed off to Cammell Laird.

HMS *Gurkha* is a wonderful ship – her Commander is delighted with her – & certainly – from the numbers of guns – torpedoes – depth charges & what not – she looks very ferocious. May God bless her & all who sail in her – may she help

---

* Mary means Giles Gilbert Scott

to bring Victory & Peace nearer . . . after lunch we spent a long time going over the ship. Pam & I started up the engines for the first time. Then left – regretfully – 'my' grand destroyer – I am SO proud & honoured to be connected with her.

Back to Adelphi – then after slight hitch – to Communal Feeding Centre – then to tea with Sir Sidney Jones (the Lord Mayor). And finally exhausted but happy back to Knowsley. I do find I get internal panic when doing anything formal – & out of shyness find it <u>so</u> difficult to know what to say to people when going round. I'm so desperately afraid of giving myself airs & being <u>THE END.</u> But I fear I'm not very good at sort of going round places & meeting people. I do feel shy – but I want to do it well – for Papa's sake. It is a small service – but one I should like to render him.

Thursday 13 February

. . . News all these days is very worrying – I feel the war is just about to begin in reality. May God be with us.

Saturday 15 February, Ditchley*

Matinée grasse for Mummie & me. Went for walk with Mummie. News in papers about our paratroops landing in Italy. Apparently there was a hitch – anyway it's clear it was rather a flop. Roger Keyes† in state of semi-hysteria over it &

---

* Ditchley Park, Oxfordshire, home of Ronald Tree MP and used by Churchill as a country retreat during the war, as Chequers was thought to be too visible from the air, especially when the moon was full
† Admiral of the Fleet Sir Roger Keyes, 1872-1945, Special Liaison Officer to King Leopold III of Belgium, 1940, and Director of Combined Operations, 1940–41

has sent in his resignation [as director of combined operations]. Really my poor darling Papa is not <u>only</u> plagued by the <u>Germans</u>.

Cousin Venetia arrived. Diana [Cooper] looking <u>very</u> bizarre in plum corduroy slacks & shirt, scarf & hat in chiaroscu[ro] of mauve which made her look faintly violet coloured in her beautiful face. Walk with Nancy [Tree] and Mummie in afternoon – Mr David Bruce arrived (good-looking – charming & intelligent). Sarah & Judy rode over from Blenheim. General talk after tea.

After dinner saw lovely films. *Escape* (v good!) – a wonderful news film of the return of Haile Selassie to Abyssinia – very moving. German propaganda film (for Portugal). It showed the defeat of France. The swastika fluttering over Versailles – O France – where is your soul – your genius. Are you indeed broken – worn out – And yet I dream of the tricolore over Versailles again. '*Que Dieu protège la France*'.

Sunday 16 February

Went to Blenheim for lunch with Mummie . . . Was ragged about my photographs. I am likened to Grandmama Jennie Jerome – so far so good – BUT – they say 'we print a photograph to show striking likeness' – the said photograph is one taken when she was at LEAST 53 & rather tipsy looking. WE ARE NOT AMUSED!

Sunday 2 March, Chequers

Church. Long walk to monument with Mr Menzies* – I think he's delightful – just couldn't be nicer. Dr Dalton to lunch.

---

* Robert Menzies 1894–1978, prime minister of Australia

Papa talked largely about socialism & capitalism – he stressed how important private enterprise is. 'I'm afraid' he said 'you will not get much work without profit.' Discussed nationalisation of railways for instance. Papa said he had been very much for it – but found it had answered little better – in fact considerably worse (from point of view of strikes, efficiency etc).

Mr Menzies said that in Australia the railways were already nationalised but he had no doubt under private enterprise they would run more efficiently & profitably – especially as at the moment they rather 'fell between 2 stools' for railways <u>are</u> nationalised & road transport is <u>not</u>. The latter [therefore] is always trying to cut out the former – often with considerable success.

Saturday 8 March

To London. Shopped happily with Judy. Bought pretty night-dresses & lovely dressing gown. I do find London shops <u>so</u> gay & pretty now . . . Rehearsal for Queen Charlotte's [Ball]. I must say we all agreed this year's 'debs' aren't much to write home about. Tea with Ally at the Dorchester. Great fun. Manicure. Dressing for the Ball!! Wore blue chiffon. Lucia looked LOVELY & glamorous. <u>Air raid</u>. My first London blitz.

3 loud bangs before going down to dinner. But in the Ballroom one could hear nothing. There everything was gay & carefree & happy. It seemed so easy to forget – there in the light & warmth & music – the dark deserted streets – the barking of the guns – the hundreds of men & women ready at their posts – the bombs & death & blood. Somehow these last did not seem real – of course it is only a terrible dream, a figment of the imagination. But no – it is real – the Café de

Paris hit* – many fatal & serious casualties. They were dancing & laughing just like us. They are gone now in a moment
from all we know to the vast, infinite unknown. Oh it was so
gay our party . . . & suddenly it all seemed wrong & a mock-
ery. But Tom said – 'If all those people who have been killed
at the Café suddenly came back & saw us all here – they
would all say "Go on – strike up the band – carry on London".'

We danced on – we laughed & joked – we enjoyed ourselves.
The Duchess of Richmond's ball <u>before</u> Waterloo was nothing
to this. This was the ball <u>at</u> Waterloo – & we were the soldiers.
I suddenly thought of those lines – 'to court wild laughter in
the jaws of death'†. All Clear . . . – Bed 4.30. This is one of the
most dramatic & ironical evenings of my life. It is the night of
March 11th as I write this – & overhead for nearly an hour
there has been the throb & purr of enemy planes going North
– I cannot stop them. I can but listen & pray for those to whom
these planes mean death & cold – blood & tears.

Saturday 15 March

M Dupuy – Canadian minister to Vichy to lunch. V interesting & sad. I gather – Great interest displayed throughout
France in GB's war news & BBC programmes. Increasing
pro-British feeling – food scarce. More & more young men
from 'occupied' France are crossing the frontier & joining
Gen Weygand in N. Africa. Petrol v scarce (on road from
Vichy to Marseilles he only met 2 cars in a day).

Most beautiful Spring day – balmy. Papa looked at some of
the new guns defending Chequers, which is becoming more

---

* 34 people were killed when the Café de Paris suffered a direct hit
† From Shakespeare's *Loves Labour Lost*, Act V Scene II, 'To more wild
laughter in the throat of death?'

& more fortified. In evening arrived Nancy Tree & Beatrice Eden (both suffering from ill effects of flu), Mr Winant, American ambassador, Mr Averell Harriman. Both good-looking – charming & most inspiring.

Monday–Tuesday 17–18 March

Work *comme toujours*. The weekend was thrilling. Here was the hub of the Universe. For many billions of destinies may perhaps hang on this new 'axis' – this Anglo–American, American–Anglo friendship. Papa recently recited Arthur Clough's 'Say not the struggle naught availeth' – I did not know it before, but I think it is a very beautiful poem. 'And not through Eastward windows only, When daylight comes, comes in the light, In front the sun mounts slow, how slowly, But Westward, look, the land is bright'.*

Thursday 27 March

1. The Revolution in Yugoslavia, wherein 'Yugoslavia has found her soul'.
2. The capitulation to the Imperial forces of KEREN & HARAR.†
3. The signing of the Anglo–American agreement on the naval bases

What a day. It seemed quite an ordinary day for us here – work – wards – & then in the evening this wonderful news.

---

* Churchill would later use this quotation in his broadcast of 27 April 1941. The lines can be seen gestating here

† The capture of Keren in Eritrea and Harar in Abyssinia, from Italian forces

Saturday 29 March

. . . Arrived at Stansted at tea time. The party consisted of Lord Bessborough – g. looking, delightful – Lady Bessborough – v beautiful & charming – Moyra [Ponsonby] – attractive – I was rather alarmed by what I had previously been told – but she turned out to be the best of company, reserved – but gay. Eric Duncannon* – good-looking in rather a lyrical way – very beautiful grey, wideset eyes, melodious voice. Charming & easy. Capt Lagimodière (believe it or not but it's true – & subsequently became the 'Maginot Line') – good-looking Canadian but faintly dumb.

'*La jeunesse*' proceeded to a RAF party at Tangmere. Our set out was delayed by sudden activity of guns etc. However after it had quieted down we went. The party was the greatest fun. But it was distinctly an orgy & rather bizarre – But in one way or another a good time was had by all! Eric & I got whisked off to supper with a boring, tight station commander (Redhill) & his partner. A highly coloured, dark haired young woman who kept on saying to s.comm† 'Oh Barry . . . etc'. I must say I frankly thought she was the end & couldn't think of a word to say. Eric & I both were seized with subdued giggles. I was introduced to the famous legless Sq. Leader Bader.‡ He's marvellous – I danced with him & he's so extraordinarily good. He is exemplary of the triumph of life & mind & personality over matter. Danced a lot with Eric . . . Lights

---

* Frederick Ponsonby, Viscount Duncannon 1913–93, later 10th Earl Bessborough
† Station commander
‡ Douglas Bader 1910–1982, British WWII RAF ace who had lost both legs in a crash before the war, played by Kenneth More in *Reach for the Sky* (1956)

failed in middle – not an altogether unwelcome event to many I think.

Sunday 30 March

Stupendous news about a great victory over the Italian navy.* 3 8" gun cruisers sunk, 2 destroyers sunk, 1 Littorio class battleship badly smashed. After the 1st National Day of Prayer we were delivered from Dunkirk & now in a week – what news – may God be praised. All day we felt jubilant – lovely day. Walked in morning. Long walk with Eric in pm. I think he is charming. He said as he left 'May I ring you up?' I do hope he will.

This news is too wonderful. But also there is a squalid incident off Algiers with French ships – they seem not to have fought with the Germans half as bitterly as they now seem to attack us. O France – France where is your greatness – your genius – your SOUL?

Monday 31 March

Clear, cold day. Left Stansted after a weekend I enjoyed completely. Arrived in time for lunch at No. 10. Mr Loveday (Principal, Bristol University), Papa, Mummie & self. Papa read us Sir A. Cunningham's report on the Battle of the Mediterranean.

Speaking of Chamberlain Papa said 'He knew nothing about Europe & nothing about war – & he had to deal with both.' One could not find a more generous explanation – nor think of a deeper condemnation.

---

* Battle of Cape Matapan

Thursday 3 April

Bed 4 – Called 7. Hey diddle diddle! Rushed madly & (alas) unavailingly to catch 8.15. Caught 9.04. Nana met me, went straight to work. Had letter from Eric – a very sweet letter at that. Now – Mary – take a hold on yourself – my little plum. 'Went to it' like mad. Did wards very thoroughly. Very early bed.

Friday 4 April

We have evacuated Benghazi. Depression.

Saturday 5 April

. . . Letter from Eric inviting me to dine next Thursday or Friday. O heaven . . . Papa not too depressed about Benghazi. Further successes in Eritrea. Rumours that invasion of Yugoslavia will start tomorrow morning.

Sunday 6 April

Bitterly cold . . . Eric rang me up & I talked to him for about 20 mins: he is v charming I think & has a very beautiful voice. Oh dear – have I fallen or have I? Anyway, DV* he's coming to drinks on Thursday . . . Saw photographs of new bomb. V satisfactory – 20th Century – o glorious civilisation!

---

* God willing (from Latin, *Deo volente*)

Monday 7 April

Family & guests left. I went to say goodbye to Papa – he was sitting in his room reading some papers. He looked tired, I thought – grim – sorrowful. He told me he thought this would be a week of bad news. He told me to keep up high morale. Darling – I will try, perhaps I can help in that way. It is thwarting to feel so ardently about our cause & yet to be so unavailing. And so weak – for I – who am really very happy & comfortable – have gay friends and rather a butterfly disposition – little or no cares – allow myself to feel despondent – gloomy.

I did a lot of work & stayed to lunch in the library. I wish I knew whether I am in love with Eric rather – or whether I simply have a crush.

. . . News not too bad really. It is terrible to feel that we hold a great responsibility for all that is happening now in Greece & Yugoslavia & the other Balkans. They might have stood together if only France & England hadn't gone around putting them all wrong & then backing out of real moral obligations. According to Richard Stanley Lord Baldwin said the other day (R was present) 'In 1934 I saw Ribbentrop & I saw what they were up to – so I began rearming the country.' <u>NO COMMENT</u>.

11 April, Good Friday

Tour of Swansea. The devastation in parts of the town is ghastly. Never have I seen such courage – love – cheerfulness & confidence expressed as by the people today. Wherever he went they swarmed around Papa, clasping his hand, patting him on the back, shouting his name. Not just fairweather friends these – he has through many years earned their gratitude – won their confidence – been rewarded with their love. It is rather frightening how terribly they depend on him. It was wonderful their spirit 'grim & gay'. The triumph of the Spirit of Man above the fear & squalor of material sorrows.

News today: 1. Hungary stabs Yugoslavia in the back. 2. 10 German planes shot down in Libya. 2 of our own missing. 3. During the last 4 nights 38 raiders have been destroyed over here (30 by fighters).

Duncan is v badly injured – it will be many months before he can walk. He may even have to have a foot amputated. What a cruel blow! Just when he was doing so brilliantly. Saw Kenneth Post in pm at demonstration (I cannot write about the latter – except that it was interesting – exhausting & deafening).

Saturday 12 April

Bristol. A cold grey morning – men & women going to their daily work – not after a quiet night's sleep – but after a night made ghastly by the enemy. Rather strained pale faces – weary – quiet.

As we drove through the battered streets – people turned in surprise – & slowly through their sorrow – weariness & fatigue broke a smile & a light of faith – & joy. We went to the newly bombed areas – rest centres & finally came to Bristol University. The ceremony was most moving. The dignity of the proceedings – the brilliant colours of the robes. And after-wards – when Papa as Chancellor had conferred on Dr Conant (in absentia), Mr Winant & Mr Menzies degrees – he drove away cheered by a huge crowd of men, women & children – laughing – cheering – waving. And the sun had come out.

These are not mere fairweather friends. Papa has saved them with his heart – his mind always through peace & wars

& they have given him in his finest & darkest hour their love & confidence. O please dear God preserve him unto us – & lead us to victory & peace.

We then went to Cardiff – which gave Papa a stupendous reception. I drove mostly with Mr Harriman. I think he is charming – he has the root of the matter in him. He feels & works for us so much.

We arrived home at Chequers late – exhausted but happy . . . I found out that my diary was left on the train. O Calamity! It was recovered later however. I am writing this a week later or so.

Sunday 20 April

. . . *Major Barbara* in evening. (Major Barbara is apparently modelled on Lady Dorothy Howard who Papa nearly married. Thank my lucky stars he didn't – that's all). I think Mr Harriman is <u>charming</u>. I am very dissatisfied with my behaviour.

Sunday 27 April

. . . The daffodils at Cranborne are the loveliest I have ever seen – masses and masses & masses of them – but all arranged quite exquisitely & naturally in the best way possible.

The Germans have occupied Athens. We all felt gloomy & depressed & then – Papa spoke to us all. And then – We were all courageous again & ashamed of our fears & gloominess – here was strength – determination – just appreciation of the situation. He gave us back our perspective. I listened with mingled pride, wonder, humility & love.

Sunday 4 May

This evening Eric proposed to me. I'm in a daze – I think I've said 'yes' – but O dear God I'm in a muddle.

Monday 5 May

I've struggled all day within myself. Mummie came back again – Nana came. I must keep calm. Long walks in garden – finally succumbed to tears – but happy.

Tuesday 6 May

Felt calmer today. I really can't write all I think and feel. I only know I am most seriously & deeply looking at every aspect of it. The trouble is I have so little to judge by. And yet I do love Eric – I know I do. The family have been quite wonderful. So helpful & understanding. I wish I could write about all that has happened in detail – but somehow – it all seems too unreal & strange. And too important & pent up to write about calmly.

Friday 16 May

It is 10 days since I last made an entry – they seem to have been 100 yrs! And they seem strange & unreal. I still don't feel quite right. This is the record of those last 10 days – v critical ones in my life.

Wednesday 7 May

Worked at library – told Mrs Dickson & Mrs Winterton. Had made up my mind. Eric rang in pm.

Thursday 8 May

Wards. Rushed up to London. Eric to dinner – felt v happy. Mummie anxious for wedding to be put off for 6 months – clearly she is not v taken with Eric. Went to bed feeling perplexed – doubtful – sleepy.

Friday 9 May

Felt miserable – uncertain. Had hair done. Eric came & we walked round St James's Park – lovely day. 'Sweet lovers love the spring'!* Once with him – somehow all fears & doubts seemed to go. Returned to lunch happy – confident – decided.

Lord & Lady Bessborough to lunch. Families confer – engagement to be announced following Wednesday. Joy – Lady B – gave me beautiful brooch. Ally came round & saw me – very sweet. Tea with Diana – Eric joined us. Then we two went to Leatherhead to General & Mrs McNaughton – charming. Moyra there – she was pleased. Everything looked WONDERFUL.

Saturday 10 May

Still WONDERFUL. Eric took me over to see Mrs Ronnie Greville† – v extraordinary. Vast tea party of Brig-General etc – all v sweet & saying delightful things. Met Lord Beaverbrook riding in lane – he did not seem v pleased. Then rang me up – v sweet. Pamela came over bearing 2 lovely brooches from

---

* From Shakespeare's *As You Like It*, Act V Scene III
† Dame Margaret Greville 1863–1942, renowned society hostess and philanthropist. In her Will she left her important jewellery to the Royal Family and much of it is worn to this day

him*. She looked grave – & said 'Don't marry someone because <u>they</u> want to marry <u>you</u> – but because you want to marry them.' I didn't pay much attention at the time – & yet it stuck & I kept on thinking of it.

Brig-General & Mrs Loughton gave small party, our health was drunk in champagne. Papa's too – today a year ago he became Prime Minister – what a year – it seems so long. And standing there with everybody around I remembered how last ycar I had been at Chartwell & heard Chamberlain's voice telling the world that Papa was Prime Minister. And I remembered the orchard at Chartwell – & the blossoms & daffodils glimmering through the quiet twilight & how I cried & prayed in the stillness . . . Talked for a long time to Eric alone at McNaughtons'. Slight doubts assailed me. Late bed.

Sunday 11 May

Left early for Ditchley. V bad blitz in London – stations closed, so v devious journey to Oxford. During this journey I became aware of <u>very</u> <u>definite</u> <u>misgivings</u>. 'Don't marry someone because they want to marry you.' Eric v delightful & tender. Misgivings soothed by his sweetness.

. . . Immediately on our arrival Mummie whisked me off to her room. She said she & Papa had suddenly been seized with gr[ave] doubts & fears – she was sorry, v sorry she had let the whole thing get so far without saying anything – but she wanted the entire question of an engagement to be put off for 6 months. BOMBSHELL. And yet – through my tears I became aware most clearly of her wisdom – and all the doubts – misgivings & fears I had experienced at various times during

---

* An inkblot obscures the word assumed to be 'him'

the last few days seemed to crystallise – She asked me if I felt certain – in all honesty I could not say I did.

Mummie went to talk to Eric. I feeling crushed & miserable & rather tearful went for a walk with Mr Harriman. I can never say just how sweet & sensible & sympathetic he was. He said all the things I should have told myself – Your life is before you. You should not accept the first person who comes along   You have not met many people. To be stupid about one's life is – a crime. All these & many more. As we talked I became more & more conscious of how right M's decision was – & more & more conscious of my own unintelligent behaviour. My weakness – my moral cowardice. What would have happened had Mummie not intervened? I have an awful feeling I might have let it be announced & then having appeased to the last ditch made a passionate but illogical stand to everybody's consternation & surprise. Thank God for Mummie's sense – understanding & love.

Eric was absolutely kind about the whole thing – but angry with Mummie. Hectic telegrams sent off. Tears – unhappiness. Went for walk by myself – felt calmer. Nancy Tree SO kind & understanding. Archie then congratulated me – which made me laugh instead of cry . . . Had a lot of cider cup – felt better. Wrote letters till v late – went to bed crushed – humiliated but fairly calm.

Monday 12 May

To London with Mummie who is unfailingly comforting & robust. Sweet letters from Lady Bessborough. One written before postponement saying such wonderful things & so welcoming – I felt a worm. Lord Beaverbrook to lunch where I mingled tears & curry! He was sweet – & said our decision was right. How wonderful everyone is when one is unhappy.

Lord Bessborough to see Mummie. In awful state about leakages to press. Rather wanting announcement & then later cancellation if necessary. But Mummie adamant & protecting! Inspected with M & P ruins of House of C[ommons] & St Stephen's Hall. Then bought in a haze of gloom dinner dress at Harvey Nichols. Fiona & Nana arrived. Mummie saw Duff about press question. Drove to Chequers. Dead tired.

Tuesday, Wednesday and Thursday 13–15 May

Rather gloomy days – but calm on the whole. Deep realisation of my vanity, weakness, pride. Went to Communion on Wednesday. *Daily Sketch* says 'engagement will be announced today' etc etc & half witted photographs. You can of course <u>always</u> trust the Kemsley press . . . What I feel about Eric now I honestly don't know – these days have seemed so unreal – & yet I don't think I have ever before been so unhappy or so deeply shaken. I can only pray that I shall come out of this stronger, humbler & wiser.

Saturday 17 May

Left for Edinburgh. Eric wanted to come & see me off – but I said 'no'. I am looking forward to Scotch visit, but I still feel v dazed mentally & spiritually . . .

All last week tremendous Hess sensation.* Papers tried a little bit to make out – 'this idealistic German' etc etc. All I can say is I think he's a bloody Nazi & deserves everything he gets.

---

* Rudolf Hess 1894–1987, deputy führer to Hitler, who flew to Scotland on 11 May in an attempt to negotiate peace

Tuesday 27 May

. . . Heard news of sinking of *Bismarck* – thank God.

Thursday 29 May

. . . Before dinner tried hard to write letter to Eric – for I made up my mind – I do not want to marry him.

Saturday 31 May

Arrived home – & was <u>so</u> pleased to see Mummie. She reproached me v gently for not letting Eric hear a word. I <u>know</u> I've been naughty – oh dear – but somehow I <u>couldn't</u> write – just couldn't.

Sunday 1 June

. . . I feel unsettled & depressed. Wrote the letter to Eric for Monday 2nd.

Sunday 8 June

. . . Spent indolent morning conversing with Portals, Lytteltons & Aunt Nellie. Slogans for clothes rationing. 'Less for knickers – more for Vickers' & 'Smaller combs – bigger bombs'. Growing anxiety in press about Crete.

Oh – MOST important   at lunch Papa had announced that our forces & F[ree] French forces had marched into Syria. Great excitement & aching anxiety. Germans declare they have no planes or troops there – oh get along, do.

Mummie arrived at tea time – having been at Chequers with attack of lumbago following violent use of stirrup pump in fire practice – poor sweet!

Saturday 14 June, Breccles

Matinée grasse – messed around. Painted my nails red – result rather shattering – removed polish! In afternoon went to a loathly fete – or as Judy remarked rather wittily – a fete worse than death.

Midsummer day

A really beautiful day. Mummie & Judy & I went to Springfield to play tennis with Sir Richard Peirse . . . V enjoyable. Stayed to lunch. On returning home Judy & I lay in the shade and gossiped & played records. A perfect, lazy warm afternoon.

Sir Edward Bridges – Papa – Jock – Edens & Winants arrived in time for dinner. After dinner we stayed in the garden.

<u>3 bits of news today</u>
1. Free French enter Damascus.
2. RAF sally forth over France – about 180 fighters 2 bombers & are challenged. We have air victory – thank God. 28 of theirs down for certain – we lose 6 & 1 bomber.
3. News that Bob Laycock's Commando have been cut to bits – I pray Randolph is safe. Also Julian Berry & George Jellicoe – & Bob Laycock.

Mr Winant had only arrived back today – having left the States yesterday! He says Harry Hopkins sent me a message – <u>Most</u> gratifying – for reference in moments of gloom I quote it: 'Girls as attractive as Mary should get engaged <u>at least</u> 3 times before marrying – & I send her my best love.' Well – if that isn't gratifying what is?! Ho ho!

Sunday 22 June

<u>Russia invaded by Germany – she resists.</u>
For lunch came: Mr Fraser, PM of New Zealand, Lord Beaverbrook, Sir Stafford* & Lady Cripps, Lord Cranborne. Heavenly hot day. Spent afternoon talking to Lady Cripps – she was fairly interesting, but interest waned after an hour – & then I suddenly was seized with a desire to sleep. Luckily Jock arrived & helped me – by carrying on well informed conversation about Russia – Russians etc etc. I sank into a coma – & said 'yes, yes' or 'No, really' at – I hope – appropriate intervals. Slight diversion caused by my fancying I heard Lady C say 'Of course we couldn't go to the Opera much at first as we hadn't enough black <u>rubies</u>.' I awoke with a start & enchanting visions of svelte Slavs in scarlet boots & <u>dripping</u> with black rubies, all listening to opera immediately took form in my mind – I must say I had formed hitherto a rather gloomy opinion of Russian life & modes – but this revolutionised my attitude. I said breathlessly 'Black RUBIES?' Lady C 'Black <u>roubles</u>' (disappointment – but still curiosity – <u>why</u> black?). Lady C – before I could ask – rather crushingly said 'But we don't mention it of course.' Well <u>I</u> didn't – but I pine to know (a) What <u>Black</u> roubles are. (b) Why one can't go to the opera without them. (c) Why are they taboo. Is it something to do with white slave trade – but looking at Lady C I decide NOT.

Jock enlightens me – Black roubles are obtained on the 'black exchange' where one gets a more favourable rate. And the government doesn't recognise it. Am <u>bitterly</u> disillusioned – & former gloomy impression of Russians returns redoubled.

---

* Sir (Richard) Stafford Cripps, 1889–1952. The Labour MP and lawyer was another vehement opponent of the appeasement policy. Cripps was ambassador to the Soviet Union from 1940–42

Am in exhausted condition by tea time as Lady C was rather a trial – she is red & rather apt to look at one in an inspired way say[ing] 'The future of the world depends on you – <u>what</u> a terrifying prospect – but what a SPLENDID opportunity.' Actually I really <u>do</u> feel the responsibility at lunch & appreciate the grandeur of the task before us – but somehow I felt contrary & longed to say I didn't mind who won the war as long as I could have my special face cream & eat caviare & live on sweated labour. Diana, Sarah, Duncan (better but limping), Phyllis to tea. Long walk & talk with Judy afterwards. Discussed – the future – class inequalities – happiness & unhappiness & young men.

Papa broadcast – superb.*

Sat between Jock & Lord Cranborne at dinner – <u>Very</u> pleasant. Sir Stafford & Lady Cripps are not what one might call a very attractive couple – their personalities are not v sympathetic. Good air news.

Friday 27 June

M[ummie] & I drove to Seer Green and dined with Mr & Mrs Winant at the house they have rented there. It belonged to a very rich American before the war & it is <u>exactly</u> like a film. Ghastly pseudo-Tudor, v heavy mahogany furniture – stupendous bathrooms – ye olde fires (electric – sham logs), beams. Very set out garden with very well trained artificially pumped trout stream being propelled into elegant cascades & ripples over rockery crockery (well cemented) – engine house carefully concealed behind rhododendrons. In fact, the American millionaire's concept of a cute Elizabethan country house.

---

* Broadcast on Germany's invasion of Russia

And how unlike this setting are the Winants. They are so real while the house is unreal – so cultured & civilised where the house is garish & in bad taste. So full of all the lovableness & charm & simplicity & humour of which the house & garden are totally devoid. Spent v agreeable evening. During which Sukie distinguished herself by walking unwittingly into the lily pond!

Thursday 3 July

Worked with unwonted energy. Was v nearly late for dinner in the mess as was buried in entrancing book about Jack the Ripper! <u>My dear</u>. It just shows how careful one should be. Pleasant dinner – Claude Crawford v charming – married – middle aged & fascinating. Rest nice but unexciting. Scenario over Maud the mess kitten who had been seized by NAAFI girls & had to be re-kidnapped.

Friday 11 July

Worked in library. Nana & I left for <u>HOME</u>. A hot, thundery, sweaty evening. Wrote speech for Breccles all way home & read S. Maugham *Mixture as Before*. Found Mummie, Papa & the new PPS (Mr Rowan*) precise & charming – at Chartwell.

Chartwell – how could I for one moment have been unfaithful to you! For I have been sometimes – telling myself I didn't <u>really</u> love you – & then in the middle of this week I suddenly had a great homesickness for you. And when I came – although the swimming pool is no longer a limpid, cool,

---

* Sir (Thomas) Leslie Rowan, 1908–1972. Assistant Private Secretary and later Principal Private Secretary to Churchill, 1941–45

glittering glass, but covered with brown splodges – although the middle lake is piled high with dead branches – although the soldiers have dug trenches & worn bald patches on the grass – although the lawn is unmown – the tennis court looks as though it's got eczema & the rose garden & flowers are running wild – & though the house looks so sad with its uncurtained & shut windows – yet I knew I'd come home to the place I love so deeply.

The roses were blooming & the clematis & the syringa by the tennis court. Was it all a dream? I wonder if I ever really appreciated the life I lived before the war – I think & believe I did – although I took so many things for granted – I did enjoy & love it so – and I shall never forget it, never never never. It was so gay, luxurious, pretty – lovely, scrumptious, spoilt – selfish perhaps. Perhaps it will never come back – but one must not cling too passionately to the past – and I feel that perhaps it never will come back – perhaps it is not right that it should. And although I hark back to the old days & have a nostalgia for them – yet I feel – & hope   that I can face the New World. We must do that – we who have had so much – I feel that most sincerely.

Dear old life – we will never forget you – but you mustn't shackle us. And my memory of you is not a peevish one that you can be no more – faint regret – a little sorrow – but I must find – & I mean 'we' – the jeunesse dorée who have lived so comfortably – we must not & will not cling to you – gay & tantalising tho' you may be.

Sunday 13 July

Early church – satisfying . . . Long ride – got drenched in thunderstorm. It is so lovely to be en famille – Papa <u>rather</u> disgruntled – but sweet on the whole & v funny. Mummie

funny & charming & good company. I am so happy with them
& love them both most dearly.

Took dogs for walk & got chased by cows . . . Went up to
London after dinner latish. Slept at annexe.[*]

Tuesday 15 July

. . . On Monday I had lunch with Sarah – she was v sweet &
wise & gave me a well needed lecture. Greater poise – not so
much '<u>mental undressing</u>'. Be 'mentally dressed'. Must try.

Thursday 17 July

Wards. Sarah to lunch. Opened Wendover Waifs & Strays
fete in pm. In middle of speech large bomber flew over,
drowning most touching part!!

To London in a rush. Mummie & I went to Lady
Cholmondeley's cocktail party. SCRUMPTIOUS food & the
Duchess of Kent – what an exquisite peach. Gazed in rapt
admiration. Also there, Averell Harriman, Quentin Reynolds.
Went to news theatre – headachy. Supper with Mummie.

Then took myself off to party at the Savoy – which in a
series of whirlwind conversations & illegible notes Robin had
fixed. Party in its entirety included Robin[†], Kate, Mary, B &

---

[*] Annexe to 10 Downing Street, which the Churchill family moved to
following near misses to Downing Street by bombs in 1940 (though
Winston Churchill disliked living there and continued to work and eat at
Downing Street). The annexe was a converted flat in nearby Storey's
Gate, directly above the underground Cabinet War Rooms
[†] Robin Maugham, the novelist, playwright and travel wrtier. One the
Kates assumed to be his sister Kate Bruce. Gladys Bronwyn (born Bertha)
Stern, 1890-1973, was the author of over 40 novels, short stories, plays
and works of non-fiction

'godawmighty Kate' B, Self, G.B. Stern (who was v nice but slightly gave me the impression she felt it incumbent upon her position as an authoress to make v profound & scintillating & well got up remarks – which seems OK but it's a pity to try so hard), H.G. Wells (oh charming), Roger Keyes (I yawned by the time we'd been through his sons & King Leopold), Prof & Mrs Drummond & a young unmarried woman.

Tried new campaign & was I hope 'mentally decent'. Robin kept on saying I'd changed – must have suffered – now tell me all about it – and I had to soothe him down about not letting him know of my engagement & subsequent debacle of same. However I disclosed v little.

Sunday 20 July, Breccles

. . . Judy & I spent this afternoon lying flat on our backs in a field having v enjoyable conversation. Discussed – Beauty, male & female, 'coming' young men & 'coming' girls, opera & ballet, decline of art & otherwise etc etc.

Judy & I gossiped ourselves to bed – & also discussed our futures with Cousin Venetia.

Monday 21 July

Back to London. Judy & I seriously contemplated joining the ATS. Read various appeals etc. At lunch were Papa & Lord Moyne – discussing new Governor for Bermuda – (Trees, De la Warrs etc). I broached the subject of joining the ATS as member of a gun crew – Papa seemed v favourable.

I find it difficult to see my duty clearly. I know I help Mummie by being at home – also in a queer way Papa – & I have a duty at home. But is it right that I – strong, healthy, happy – with every opportunity in life should be living in great comfort & happiness at home, doing a job which could well be done by someone older & less strong than myself – having luxuries & pleasures – IS IT RIGHT?

And I do care passionately about the war. Please God – what is my duty. Would I not be also helping Mummie & Papa if they could feel rightly & genuinely proud of me? Can I help my country more in the ATS? If I <u>really</u> feel so ardently about the war as I think I do – then surely I must give more. O God my selfishness appals me sometimes – I think I see my duty clearly.

And so I am going to join the ATS. Mummie was wonderful about [it]. Darlings – 'I don't want to leave you – but I think I <u>ought</u> to go.'

Sunday 27 July, Chequers

<u>Terrific day</u>. Went to church at 8. Pouring with rain. Spent afternoon talking to Mummie – who was feeling low & tired. I am much exercised about going into ATS. Discussed it with Horatia – she agrees I should – but I have obligations at home – important ones. And yet I feel I would like to have the guts to go right out to leave my home where I am so happy, comfortable & sheltered & stand on my own feet & do something real for something which I sincerely & passionately believe in – victory. I pray most fervently for the courage to do it & what is more <u>stick it</u>.

Mummie stayed in bed. Wore new white linen skirt with pink & white striped shirt. Mr & Mrs Winant & Prof (Hail Lord Cherwell) to lunch besides house party. Mrs Winant <u>sweet</u> & said she thought my decision was right. I made awful 'Lady B' patronising remark & blushed for rest of afternoon over it. O God!

Winants left before tea. Averell Harriman & Kathleen

arrived. Played croquet with Kathleen. Mummie came down for dinner looking exquisite as always & in terrific form despite fatigue.

For dinner in addition to already existing party came Miss Dorothy Thompson (handsome looking – & a little formidable),* Sir Maurice & Lady Violet Bonham Carter (charming & such good co[mpany]), Col Harvie Watt (Papa's new PPS). Dinner (15!) was tremendous success. Papa in best spirits & delightful to everyone. Listened to flow of Miss T's stories including 'cute' sayings of her only child. I sat next Averell who told me he thought Miss T was a 'bore'. It was v amusing because all 3 Americans i.e. Thompson, Harriman & Hopkins were terrifically on guard. Said D. T. to H. Hopkins 'Why hello Harry – I have to come over here to see you'!!! After dinner M. & H. Hopkins made moderate broadcast 'good in parts like curate's egg'. And then we all strolled on N. lawn in beautiful gloaming everyone in good & amusing mood. Papa said 'And why are we in such good spirits tonight? Because they're not at our throats.' How true – one feels one can breathe for a bit. But even the break is a bit breathless – one knows so well it is only a pause.

When I am old I shall remember all this wonderful life. They say 'Distance lends enchantment' – I cannot imagine any future memory being more enchanting – interesting & thrilling than the actuality. And I am renouncing this life – so varied, interesting, free, luxurious, happy, full of colour & excitement. Renouncing a unique opportunity – am I crazy.

O God, please help me & guide me. But I feel – much as I know I can help Mummie – that I am not doing enough. Where are the Blood & toil, tears & sweat of my existence. It is a luxury for me to weep – to look agonised at the news. I am only seeking

---

* Dorothy Thompson 1894–1961, American journalist and writer

1 Sunday (1-364)

1st after Christmas. New Year's Day
Dog and Annual Motor Licences renewable

Saw 1938 out & 1939 in with Punch at Breccles. Self, Nana, Goonie, Clarissa, Juliet Blanche Leopold, Sylvia Lord & Lady Moore & Judy (house party) + Barbara & Victor Rothschild, were there.

Went for longs walks in a.m. with Nana.

Walked again in p.m. Great fun & most energetic.

Read mainly after tea.

My resolutions are (1) to say prayers much more carefully.
(2) to be much more regular re letters, accounts etc & especially my zoo is to be attended to.
(3) to have greater strength of purpose. Not to procrastinate.

(4) to keep a diary.
(5) to read lots of good books

I am really going to try to keep these.
May God bless my year & be with all those I love!

The first entry of Mary's diary on 1 September 1939.

Mary with her father in the audience at Bertram Mills circus in Olympia. The photo was taken on 22 December 1938, just days before Mary began keeping a diary.

Mary with her brother, Randolph, at his wedding to Pamela Digby, which took place at St. John's Church, Westminster in October 1939.

Mary with her horse, Patsy, at Scamperdale Horse and Pony show in 1939.

DECLARATION OF WAR.

3 Sunday (246-119)
13th after Trinity

At 10 a.m. came news of our ultimatum to Germany expiring at 11 a.m. Went down to Scamperdale via Elizabeth's.

11.15 a.m. Announcement by the P.M of a state of war between Great Britain & Germany

Good — I thought, I hoped, I prayed that our generation would never see again a war, and that those who fought last time would never have to face the ordeal a second time. Standing in the sittingroom at Scamperdale and looking out at the blue sunny sky, just as blue and gay as ever with great white clouds floating slowly by, I found it impossible to believe that war has come —

WAR HAS COME

Still I cannot believe it. Everyone one was rather tense & alternating between precarious

War is declared on 3 September 1939. Mary writes, 'I hoped, I prayed that our generation would never see a war'.

The war didn't dampen Mary's excitement for her debut on 29 February 1940, an evening she described as 'a dream of glamour & happiness'.

The Churchills, including Mary, moved into 10 Downing Street on 18 June 1940. That same day Antony Beauchamp photographed Mary, 'I felt and looked a mass of affectation but HOW I enjoyed it'.

While the Blitz raged, Mary spent much of summer 1940 at Breccles, the Norfolk countryside home of her friend Judy Montagu. On 6 August they were joined by Cecil Beaton who took photographs of them for *Vogue* 'at tea in most unaesthetic attitudes'. Mary is pictured above with Judy and another friend.

Mary at Ditchley with her less-than-loyal poodle, Sukie, who was occasionally a source of embarrassment.

Mary's first solo engagement, the launching of the naval destroyer HMS *Gurkha*.

In February 1941, Mary opened Westerham War Weapons Week. A nerve-racking experience for the nineteen-year-old, Mary was anxious to do her father credit, but discovered she had a natural flair for public speaking, writing 'strangely I didn't feel nervous – just elated and determined'.

Longing to do more to help the war effort, in 1941 Mary and Judy joined the Auxiliary Territorial Service (ATS).

Mary with three other ATS recruits. This photo was taken on 27 September 1941, when the press descended upon the camp, causing much embarrassment and misery for Mary.

Mary writes, 'Parading, Drinking tea, Eating bread, Sitting up on bed, Making bed, Writing letters, Polishing boots & buttons, Scrubbing floors & doorsteps – Emptying dustbins, Saluting – O God taking a bath was about the only portion of my day omitted.'

Mary on leave, but wearing her ATS uniform, with her mother Clementine and Clementine's cousin Nana, who came to Chartwell in 1921, and who brought Mary up and remained one of her closest confidantes.

Mary's diary entry from 28 July 1942 describes her exhilarating experience of going into action: 'This is the moment to which I have been called'.

Mary and her sister Sarah – both in uniform – with their parents on the way to receive the Freedom of the City in London, June 1943.

In July 1943 the Queen visited 481 Battery in Hyde Park.

to translate all my purest & deepest emotions & ideals – illusions, if you like – into reality. Seeking to make all the passionate love I feel for our cause an <u>actuality</u> & not a luxurious emotional indulgence. Can I? Can I make? Can I take it?

'I will not cease from mental fight, Nor shall my sword sleep in my hand.'

Wednesday 30 July

Hoorosh about ATS. Oh dear.

Thursday 31 July

Mrs Knox * came to dine with Mummie. She is 100% feminine, <u>very</u> attractive – & a most compelling personality.

Tuesday 5 August

Returned home – long journey. Thought very much of Papa – felt fearful & anxious and yet I know that he must go [to Newfoundland] – and I hope it will be a great turning point in the events of the world.†

Friday 8 August

Went up with Nana to London. Met Judy at ATS recruiting office at 2.30. She burst out of taxi with Brucc – looking quite lovely & radiantly happy. I hope so much it will all turn out

---

* Jean Knox, chief controller and director of the ATS -43, later Lady Swaythling
† Churchill's 'Atlantic Charter' meeting with Roosevelt at Placentia Bay, Newfoundland

well for her. I am anxious about it. But I think Bruce is very delightful.*

Medical examination and interview passed off successfully. Both of us passed Grade 1, 'Fit for anything'. Curiously enough Dr Winder from Westerham was the MO! Felt besieged by rather ignoble fears. Felt depressed & chilled. I so want to do well – to do something real. Am ashamed of my fears. But it is <u>entirely</u> my own wish – & I am proud & pleased that I am needed. But my fears are of my own insufficiency. But apart from my desire to serve to the utmost a cause for which I sincerely feel I could die – I feel I shall be a 'bigger' person for it. Because I am so <u>terribly</u> happy at home with Mummie & Papa and very much bound up & interested in my home life I feel perhaps that my outlook is rather narrow – my experience extremely limited – and unconsciously I feel I have become too 'name bound'. I have never really had to stand on my own feet – or to fight a battle of my own. And I feel that in these days when so many people are living saddened lonely lives – their homes broken up – many of them living in great discomfort – that it is wrong for me to whom life has given so much – to whom nothing has been denied, should be living in great comfort & happiness at home – still able to see my friends – to go to dances. And I believe that thinking & feeling as I do passionately about the war I shall feel happy in being able to give up a lot in order better to serve the cause.

Sarah was wonderful about it. She said '. . . and I will not insult you by sympathising with you for what you are giving up.' And that is true. With my whole heart I am proud & glad that I can offer my whole service & that in offering it I can make a sacrifice. I only pray for courage & perseverance.

---

* Flight Lieutenant the Hon Bruce Grimston, DFC, died aged 28 13 July 1944 when his Wellington crashed into the sea

Returned with Sarah & stayed the night at Stone after visiting Mummie who is having a rest at Champneys. Sarah talked to me about her sorrows. I feel most deeply for her.

Saturday & Sunday 9–10 August

Spent quietly alone at Chequers with Monty.* Began tidying away my things. Spent a good deal of time with Mummie who is feeling much better & looking better too. I am SO glad. Praying most constantly for the safety of my darling Papa.

Wednesday 13 August

Drove with Mummie to London and saw Sarah act exquisitely in harrowing play at Q [Theatre] called *The Trial of Mme Conti*. Mummie returned to her madhouse, I went & rested at annexe. Began reading *And No Man's Wit*. Ally called & stayed for about ¾ hr. Very entertaining but old devil tried to pump me about Papa. For once however I remained inscrutable – & knowed nuffin.

Dolled myself up like mad. Tony† came and collected me at 8.45 & we started out in his most glamorous car (he calls it his Sex Appeal car!) on what was one of the most gay & enjoyable evenings of my life. We started by dining at the Mirabelle: Hors d'oeuvres whitebait, a delicious Russian dish, 2 ice creams, coffee AND CHAMPAGNE!!!!! All to the accompaniment of gay music. We stayed & danced at the Mirabelle until about 12.30, when we removed to the Embassy.

---

* Miss Lamont, administrator at Chequers

† Tony Coates, cousin of Churchill's private secretary Jock Colville. Mary had met him at Chequers when he was stationed there with the Coldstream Guards

Which is a VERY elegant night club – decorated in pale pink – mirrors & candles. Saw 'Dopey' Dick there with a pretty blonde (*on dit* from the Palladium!). At 1.45 we went to the Palm Beach – which we found was closed (it could not apparently survive the scandal of having its manager murdered about a month ago on the premises). Tony [Coates]'s 'Sex Appeal' car we had to abandon in Bond St owing to its batteries giving out!

We went to the Nut House – where a v ugly girl took all her clothes off to an inattentive audience. One Free French pilot completely passed out – & was removed amid delighted cheers. Michael Tree, Susan Winn (charming, I think), Ann Lloyd Thomas (rather tight & boring – but distractingly pretty). Danced wildly & energetically with Tony till 3.45 – when we said 'Let's call it a day' BUT at the door we met Michael who said 'Home?!! NONSENSE. We must all breakfast at the Coconut Grove.' SO bidding an affectionate farewell to Alma* who was rather annoyed at us leaving 'so early'! we walked in the clear moonlight up stately (very stately at night – & silently dignified) to the more calm atmosphere of the Coconut Grove where we ate an enormous breakfast of fried eggs, mushrooms, chips & coffee. We read the morning newspapers – which said 'important govt announcement will be made at 3 pm'!!! Great speculation – 'America will declare war' said some. I just sed nuffin – but thought plenty.

Well about 4.30 Tony & I went home – walking through the quiet streets to Bond St where we picked up his car (which condescended to start) and with the stars slowly paling and the sky turning from midnight blue to a soft silvery indefinite glow – against which the Horseguards Buildings stood out a chalky white – we came home. I think

---

* Difficult to make out in diary

I shall always remember this as one of the gayest and most lovely evenings of my life.

It is strange – thoughts of marriage & of 'settling down' – even romance or a wish for it have for the moment left me. I feel strangely calm & aloof. I care for no one – & no one (at least I <u>think</u> no one cares for me?)

Thursday 14 August

I slept for 1 ¾ hrs – & caught the 8.15 in good time. Did wards rather strenuously. Announcement at 3 by Mr Attlee told an already speculating world about Papa's meeting with FDR and their 8 point Declaration. Their meeting & this declaration to me seems like a glimpse of the Brave New World – We say 'It will not happen again,' 'Things will be better,' 'Not another Versailles' and 'Oh Brave New World.' But sometimes little sneaking fears crept in – quislings to the fortress of one's soul whispering 'Will it be better?' 'As things have been so they remain' . . . 'perhaps your Celestial City – your Brave New World that above the squalors & miseries heroisms & strange happinesses of these days shines so brightly – will it not dim as you get nearer – will this delusion not shatter to bits – WILL YOUR WORLD be BRAVE & NEW?'

I strove to fight these thoughts as cowardly & unworthy – but still they were there. But now they are banished. There <u>is</u> going to be a New Deal, a Brave New World – there must be – if the future does not break faith with the past.

Sunday 24 August

Although it is so late this has been such a full and interesting day that I feel I must write about it while it is still fresh in my mind.

I went to early church. Breakfasted in Mummie's room ... Mummie Sir Pug & I went to matins at Wendover. Quite appalling sermon. In addition to house party for lunch were Dolly & Jimmy de R[othschild], Lord & Lady Bessborough (This was my first meeting with them since I broke off my engagement. They were v friendly & sweet. I felt shy) & Flt Lieut. Coward. So nice. Spent afternoon in garden talking.

After tea Cpt. Elliott Roosevelt* arrived. Also Lord Beaverbrook (who left America only yesterday!!). We all sat in the Long Gallery for Papa's broadcast.[†] I think it was the best he's done. No words can express my love and pride.

Dinner was v pleasant. Sat between Sir Pug & Lord B – what could be nicer! After dinner Mummie went to bed – but Horatia (suffering from nettlerash – poor sweet), Lady Cranborne & self stayed up v late. (At dinner Papa jokingly said 'I have been enlisting two new allies – the Republic of America and the Kingdom of Heaven.') Cpt Roosevelt obviously 100% interventionist. Whoops. Had long & interesting talk with him. Papa SWEET to me – so tender & loving. Papa said as Persia wouldn't boot the Germans out – tomorrow we go in.

After dinner Papa & Cpt Roosevelt just put a call through to the President – who is delighted with the speech. Apparently, he was having a bathing party for the D of Kent – & listened to it!

Lantern slides. Bed. What a day!

Monday 25 August

Mummie & I drove to London. Papa & Uncle Jack at lunch. Papa in one of his best moods – gay & a little wicked. How

* Captain Elliott Roosevelt 1910–90, son of the American President Franklin Roosevelt
† On the Atlantic Charter

proud I am that <u>he</u> is proud I am joining up. He has been so sweet about it. Somehow it has brought us closer together than I ever hoped or imagined we could. I have often felt so unavailing although I love him with my whole heart. And of Mummie – I think one of the very happiest things in my life is our companionship – I love her very dearly – not only because she is my mother – but as a person – I shall miss her so much.

Until I lived with her I never appreciated how fine & exceptional her intellect is – how compassionate & understanding of human griefs she is. Nor how much she has contributed to Papa's greatness, goodness & charm. I do appreciate these now.

... Came home to Chartwell (travelled down with Horatia) and found Nana waiting for me having got the house looking like a new pin & with a scrumptious tea of peach jam, brown bread & ginger biscuits! Spent quiet enjoyable evening.

<u>The Life of an AT.</u>
Here begins the account of the military
career of <u>Private Churchill ATS</u>

Friday 5 September

Caught 11.20 from Paddington. Terrific farewell scene. Rosemary S-E, Fiona, Ronnie, Nana, Mummie, Cousin Venetia & Cousin Sylvia to see us off. Judy & I bore up – & went away saying firmly 'No regrets.'

Army vans to meet us at Aldermaston. Lunch. Medical inspection. I & Judy are in Clive Hut, beds nos: 13 & 14. Macs, hats, mufflers, badges & buttons issued. Tea – Free – Supper.

10pm Weary – but happy on the whole & not too homesick – bed.

Saturday 6 September

6.15 Reveille.
7.20 Parade for breakfast.
9.00 Hut inspection then tour of the depot.
Dental inspection (Most gratifying my teeth were
   pronounced 'perfect'!). Lunch (mince, veg & ginger pudd).
Initial lecture. Our platoon (!) detailed to duties – I was free.
   Except for handing over food cards. Sat outside hut &
   turned up hem (with great difficulty I may say) of overalls.

Tea –
Free –
Supper
Bath
Bed
Lost cap badge – damn.

Sunday 7 September

7.30 Reported as officer Orderly. Did Chief Instructor's office – swept passage. Emptied dustbins – did front & back stairs with Judy & Staff ante room.

Lunch – mutton & rice pudding. Afternoon off. Snoozed. Began *Jennifer*. Got raspberry for making noise after lights out. Oh.

Monday 8 September

Was cold in night, got up at 6.30. Hut scrubbed out. Hut inspection after breakfast (bacon & potatoes, jam & bread & butter). First ack-ack tests – I was completely bamboozled by them. They were all catch outs & sort of jigsaw things. Clothing lecture, lunch (shepherd's pie & choc pudd). Clothing issued whoopce. First drill. Watched drill competition, tea. Read. Polished buttons, M[inistry] of I[nformation] films.

Tuesday 9 September

I'm afraid the cat's out of the bag, blast it, about me. Still *c'est la vie.*

Letter from Mary to Clementine on her interview with 'the Chief' on remaining incognito at Aldermaston, 5 September:

. . . She saw me alone & said that if I agreed she thought I should remain <u>entirely</u> incognito. I am pleased about this – & would you please if you do write to me and send plain envelopes without the Downing St address? I think it will – anyway for a little while be better that way. And would you please address me Private M Churchill!! Ahem!

Sunday 14 September

Wore uniform for first time. Felt v conscious of it.

Church parade. Sermon by Army Chaplain – <u>v</u> good, 'teach me my God & King; In all things thee to see'. After lunch Mummie came – & was I pleased to see her! Spent LOVELY afternoon with her & Judy. She brought a cake & fruit & flowers. Felt v homesick after she left – went to evening service & succumbed to tears.

Monday 15 September

My nineteenth birthday telegrams from Mummie & Papa, Sarah & Vic, Phyllis, Ronnie. Ponds [cream] & f[ountain] pen from Nana & the dogs!

Friday 19 September

6.45 Reported at HQ as Officers' Batman! Cleaned shoes, rousted officers. After breakfast 'did' their rooms – made beds & swept floors that seemed interminable.

PAY PARADE. I DO feel so grand drawing an '<u>earning</u>'. 11/6d in cash – 'O thank you ma'am!' Lecture on Ranks & Privileges.

Rather dreadful concert in the evening – a trying young woman with a bad figure tightly draped in silver lamé had the nerve to sing very indifferently not only 'Ave Maria' & 'Largo' BUT also 'The Last Rose of Summer' & 'Home Sweet Home'.

Felt coldy.

Saturday 20 September

5 am Mary rose.

5.45 On duty in kitchen (knicker elastic collapsed). Ruth & I scrubbed & scoured – polished & scrubbed etc all morning. Reported sick. Had new vaccination dressing & an inhalation – both which operations took over an hour. Polished taps. Ate huge lunch, scalded right hand. Feel rather weary. Went off at 1.30 – tired. TAB inoculation. Off duty. Wonderful unorganised afternoon.

Cleaned buttons, shoes – Judy washed my things for me – ironed – mended. O <u>what</u> a little dove I am – I am so <u>longing</u> to see Mummie tomorrow. There is now a large new intake. We are now <u>old</u> intake. O my my.

Thursday 25 September

Frantic preparations throughout camp for Mrs Knox. Volunteered to replace somebody in HQ pantry – cleaned windows & washed up. Cut finger.

Marched for ½ hr. Practised singing for concert. Talked in hut to Sergeant Cross. Charming & so interesting. Feeling tired.

Friday 26 September

What a terrific day!!

12.30 Officers' Mess Pantry as waitress. The distinguished visitors had by this time arrived. The Princess Royal,* Mrs Knox. There were 8 of us waiting. Lunch passed off – thank goodness – successfully. HRH did not get gravy down

---

* Princess Mary, only daughter of George V and Queen Mary

her august neck. They had the same menu as us – pie & Summer Pudding.

After lunch the inspection began. The whole depot was on its toes in the excitement. And the Chief afterwards told us she was pleased with us all. Our platoon drilled frantically all afternoon up & down in front of the Library! For about an hour we marched & checked, turned & wheeled till sweat dripped off our brow – but at [last] the party did come & watch us for a little while, & I hope we did quite well.

Just before this Judy, Ruth & I had been sent for to the Chief. Mrs Knox was in the passage & came up & talked to Judy & I, who gave her a 100% salute & heel click! I really do think she has the power to inspire me with a tremendous personal devotion to her & a feeling of love & pride in the service. When she stood opposite to me she said 'Well Mary – I hear you're doing frightfully well – frightfully well & I am terribly proud of you.' I felt so proud & happy that I, as usual, silly fool, went all choky & swimmy & could only mutter 'Thank you ma'am.' Then the Chief emerged & said that the Princess Royal would like to see me. By this time my hands were hot & sticky with excitement & nerves & I was all of a doodah. However I bundled in & saluted & she asked me to sit down. I thought she was very kind & charming. She asked about Mummie & Papa & whether I was happy & whether the food was good – the beds comfy & the uniform nice to wear. We talked for about 10 mins. Then we rushed off to drill.

We all waited again at tea, Judy & I were by this time rather weary & heaving with giggles as dear Cecil Beaton had appeared on the scene – looking v elegant & <u>completely</u> out of place in this galaxy of determined khaki clad women! We rushed out to cheer them as the party left. Then I & Judy went & ate a <u>colossal</u> tea.

Afterwards we met Sergeant Cross & we went down to her cubicle where she sat us down on her bed – placed pillows behind our heads & bade us relax. Which we did. Our pleasant conversation was interrupted by a summons for me to attend Company Office. And there the bombshell fell. Miss Russell told me that the War Office announced that I was in the service & the press were coming to see me. An awful feeling swept over me – and for the second time today I felt v choky – but not with pride & happiness this time, but with disappointment & fright & rage. Oh how I had hoped it might not happen. That I really could be a person & not a name – that I might be just a perfectly ordinary Private.

I just said 'Very well Ma'am' and went miserably to my hut. Where I shed some bitter tears. When I calmed down a bit, I felt better. <u>Personally</u> I am sad it has happened this way, but if I can help the service – if there is anything I can say or do to make people realise what a wonderful opportunity it is & how much needed one is – then I will do it. And if there is anything I can do to help my Papa – then I will do it.

The Chief came all the way up to the hut & was absolutely sweet about it. And Judy & I bundled down to her office. Here we remained from 7.30 until 10.15 while at intervals people flitted in & out & asked rather silly questions. Tomorrow there is to be an orgy of photographing – It is a solemn thought that the delectable sight of Private Churchill (rather cross in the early morning) stuffing toasties & condensed milk into her mouth will send up the recruiting. Perhaps it won't another even more solemn thought. I retired to bed <u>completely</u> exhausted. What a day. My feet ached – oh – something awful. <u>But it was wonderful.</u>

Saturday 27 September

This was quite one of the BLOODIEST days of my life.

From dawn till dusk I was pounced at by photographers. Pte. Churchill – Parading, Drinking tea, Eating bread, Sitting up on bed, Making bed, Writing letters, Polishing boots & buttons, Scrubbing floors & doorsteps – Emptying dustbins, Saluting – O God taking a bath was about the only portion of my day omitted. I couldn't have felt more mortified, embarrassed or miserable.

The crowning blow came at lunch when I was told I must not go to Reading. Judy was an angel & stayed with me. I dissolved into tears & then had to have a close-up taken for the USA – I tremble to think what it must have been like. The other girls were absolutely charming & understanding about it.

Rehearsal for concert. Then bed – crushed, exhausted & rather miserable, but for the fact that I was granted a luncheon pass for tomorrow. Yippee. Rang up Mummie.

Sunday 28 September

Early church. Feeling calm & rested. Last Church parade. Harvest festival. Mummie, Nana, Cousin V came (got raspberry for saluting officer on the run). Met them afterwards outside gates. They had arranged lunch at Marlow – pass expired at 2 – this impossible. Nana, Mummie & I stayed in Reading at hotel where we met Sarah, while lunch was collected by Judy & Cousin V. Mad dash to camp. Had delicious picnic with grouse & cider, jam tart & figs in grounds. Never have I enjoyed a picnic more. Fooled around, showed Sarah & Nana the camp. Sukie was there too – but – faithless little bitch, had forgotten me. Tea in Chief's office. She talked to Mummie & Cousin V – apparently we've done well.

Waved all the darlings goodbye – feeling a little blue – Oswestry is <u>so</u> far away. However – <u>no</u> tears! Rehearsal of concert <u>tremendous</u> fun. Bed – tired & happyish.

Monday 29 September

Oh horrors – news reel companies descended on me in force. Gloom.

Drill competition made doubly hysterical by presence of cameramen shooting from all angles. However, Platoon 3 won – whoopee.

Last rehearsal of concert.

Tuesday 30 September

Last day at Aldermaston. Concert in evening – great success & immense fun. Rowdy & hilarious party afterwards in Sergeants Mess – & bed after much screaming & yelling.

Wednesday 1 October

Left Aldermaston. We marched to the station. It was a very calm morning – with a thin mist over a clear blue sky. The country looked so peaceful & beautiful – so 'green & pleasant' and I felt full of hope and courage & pride. The journey was tedious, long & hot and by the time we had reached Park Hall camp & in the dimming evening light saw the vast waste of the barrack sq[uare] & the row upon row of corrugated-roofed huts – and the many strange faces – our pride, confidence and courage had ebbed & the self-confident Privates found themselves rather frightened – very tired new gunners. I felt very, very miserable.

Thursday & Friday 2–3 October

Days of loneliness & gloom. Strange faces – Strange customs – Strange places – & I summoned all the courage I could to face it – & suddenly by Saturday it began to get better – we began to know the people in our room – so nice & gay – tough & fun. We began to catch on to the new rules & regulations. Our plans straightened themselves out. We are to do 1 month as gunners then 2 or 3 on NCOs' course – then posted to practice camp & subsequently gun site.

Judy & I feel happy & begin to settle in contentedly. We went – feeling nervous – to the 211's regimental dance. Greatest fun. I danced with several charming people – & a particularly fascinating sergeant Berry escorted me most considerately 'to my lines'.

Sunday 5 October

Church parade in Oswestry. Marched in with the band. Very exhausting – but wonderful.

Monday 6 October & de suite

We have begun our predictors course. It is complicated & <u>terribly</u> thrilling. Our Sergeant Instructor is called <u>Trutch</u> & both Judy & I have developed for him a deep devotion. He is 100% natural charm – besides being an excellent instructor. An old RA saying is 'When you are in the Artillery, you don't walk – you don't run – you BLOODY WELL FLY!'

<u>Army grouses</u>: <u>NAAFI</u>, the MO, the food – & waiting!! But I think – on the whole – we are all happy. All the complaints – grievances & grouses are so tangible & explicable – but all that is fun – interesting, absorbing – is somehow difficult to

formulate but it is very real & as long as I live I shall never, never regret joining the ATS.

Mummie & Nana are wonderful & send a constant flow of letters & parcels. Time flies – there never seems to be a moment to write or read – (This is written in the train on my way home on my first 48 hrs). But it is a <u>wonderful</u> life & I only pray for courage to stick out the black moments.

Thursday 16 October

W/78871 Gunner M. Churchill becomes W/78871 Local Unpaid Lance Bombardier!! Begin NCOs' course.

Letters from Mary to Churchill about her posting to Enfield, 18 December:

My own darling Papa . . . Today Judy and I join our battery, which is situated near Enfield, I am so much thrilled by the thought of being in action. And the fact that I shall be so near home makes me very happy indeed. Please take care of yourself and come back soon. With love and kisses from your own kitten, Mary

And 20 December:

I was on duty at the gun site from one o'clock yesterday until one o'clock today. The 'manning team' sleep in a little concrete warren – ready (fully dressed in battle regalia!) to rush to the instruments. Twice during the night Judy and I took our turn to do an hour's stretch at 'spotting' – and watching for anyone suspicious on the gun site. The battery I am with seems very agreeable. There is a great deal of work to do, for besides manning the guns we have fatigues and guarding duties to do. I am sure I shall be very happy here, and I am thrilled and proud to be part of the <u>aggressive</u> defences of London.

1942

Growing Pains

'This is the moment to which I have been called.'

Tuesday 16th [16th]
June 1942

Monday 15th (cont)
Went home to dinner.
Mummie & Papa alone.
The news is bad &
he was in very low
spirits. He was
unhappy & tortured:
& Mummie & I tried
so hard to comfort him.
He may go to America
on Thursday.
Brendan arrived at
the end of dinner &
was cheerful & encouraging
I left with a very
heavy heart — but
Papa's last words to
me were — "... now
not a word — & no one
must see in your
face how bad things
are"
They won't.

This period sees Mary growing into battery life, albeit with occasional bouts of depression and nostalgia for her lost childhood. The reality of what she was doing would have been brought home by the death of Nora Caveney, the first ATS to be killed in action, though this is not mentioned in her diary.

1942 does not start well for the Allies. While the Japanese attack on Pearl Harbor brings the United States into the conflict, it also leaves the British Empire in the east dangerously exposed to Japanese aggression. Churchill describes the subsequent fall of Singapore in the broadcast that Mary misses as a 'heavy and far-reaching military defeat'. In fact, it is the largest single capitulation in the history of the British Army and comes on top of reverses in North Africa and the escape of German warships from Brest through the Channel. These events lead to much criticism of the war direction in parliament and the press. Mary's diary is very clear about the heavy personal impact on her father. She seeks solace in her work and, in spite of her denials, clearly develops a crush on Mr Green, her section officer.

There are also tricky family tensions to navigate as Mary becomes embroiled in the breakdown of the personal relationship between her parents and her brother. Randolph accuses Winston and Clementine of colluding in Pamela's affair with the American envoy, Averell Harriman. Fearing the negative publicity it would generate for her father in London, Mary writes Randolph a letter begging him to rejoin his regiment. But she is then castagated for doing so by Churchill who demands she apologise. His reaction upsets Mary, who wants her father's love and approval, but she demonstrates her growing independence by refusing to back down straight away.

Meanwhile, the government continues to face heavy criticism and Mary is in the gallery of the House of Commons at the beginning of July to see Churchill face down a vote of no confidence in his government.

Then, after almost a year of training and waiting, Mary sees action for the first time and proves that she has inherited her father's calmness under fire. After some heart-burnings about leaving the ranks, her acceptance for officer training coincides with a mortifying story in the American press about her being spanked by a US private at a party for teasing him about his big feet. Events lead to a low period in which Mary questions but ultimately refinds her faith. There is also the first mention of Ed (Conklin), a new American flame.

Meanwhile Churchill travels to the Middle East to sack General Auchinleck and from there to the Soviet Union for his first meeting with Joseph Stalin. He confides in his daughter before setting off, making her one of the very few to know the truth about his whereabouts.

In October, Mary and Judy travel to Windsor for a two-month course. This puts Mary within easy distance of her parents. She is at Chequers to help entertain the First Lady, Eleanor Roosevelt, and attends a celebratory lunch at the Treasury Annexe to mark the victory over Rommel at the second battle of El Alamein. Here she hears her father call for the church bells to be rung throughout the country (it does not happen until 15 October). Ed raises the question of more church bells when he proposes but a visit to Chequers on the eve of Operation Torch (the combined Anglo–American landings in French North Africa) convinces Mary that her own Anglo–American liaison is now over. The year ends with two parties, a formal Thanksgiving Day celebration at Buckingham Palace given by the King and Queen, and a private family celebration of Churchill's 68th birthday.

Undated

I must keep a diary again. The days pass so rapidly and merge terrifyingly with the past. And life is such a strange mix-up – & I feel I am living such an adventure – not just existing.

I wish I knew what I really felt and thought. My thoughts are legion – half-formed – incoherent –

Monday 16 February

Infuriated to discover I had missed Papa's broadcast.[*]

Home in evening. Shadow of Fall of Singapore and troubles at home hanging heavily over house. One feels torn – anxious – perplexed.

Thursday 19 February

Course. Judy and I home in evening. Cousin Venetia – Uncle Jack to dinner. Papa came in late and was full of the cabinet changes. They are to be announced tomorrow. Feel relieved.

Friday 20 February

Course. Judy on duty. So went home alone in evening. Mummie and Papa gone to Chequers. Spent a deliciously lazy evening. Pevolled[†] hair – had scented bath – and then relaxed in Mummie's black and pink satin quilted dressing gown in front of sitting room fire and ate comforting supper; onion soup, omelette (!), chips, carrots – stewed peaches and café au lait. Rang up Mummie and Nana. New cabinet seems

---

[*] Broadcast on the fall of Singapore, 15 February 1942
[†] Presumably some kind of hair curling

to be well received in press. Feel much relieved personally. Somehow this quiet evening by myself has given me a sudden reserve of peace of mind and calm.

Thursday 26 February

Busy. Home in evening. Papa weary and sad. Mummy tired. Feeling tired and overborn myself.

Friday 27 February

24 hours – Hooray. My own to do what I like with.

I feel this is a very awkward moment. But I will NOT give in – I will try to be calm, just generous.* Finished *Weather in the Streets*. Arrived home 10.10. Rushed to Marshalls – hair and nail do – shopped – Bumpus. Luncheon alone with Mummie and Papa at No. 10. Papa is at a very low ebb. He is not too well physically – and he is worn down by the continuous crushing pressure of events. He is saddened – appalled by events. Pray God he may be renewed with strength and freshness. What would our cause do without him? Here now is the blood, toil, tears and sweat.

And no one must know – 'Oh he's very well – full of confidence and hope – yes, yes – No, not tired.' Ah God, you are being worn down – your vitality sapped and we who love you so passionately can do so little. Averell said yesterday 'I think of him only as a star that shines in the hearts of all of us.'

---

* This presumably refers to family tensions over Randolph, then home on leave, who was not only making life difficult for his father politically, by publicly criticising Winston's colleagues and the conduct of the war, but had also just found out about Pamela's affair with Averell Harriman (whom she was much later to marry)

After lunch Mummie and I and Nana went to see *Hellzapoppin'* which is the TOPS! Judy came up for evening. Mummie went to bed for dinner. After supper we spent a perfectly peaceful evening – my idea of bliss. Writing, talking and listening as a background to Ravel's subtle, sensitive music.

Friday 27 February

At midnight hectic message from Judy telling me not to return until Sat in order to avoid vultures of the press! Slept till 12.30. Lunched with Mummie, Papa and Nana. Papa still sad, tired and worn. Left about 4 with Mummie for Ditchley. Such a beautiful afternoon. Countryside bathed in pale, remote sunlight. I think Ditchley is perfectly beautiful. Rested till dinner and read.

Am heavy hearted at leaving Papa and Mummie in this sad and forlorn time. What a war – and how it tears and wears people. O darling Papa you must not weaken or despair. You are our rock and guide, our inspiration.

Saturday 7 March

Manned*. Had <u>very</u> trying time with girls. But clung violently to my guns. Eyes began to give trouble and by evening were <u>very</u> bad and looked lousy. Had long conversation with Mr Green about NCOs etc – but was interrupted at crucial moment. At about 9.30 he returned from supper and from then until 12.45 we sat by the fire in the Command Post and talked.

I hope it didn't drag for him – for me the time flew. It was perfect, the conversation just flowed on easily and without

---

* Was on duty

effort. And real conversation – not just nattering. We talked about poetry – quoted Horatius, Gray's *Elegy*, D.H. Lawrence, Rupert Brooke, Rhys etc etc etc. books: (*Memoirs of a Fox-Hunting Man*, *Vanity Fair*, Shakespeare and so forth and so on etc etc). Life – he told me a little bit about his wife – he was utterly charming and we talked on oblivious of time. He is such good company – it was a heavenly evening – cosy, companionable, civilised and so restful. It made army life recede for a while with its racket and wear and tear.

I don't know how to analyse my feelings for Mr Green. I haven't got a crush on him – it's more than that. I'm not in love with him – it's less strained and violent than that. I genuinely honour and admire him – enjoy his company – and I find in him a kind of reassurance and support. He is very wise and very good too – I think. I don't know whether I should fall if he weren't married – he is very fascinating. At the moment I love him without being in love.

I think I shall always remember him as one of the people who influenced me most and wisely. He is a superb officer – there is no one I would sooner work with.

Sunday 8 March

Eyes terribly gummed up in morning but less painful. They feel tired.

Orderly NCO.

Diana came to see me and said I've got pink eye*. Damn. Spent a lovely afternoon talking to her. Suddenly I'm beginning to get on with her so well. I do love her. Slept till roll call time.

---

* Conjunctivitis

Monday 9 March

Very busy. Saw MD. Pink eye.

Got straight into bed and slept all afternoon and all night. Was cosseted and petted, hot water bottled, given hot drinks. Oh heaven. Am not allowed to read much.

Friday 13 March

Felt bored and cross. Eyes not right yet. Yearn for battery. Lovely afternoon, Nana and Sukie came. Walked down to battery. Found our section and Mr Green doing visual shoots. Felt green with envy and felt a pang at suddenly being a spectator. The work is such a part of me – I do love it passionately. 7 other people, including Mr Wade, have now caught pink eye. Oh dear!

Tuesday 17 March

Eyes peculiar again – apprehension. Apprehension dispelled after sick parade – pink eye again. Postpone leave. Bugger – felt tearful but resigned. Rested dutifully in dark room all afternoon.

Sunday 22 March

Odd jobbed in morning, busy. Packed in afternoon. When Mr Green signed my pass he said 'It gives me great pleasure to sign this Cpl. Churchill – you really have deserved it.' I value praise from him. And I go on leave with a warm feeling. And a determination that when I return I shall continue to disregard personal popularity and to try to fight desperately for the things I care about. I'm so ignoble – I find I mind quite terribly that the girls don't like me and are annoyed and aggravated with me. I am so genuinely fond of them. But I won't give in – I swear I won't.

And so after 3 months I come home on leave. I am very happy. Short walk in park. Met Uncle Jack talking to Sir Alexander Cadogan. Delicious bath, scrumptious supper (chops, chips, sweet pancakes and coffee) and now BED.

Monday 23 March

Luxuriated in bed till quarter to nine. Boiled egg and honey for breakfast. At 10 went to Marshalls for perm, manicure and eyebrow trimming. Late for lunch. M and Mme Moisiewitch[*] to lunch, Papa and Mummie. Set forth with Nana and Sukie in search of cocktail dress AND MET A HONEY.

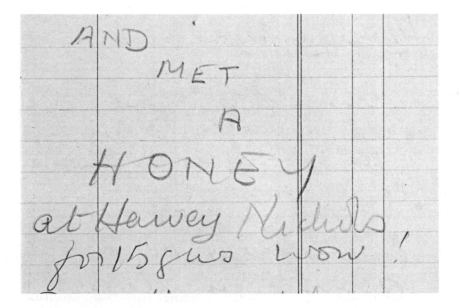

---

[*] Renowned Russian pianist Benno Moisiewitch and his wife

at Harvey Nichols for 15 gns. Wow! Dorville model navy blue and white striped coarse net over navy blue taffeta slip. Shirt waste [sic] – long full sleeves gathered skirt and red waistband. Whoopee.

Went with Mummie and Nana to see Vivien Leigh in *The Doctor's Dilemma*. I did enjoy it and how exquisite VL is. Home to join Papa, Diana and Duncan who had already started dinner. Evening from here on was <u>not</u> a success. Papa tired, low and cross had row with Mummie. Then battle royal ensued between Papa, Mummie and Diana over Randolph.

Randolph must go and rejoin his regiment if he is to save Papa from public resentment and disapproval which just at this moment he can so ill afford. Partly because of Duncan's advice (which I trust) and partly because I completely agree with Mummie, and out of fear of Papa and Randolph I have always kept myself weakly neutral. I wrote to Randolph begging him to rejoin his regiment and then went to bed.

Wednesday 25 March

Shopped and went to the dentist. He hurt. Met Fiona. Raced back just in time to get set to go with Mummie to lunch at Soviet Embassy. Wore blue dress, fur coat and new hat. Arrived at 13 Kensington Palace Gardens at same time as the fighter pilots who were being given the Order of Lenin. They were rather dreary looking and married or engaged. Mme Maisky* was looking full blooded in a bright red dress but rather untidy.

At luncheon, which was in a huge conservatory, I sat between a colonel in the Russian army who could only speak very little English and a major in the Russian Air Force who was fascinating. There was delicious smoked salmon,

---

* Wife of the Soviet ambassador to Britain 1932–43, Ivan Maisky

otherwise the food was not remarkable. But the drink was wonderful. VODKA, WHITE WINE, RED WINE and after the investiture CHAMPAGNE CUP!!! I felt wonderful. M. Maisky made a speech – urging that 1942 was <u>THE</u> year for winning the war etc etc etc. After the investiture (during which the airman looked <u>very</u> miserable and self conscious) I was given some restorative in the form of champagne cup. And then after warm farewells from my lunchtime companions and Mme Maisky and after gazing at an impressive full size portrait of Stalin – and clutching feverishly for something suitable to say – we went away.

I felt rather headachy but I sallied forth and shopped. Had a field day at Bumpus and overspent myself there. A book of Augustus John's drawings, *Lust for Life* (Van Gogh's life), Siegfried Sassoon's trilogy, *They Die With Their Boots Clean*, *Importance of Living*, Lin Yutang.

Bundled home in a taxi just in time to change to go to see *Old Acquaintance* by John van Druten with Edith Evans, Muriel Pavlow, Marian Spencer, Ronald Ward with Mummie. It was a <u>wonderful</u> play. Witty, true to life, moving and full of calm philosophy. I loved it. Papa was dining with Bendor* and Prof. Mummie and I had supper in her room. Afterwards I went in to talk to them. Bendor has aged and seems wandery. He talked endlessly about his taxes etc. I discovered Pam and Randolph were on the verge of arriving and so I nearly ratted – but screwed up enough courage to stay. After Bendor and Prof had gone Papa then told me Randolph had shown him the letter I'd written. I only said 'Oh so he's shown it to you' and then I shut up. But a cold hand seemed to be laid on my heart. Why try to explain to Papa why I did it – I terribly

---

* Churchill's old friend Hugh 'Bendor' Grosvenor, the Duke of Westminster (a family name still clearly in use)

regret Papa knowing. I must say I would have thought R would have had greater dignity than to go running to Papa. I must say I didn't know he set all that store by what I said or thought. I am <u>amazed</u>.

Papa then proceeded to show me two secret telegrams which explained how justified R was in being over here. Oh darling Papa – why explain to me – I know as well as any of us that <u>logically</u> R is in the right and is perfectly justified both in having a staff job and being over here, but unfortunately the world doesn't know these reasons and doesn't judge kindly. And R is very silly – if only he would not set all the world by the ears – it all reflects on Papa and does himself no good. I think the greatest misfortune in R's life is that he is Papa's son.

Papa has spoilt and indulged him and is very responsible, but R has never got over the disappointment of not being super remarkable, super successful and a genius. I don't doubt he loves Papa but he shows it in a very queer way.

But somehow I couldn't tell all these things to Papa. He would have overborne me and also R is his blind spot. He does not see him as we see him – we who love Randolph but know his sorrows, faults and failings. He thinks R is mistreated by the world and misjudged, that Mummie (unfeeling mother!) and prejudiced jealous sisters are all against R! It might be funny, only somehow it all hurts so much. I so much wish this bust-up hadn't happened. But I <u>DON'T</u> regret writing that letter. I took on me a responsibility and a share in family affairs I had shelved too long. But darling Papa – if only you knew how reluctantly I did it, how grieved I am you're angry with me.

Well then in the middle of Papa lecturing me in walked R and Pamela. It was a little strained but all right on the whole. I went to bed after about quarter of an hour. R leaves for

Cairo tomorrow. I said goodbye – *il y avait un peu de gêne.*[*] Papa
in a hoarse whisper tried to make me say something about it
but I wouldn't. But I weakly capitulated and vaguely promised I'd write to R about it. I went to bed feeling calm but a
little saddened. I <u>will not relent.</u>

Thursday 26 March

Got up luxuriously and slowly. Dressed to go with Mummie
and Papa to the Central Conservative Committee at Caxton
Hall. Just before we went Papa came in looking frightening and
said 'Have you written that letter?' I said 'No' firmly. But felt
sick at heart.

Papa made v good speech. I am so proud of him.

Met Judy at annexe who had arrived for 24 hours. Rushed
off with her and wolfed smoked salmon sandwiches for lunch
at F[ortnum] & M[ason] and then dashed off still chewing!
To the dentist. He hurt like hell! Met Katy in F & M. Shopped
then went to Gunters and met Judy. Mummie joined us. Saw
the Duchess of Kent looking exquisitely lovely and in no way
visibly pregnant. Ate ices and cakes. Judy and I went off to see
Katy who had subsided into London Clinic. Roared and
giggled for a bit there. Goodness I like her and how she makes
me laugh. Changed for dinner. Bruce and John B came.
Enjoyable dinner party. Papa genial.

At about 11 we walked to the 400. At 1.45hrs we walked to
the Nut House. Very empty and not in very good form. But
we were there so that was all right!

At 5, thinking the Nut House food looked gruesome, we
walked to Lyons Corner House in Leicester Square and ate
an enormous breakfast of

---

[*] 'There was a little embarrassment'

Coffee (au lait)
Sardines on toast
Waffles and butter and treacle.

Oh heaven.

And this perfect meal gave me the poetic brainwave of seeing the dawn from Westminster Bridge!!! So we walked down Lower Regent Street and down the Duke of York's steps and through St James's Park and across Parliament Square to Westminster Bridge. What a lot one misses by taking taxis at night in London. How lovely the night is and what fun walking the deserted streets. I had a pair of low-heeled shoes and John carried the others in his pocket.

Just before dawn on Westminster Bridge. It wasn't a letdown. It was still and chilly and mysterious. Rather than the light increasing, the velvety darkness faded and the Houses of Parliament emerged clearly and took shape – grey secret shape. Three dim lights glowing downstream and the Thames, broad, silent, sliding slowly with dulled steely glints slipping up for a moment and behind us on the bridge every few minutes a dawn tram with bleary lights rumbled by. I threw sixpence into the water and wished – it was a queer wish and it flashed suddenly across my mind 'That I may all my life be courageous.'

And then as the sky was growing paler we went home. Judy and I both agreed it was a perfect night and had hot baths. Mummie's comment was 'Well I don't mind you coming in at five but at six I draw the line – and what MUST the Marines have thought!' Went to bed from 8.30 till 12 and felt awful when I woke up. Nana and I bundled off to the Berkeley where gradually a large family party assembled: Mummie, Aunt Nellie, Sarah (in WAAF officer's uniform), Self, Nana and Fiona.

Delicious lunch with Glace Alaska for pudding. Yum yum. After lunch Nana and I and Fiona did a bit of shopping and joined up with Diana and searched unsuccessfully for the crystal bowl Mummie had so much admired at Goode's and which we all wanted to give her. Had tea with Diana & Nana at F & M. Left with Mummie & Nana for Chequers, slept on way down. Lovely to see Monty (Miss Lamont) again. Felt very tired and had cold coming on – so went to bed for dinner. Oh the heaven of lying warmly in linen sheets propped up with pillows with a roaring fire & someone to bring one hot orange & aspirin just before dropping off to sleep.

I was reading over my war diaries. They made me remember very vividly and they made me see myself from afar off. My God some of the things I wrote are so HOT MAKING. Terrible. They stink!!! and yet at the time they were so sincere. They seem terribly emotional. But then I suppose that's growing up – and I had never tied my emotions to any endeavour – they were luxuries pure & simple. I think I have changed – Sarah says I have grown up a lot. I do feel calmer inside & more detached. But I do get into such mental and spiritual muddles. I wish I saw life clearly & understood about it more. And God – how I hate, despise and loathe myself & alternatively how absolutely the cat's pants I think I am & how obsessed I am with myself. O bloody girl!

Saturday 28 March

Went at 09.45 with Papa who inspected the second division who are going on active service. It was a lovely drive – right on the road I used to dash along going for those lovely weekends at Ditchley. Papa talked to me for about 20 mins on and off about Randolph – he was very cross but I didn't answer back nor argue at all. Out of wisdom I hope – perhaps cowardice – & yet I somehow felt hopeless about making Papa see it at all as we see it. It's funny really because in a way I care for R more than I ever did before I knew him so well & God knows I love Papa. And now I seem to have alienated Randolph, & which grieves me to the heart – hurt and angered Papa & destroyed that understanding & sympathy that really had grown strongly between us & which alas had naturally diminished a little as we see so little of each other – & now this has dealt it a blow.

However later he was sweet to me – but I felt a little chilled inside & fearful. A gaggle of generals & the Turkish ambassador (newly arrived) & his military attaché met Papa at a wayside inn. I saluted wildly in all directions & felt rather shy. A rather 'poo-poo' staff captain in the Guards had been detailed to escort me round. The inspection was rather impressive. In the morning half a division was lining the sides of a twisting road. There were demonstrations etc.

We then went to lunch at Batsford Park. Lady Craven is a vague cousin & was very nice. We were the only 2 women there – Delicious lunch. Sat next to 2 charming cols. After lunch set out to see 2nd half of division. It was even more impressive than in the morning – there were about 4000 men drawn up on three sides of a huge field. It was a lovely early spring day – fresh sunshine with drifting clouds & a soft wind. It was beautiful driving through the countryside – it's such gracious, rich rolling country with grey walled grey roofed villages. We watched a commando raid demonstration & anti-tank guns in action – wow the noise. Then we had tea in a sweet little country vicarage. And it suddenly gave me a longing for country life & the smell of hay & farmyards – & hot buttered toast & linen cupboards & children.

Until the road to Chequers & London parted Papa drove with the Turkish ambassador & I struggled to make diplomatic conversation with the military attaché. On return rushed with Nana & Monty to Ellesborough warships week auction. Saw quite a lot of my old acquaintances. Sarah arrived. Lord and Lady Louis Mountbatten arrived for dinner. Sarah & I both fell for him in a big way!

All through dinner news of the St Nazaire raid kept coming through. <u>Thrilling</u>. Saw *Les Misérables* after dinner. I thought bloody awful – Papa – the sweet – said 'fine film.'

Monday 30 March

Lord and Lady Louis left early. So did Mummie and Nana and I – for Fulmer Chase.* It was great fun being shown over and seeing the babies. It made me long to have twins immediately!

Began feeling miserable and increasingly gloomy until at dinner I was on the verge of tears. It's been a perfect leave and I wouldn't not go back – but oh my God – how the thought of it struck cold to my heart.

Back to battery.

Wednesday 1 April

Mr Green went on leave. A long week starts.

Monday 13 April

Long ramble in pm. Beautiful day – sun, wind and faintly hazy sky.

Went home. Rang up Mummie who has been ill and is at Chequers.

---

* Fulmer Chase Maternity Hospital for officers' wives, where Clementine Churchill was the chairman

Went to see news film of Papa coming to battery. Very good programme.

Papa sent for me to talk to him while he was dressing for dinner. O heaven – something of that companionship has come back. I was able to say I had written to Randolph who has joined a sort of armoured skirmishing-come-parachute corps. O darling Randy, how terribly proud I am – we all are.

Had a sudden stab at dinner this evening (when Papa talked of Chartwell) of homesickness and of longing for the old life.

I remember breakfast at 8 on hot midsummer mornings – Sarah, Nana and me round the small table in the dining room. Outside the Weald is drowned, is submerged in mist and the sun struggles through – Inside the amber floor and rush matting make pale golden lights.

'The sea is rising' we pretend – what shall we take – I say 'my pearl necklace'. Islands are appearing in the sea – and slowly the tide recedes and the glittering dew is sucked up and the Weald stretches in clear detail to the horizon.

Papa in the water garden – cool and always there is the sound of dripping splashing water – dark secretive pools. Papa watching his goldfish-monsters and over the grey wall waves of scent from the roses come.

Cool spring evenings – dew drenched – a dim light and the apple blossom like the milky way at my feet as I stand by the aviary.

The chestnut tree with all its candles – cool, quiet and so beautiful that it hurts – O days that are gone – you can never return – never should – but you were beautiful and graceful and gay and sincere.

The grass at Chartwell, the people at Chartwell, grit in my sandals on the hot dusty drive – the lakes – the black swans – and that disproportioned irregular heavenly house. It comes back to me too strongly.

Wednesday 15 April

Orderly NCO. Long energetic day. Perfect spring weather.

Felt terribly depressed – inefficient & had moments of useless impotent hate and raging against the army life. All the things I gave up so gladly and so bravely – I suddenly longed for them and longed and longed and longed. Until I felt I was like a lost, spoilt child & I longed to cry & no tears would come.

Made hysterical bitter remarks & flounced around in a stupid fashion. But felt terribly miserable. Oh bloody – bloody – bloody.

Letter from Clementine to Mary, 22 April:

My darling Mary, Perhaps I may see you before you get this letter. But I want you to know my feelings when I read of the death in action of Private Nora Caveney. My first agonising thought was – it might have been Mary – my second thought was satisfaction & pride that the other girls on duty continued their work smoothly without a hitch 'like seasoned soldiers' – & then private pride that you my beloved one have chosen this difficult, monotonous, dangerous & most necessary work. I think of you so much my darling Mouse. I know you will never regret your choice.

Monday 18 May

24 hours leave.

Did 'good reliable' shopping jobs in afternoon. Had delicious bath. Cousin Venetia came to tea. Then Mummie & I went to see Cochran's Big Top. Bea Lillie as always was brilliantly witty – especially as Mme Récamier. But it was a v bad revue. Mr Cochran's Young Ladies either being 'Young' and looking middle aged or just middle aged – Clothes bad – décor bad. But one or two really good moments compensated.

Papa & Sir Charles Portal* were dining – Papa in a beaming mood & Sir Charles as always charming. Cousin Venetia & Mummie & I had cold supper.

Bed.

Tuesday 19 May

Wonderful sleep. Breakfast in Mummie's bedroom. Greased up.

Got up <u>v</u> slowly. Returned to camp. Felt gloomed up. Mr Green in hospital with impacted wisdom tooth. Am made messing sergeant. I do hope I'll make a success of it.

Sunday 31 May, London

Slept till 5.45. Dashed up, out & back to battery at 7.15. Met charming American sgt pilot on Tube. However early morning NOT best time for allied contacts really. Damn – walked into Major as I arrived back. Miss T later in day asked me why I returned at that time – I explained – she was <u>v</u> nice – but I shan't repeat the performance. (Query: Why is it that I <u>always invariably</u> get caught the moment I attempt anything at all – even faintly shady???). <u>V</u> unfair.

Tuesday 2 June

Miss Tyrwhit while talking to me about things I was to buy for battery – said '& by the way you better get yourself some guns.'†!! I really could hardly believe it. I am so thrilled &

---

* Sir Charles Frederick Algernon Portal, 1893–1971, later 1st Lord Portal of Hungerford. Chief of Air Staff (CAS), 1940–45

† Sleeve badge for gunnery

delighted. It naturally made Judy feel unhappy and left behind – she is getting ready to go on course at Lichfield tomorrow.

Hectic morning. We both left for home about 12.30. Just Mummie & us two at lunch. Changed afterwards into my grey flannel dress & magenta snood – blue shoes, and did terribly 'steady' shopping all afternoon – joining Judy at Fortnum's for tea – laden with curtain cord, clothes lines, tapes, guns – & HAIRPINS 1 PKT ME for the use of . . . Was lucky enough to get an appointment with Quinton at same time as Judy. This made us both <u>V</u> late for high-tea-come-supper at 6.30. Mummie was sweet about it. Arrived just a little late for *Les Patineurs* – Other ballets were *Hamlet* – *Sylphides*. *Hamlet* I thought absolutely wonderful. It tore one.

Papa and Duffy were dining at the annexe. Duff was very Duffish & quite delightful & when Papa went off to see First Sea Lord – talked to Judy and I for a while. While in bath had short but definitely severe bout of peevishness & bad temper. I felt most ashamed.

However Judy & I talked for a long time before going to sleep. I love talking until I just slip into sleep. One feels so relaxed & calm & loose & on a cloud. I think that must be awfully nice about being married. Somebody sweet & fascinating to talk to & to listen to in the velvet darkness.

Wednesday 3 June

Delicious breakfast in Mummie's bed. Face covered with grease. ORANGE JUICE! Got up v slowly. It was a lovely hot summery day. Lots to do all afternoon. Hot as hot. <u>V</u> sticky.

Went home again in the evening feeling limp & tired. Had delicious bath, and Mummie & I then walked round St James's Park. It is looking really beautiful. The tulips are over – but by the Guards Memorial there is a herbaceous border – & all round the lake the most lovely irises. Blue & some brown & yellow ones with velvety purple tongues – I hope the railings will never be put back – It is lovely for everyone to be able to sit on the grass by the lake & under the trees.

How stupid of me not to have liked London before now. I see sudden loveliness in all sorts of places. But I think I shall always love Westminster best – for one thing I know it better than the rest of London – and now it is inextricably mixed in my memory with the last 2 ½ years. The trees & lake from Admiralty House in spring – thrilling days waiting for news of naval engagements – and then before that the streets covered in snow – returning late with Mummie & Papa from Manchester (I think) & Papa throwing snowballs at me.

Went back feeling calm & exalted & happy – & not that awful dead end & 20th century blue feeling that I've had lately.

Thursday 4 June

V̲ hot again. V̲ busy again. Sweet letter from Nana because today is Corpus Christi. And she asked me to stop swearing – oh I will try – it has reproached me before now – & I must stop because I'm not like that really at all inside – or am I? Please God I'm not – Oh dear.

After hectic day's work there was a dance. Mr Green was back for the evening – & that made me happyish – because I like him. Then about 5 charming & fascinating American sergeants turned up. I got off with one rather mature one who is charming & v sweet to me. Anyway I'm going out with him on Sunday.

It's so lovely being as heartache free at the moment as I am because I enjoy people's company – like to flirt mildly if people are attractive – & enjoy so many different emotions &

learn about many people. And when one's heart is free one doesn't get hurt. I feel gay, detached & calm. And may I remain so for a little while!

The Yanks departed tight & sweet – & the Sgt Mess party spirit didn't really get going & it broke up flatly – my room however at about 1.30 was wrecked – oh dear. Shorty is back hooray.

Letter from Mary to Judy, 5 June:

Darling Judy, On Wednesday I went home again and Mummie, the Dove* and myself were all alone, which was rather heavenly. We dined in the garden at No. 10.

Papa and Mummie were both in terrific form. Discussing plans for going to Chartwell – Papa suddenly yelled in a voice of doom 'SAWYERS!'

(What was to follow? Fetch the CIGS? Summon the War Cabinet?)

'Sawyers – I desire in the first place food for my fish, grain for my birds and (long pause pregnant with fate) – in addition I do not require so many blankets!'

One or two enjoyable flare-ups during one of which Mummie said 'O you old son of a bitch.'

Dinner ended in mellow and happy silence. Papa sank into the New Yorker *– Mummie and I after 5 minutes rose to go. 'Don't leave me,' said the Dove pathetically. Mummie contemplated him with a judicial eye: 'The trouble is Winston – you like 20 people to come and watch you reading the* New Yorker*!'*

Quelle famille – and how I adore them.

---

* Code for Winston Churchill

Saturday 6 June

Boiling hot day. Inspection – woof.

Sir Frederick Pile & some other red tabs & 'P.J.'* I was told to be available – and 'P.J.' was v sweet & amusing & General Pile was also v kind. I got in a flap & saluted wildly & felt hot.

Went to ZEZO (gun site) for Sperry training. We were clearly not expected & after hanging around a while an ass of a Cpl came & gave us an inept drilling – continually goaded on by rather veiled, sour remarks from me – she kept on remarking 'Oh it's much too hot to work.' On our way back to camp we were dropped out for a delicious bathe at the Enfield Lido. Crowded but fun. And deliciously cool.

Indulged in mass washing, tidying & mending. Impromptu dance – v hot & not much fun. Took roll call – bed. Tired – hot.

Tuesday 9 June

Did lots of technical work. Mr Green back – thank goodness. Mr Cheney (now a Captain) turned up in the afternoon. He said he had recommended me as a CSM for a new mixed battery – & would I go? I was completely flabbergasted – & struggled to think clearly.

Whatever my decision – the fact that Mr Cheney suggested me has done something deep to me – because I value his opinion – was tortured with indecision & longed to talk to someone about it – but it was all too *sub rosa*.

Dance in evening to bid farewell to people going on cadre. Sergeant Philypp came and Sgt Hughes & a most wicked & impudent looking Sgt Novack – who caught my roving eye!

---

* Sir (Percy) James Grigg 1890–1964, Secretary of State for War

I talked to Charles quite a lot & danced with him – but his company palled a trifle – and I set my eye a-roving after Sgt N—. Didn't get a break until nearly the end of the evening – but made quite successful headway. He said he feared Phyl might be angry he was 'cutting in' – I couldn't altogether see what Phyl had had that Sgt N could cut in on. However returning to the bar Phyl was found rather silenced up and Scotched up. Evening became rather complicated. I behaved badly – reflex action! Seeing them off – Phyl made a determined pounce – & rather than have embarrassing scene & violent misunderstanding gave in unwillingly & cut it y short. Felt annoyed – ugh.

Also y angry with Laura & Scotty who (in front of Phyl) earlier in evening teased me a little too obviously about dancing à la Americaine i.e. cheek to cheek. So party as far as I was concerned had distinct moments of ennui & embarrassment – but it was a good party & ended rowdily enough.

Wednesday 10 June–Friday 12 June

Went on 24 [hours leave]. Mummie & Pamela at lunch. Fixed up with Pam to dine in evening. Spent afternoon looking at the exhibition in the National Gallery of 'Wartime Acquisitions of the Tate'. V interesting. Really enjoyed myself. Didn't mess around. But decided to look carefully at a few pictures. Took as main dish the Victorians & Pre-Raphaelites – & Blake.

Also looked at some lovely Johns & three striking paintings by Edward Burra. Mr Williams and Group Cpt Wilcock to tea – Wore stripey dress & looked below standard. Am too fat & red & my hands are like bits of meat.

Dinner party at Max (Beaverbrook)'s flat in Brook House. Max & little Max (Aitken), FDR Jnr – Geoffrey Lloyd – Sarah – Pamela, 'the Hairy Kit' & self. First collected Sarah, Pamela & Kathy [Harriman] at Grosvenor Sq.

Max was looking rather strained, I thought but he was in v good form. At dinner a long discussion about the growth of communism & socialism developed – and the growing power of the shop stewards. It was pointed out by little Max that the latter would cut no ice with the people fighting now in Libya & elsewhere. He said it was not true that the RAF is communistic – because it is officered & it respects men who are not for the most part socialistic or communistic. The officers of this war – will they only take it – have untold opportunities in the future. FDR Jnr talked endlessly & became a little tedious – but that I think was just Max's champagne & delicious iced white wine. FDR is fantastically good-looking, gay & charming.

As for little Max – I must say he's the tops. How pleasant people are who establish at once a civilised, gay & natural bond. But looking at Kathy – slim – competent – sophisti-cated & exquisitely dressed – & at Pamela voluptuous & furred & Sarah romantic & strange-looking – I then looked at myself & felt miserable. I look so aggressively healthy – I'm fat – my hands aren't pretty and might be better kept – and suddenly all my battery life, which for the last 4 months has been so sufficient for the day – & in which I have been so extra enthralled just lately – and which seems so important – suddenly it seemed terribly unimportant. And I felt a clod & girl guidy. Oh dear, dear, dear – it started a mood of depres-sion which lasted on & off till today Friday 12th – when I behaved badly – got a raspberry from Mr Green being back late yesterday – & finally unburdened my soul to him – he was sweet & v nice about it –

I wish I could get slim.

Last night I saw *Man Who Came To Dinner* for 2nd time & laughed more than somewhat – Mummie & Cousin Marigold [Sinclair] there. Had supper in Marigold's air ministry flat – it is lovely.

Monday 15 June

O/Sgt. Kit inspection. <u>Woof</u> the boredom. Went home to dinner. Mummie & Papa alone. The news is bad & he was in very low spirits. He was unhappy & tortured & Mummie & I tried so hard to comfort him. He may go to America on Thursday. Brendan arrived at the end of dinner & was cheerful & encouraging. I left with a very heavy heart – but Papa's last words to me were '. . . now not a word – & no one must see in your face how bad things are.'

<u>They won't</u>. At camp there was a dance in progress. 'Gee and her boyfriends' (otherwise Mrs Moulton) made the band. Mr Green asked me to dance – & began what for me was a tremendously enjoyable party. We had about 3 dances running together – interrupted by drinks in the Mess bar. Conversation flowed so naturally and easy. I felt completely calm and at ease & very happy. He said some very charming things – 'I don't know what I should do without you Sgt Churchill – & I always feel completely at ease with you.' And when – after discussing effects of army life I said regretfully how fat I was getting – 'Anyone who was at all put off by your weight doesn't at all merit knowing you.'

I am so deeply fond of him; I respect his brain and like his personality – and I'm not in the least in love with him – tho' I love his company. He showed me the ring he wears – which I thought was his wedding ring – he told me he took it from the hand of a dead German airman whose plane his gun site destroyed in France. It was rather a pathetic ring – with 1936 & 'Anni' engraved on the inside. Poor Anni.

We talked about marriage & his marriage in particular. I don't think it's altogether going with a swing – & I feel sorry. I think he can be very cold & cruel – & I think she loves him dearly. He does not believe in being 'in love' & he isn't – & I think it's writing *Finis* to their life together – But perhaps after the war it will be all right after all – I hope so much that it will. Party ended at about 2.

Thursday 18 June

Feeling frail – went home, expecting to see Papa before he went away. When I arrived I found he had gone the night before. Flying to America. Mummie & I had scrumptious cosy lunch together – salmon fishcakes – new potatoes with butter & poircs condés. And delicious drink called 'Ricardo'.

Afterwards Mummie rested on the sofa & I (after greasing up) fell into a lovely sleep till 5.

Had bath & changed into old tartan taffeta dress (short & it really looked well). Wore my turquoise – wow. I do my hair <u>out</u> instead of under now – it looked quite successful tonight.

Lady Limerick collected Mummie & they went off to Moiseiwitsch concert – & I went to a glorious High T at Kitty Bruce's.

After a scrumptious High T (which was really a full blown dinner) we repaired to the Polish Hearth in Princes Gate – feeling rather nervous. Soon however everything got going – I met some delightful Poles – with most wonderful manners. I felt how much worse the war is for them than for nearly all of us. At least we are chez nous. They were gay & sweet & danced beautifully. As for the Viennese waltzes – well – it was rapturous. I was most complimented because one of them said I was the only English girl who he'd met who knew how to waltz! Woopsi! I was flaunting a very exquisite flame chiffon handkerchief – pinched from Mummie – suddenly an airman + medals came up & said 'Mlle – your scarf – please give it me for I will wear [it] on all my flights for luck.' I was torn between the horror of confronting Mummie with the ghastly truth (<u>such</u> a lovely scarf & COUPONS) & the glamour and honour of being asked for a token in such a medieval way – The latter won hands down & I spent most of the rest of the evening dancing with the same airman who introduced me to his comrades & invited me forthwith to Northolt aerodrome – offering transport etc!

The dance was held in two large reception rooms – decorated in cream & gold – with terrifically heavy baroque mirrors – the windows on to the balconies were open & looked onto a lovely garden & trees. It was glamorous & most gay & I enjoyed every moment of it.

We subsided for a while after the party at 79 – & played gozo and fooled & larked à la Maugham-Bruce – lovely. And suddenly we all missed Robin very much – who is wounded & in hospital. David & Tony & I walked part of the way back & then taxied. It was a perfect evening.

Tuesday 23 June

News very depressing – I <u>wish</u> oh I <u>wish</u> Papa were home.*

Thursday 25 June

Feeling very 'leave conscious' . . .

Sticky dance in evening. Praise be Yanks didn't come. Danced, talked and drank with Mr Green – to – I think – our mutual satisfaction. Retreated to Command Post & larked around (the telephonists obviously thought I was tight when I proceeded to do ballet around the plotting room – but I wasn't. Just *joie de* going-on-leave.)

---

* He was in Washington meeting with Roosevelt

Friday 26 June

<u>SEVEN DAYS LEAVE</u>

Got up 06.45. Finished packing – shut case by dint of two people sitting on it. <u>V</u> heavy – practically ruined my prospects carrying it! Cross woman in tube barked her shins on it.

Lovely – lovely day. Feeling completely off my head.

Arrived home at 0900hrs. Mummie there & a kipper for breakfast. Changed into cotton dress (saxe spotted & white dress) & rushed off for hairdo at Marshalls. Did some cosmetic crawling & bought white fish net & tied my head up in it. Met Nana & Paddy at Cyclax – Lovely restful face do + glamour-full make up in velvet grape shades & navy blue eyelashes – wow! Not workaday but FUN.

Lunch at Mary Ann – Then Nana bought me 'Mikado' suite & I bought myself Tchaikovsky Piano Concerto. Then flying visit to Bumpus & bought *Coming of Aissa* by Oliver Baldwin (recommended by Mr Green), *Paintings by Van Gogh* & *The Soong Sisters*. Home about 3.30 & rested & snoozed till 5.30. Strawberries & icing sugar from Nana for tea.

Quick bath & changed into navy blue 'Miss America dress' now in 3rd year & rejuvenated by redipping. Nana & Mummie & I went to *The Mikado* at the Princes. Gay & fascinating – hideous chorus – fat & old. Walked home. Delicious supper – <u>v</u> sleepy. Bed – <u>v</u> happy.

Papa – *Dieu voulant* – arrives tomorrow.

Saturday 27 June

I was feeling so excited & relieved that Papa is home. When the train drew in Mummie & I got in to welcome him – not a very gay homecoming. His enemies have lost no time in his absence. It is strange to reflect that in the middle of world war Sir

J. Wardlaw-Milne, Roger Keyes etc etc could find nothing more glorious to do than table a vote of censure in Papa's absence & in the middle of a battle which sways to & fro & which so far has proved disastrous to us. It is stalling [sic] that when all Papa's abilities & energies should be now bent to retrieving the military situation he has got to fight a battle at home.

How our enemies must be rejoicing – wherever they are – at this vexation. How our friends must be bewildered & puzzled. What cheer & encouragement these amiable members are giving to the captive nations – I don't think. O man's ingratitude.

Monday 29 June

Slept disgustingly late. Sauntered down having had breakfast with Sarah at about 12.

Mummie, Sarah, Nana & I & Papa – in fact everyone decided to stay at Chequers. Lovely day. I spent most of it idling happily in deck chair on lawn. Went for a trial on Sarah's motor bicycle. <u>V</u> dangerous & uncomfortable. Great fun tho.

James Stuart* came for dinner to confer about debate. I thought he was rather a dream . . . Papa had bad news of the battle [of Gazala?]. He & I and Mr Stuart walked up & down the lawn. It was a soft night with high clouds & a moon gleaming through the rent in the ceiling. Papa was unhappy and anxious. It is so frightful that he has to deal with this political crisis when he should be concentrating every faculty on this battle.

I left him still pacing unhappily up and down. Oh darling – would to God I could help you.

---

* James Stuart 1897–1971, Government Chief Whip, later 1st Lord Stuart of Findhorn

Tuesday 30 June

. . . Went with Mummie to Harrods Aid to Russia exhibition. Papa lunched with the King. After lunch Mummie & I went first of all for a rather short visit to the Sickert exhibition & then went to St Paul's. The latter is a mournful sight. Battered, dusty & dead looking. But all the same one could see much of its grand loveliness.

Changed into navy American dress & hyacinth hat and gloves . . .

Ally picked me up abt 6.20 and we went to see 'Fine & Dandy'. It was quite funny and <u>v</u> well dressed. As we came out of the theatre it thundered and lightninged and we gave a lift to two other people. We dried at the Mirabelle. Ally was charming. We talked mainly *la politique* – we both disapporve violently of Sir J W-Milne and Roger Keyes. We also touched on *La France Libre* & General de Gaulle etc – Randolph – & the scenario about the letter – Ally took my side.

We then went to the 400 [Club]. We were joined by Sarah looking a knockout in a Strassner dress – (brown with emerald green embroidery at the waist of the jacket & on the pockets) and Dr Malcolm Sargent* who is fascinating. Lovely evening. I behaved like a spoilt child when we went home and tried to make everyone stay later – Ally took me home.

On contemplating my conduct I wept with shame and felt 'mis'. For I have the responsibilities & do the work of an adult. I had been behaving in a <u>v</u> grown up sophisticated way and then suddenly – like a façade – it all crumbles & I am awfully idiotic and young and ingénue – and bloody. Retired weepily to bed at 2.30.

---

* Malcolm Sargent 1895–1967, conductor of the Hallé orchestra and Liverpool Philharmonic

Wednesday I July

Dentist. Went with Nana to opening of House of Commons debate. Very crowded and attentive house. Sir John Wardlaw-Milne started off – with a long & unnecessary preamble about <u>why</u> he was moving a vote of censure. He then stated that Papa (veiling this by the words 'central direction of the war') interfered too much with the generals etc. The rest of his speech, which was not outstandingly composed or delivered – (in fact I thought it rather poor, considering how easy criticism is to make) dealt with production and also contained the suggestion that the Duke of Gloucester should be made Commander in Chief of the Armies. Wow! The House laughed loud & long.

He also went on the old hobby horse of separating the offices of PM & Minister of Defence saying we should have a strong Minister of Defence 'who would resign immediately' he failed to get his own way – but subject to the War Cabinet. (I <u>don't</u> get such reasoning myself).

He was followed by Roger Keyes and his effort was really PATHETIC. He seconded the motion by contradicting Sir John & saying – on the contrary Papa was set about by incompetent persons who kept him from organising & arranging affairs and that he <u>should</u> interfere with officers in the field. Then came an attack about the Admiralty administration (meaning the 1st Lord and the 1st Sea Lord). This was followed by the friendship stunt – the PM 'my political godfather', life-long friend etc. A member from the Opposition benches said did he realise he was contradicting the proposer of the motion & another Opposition member very logically pointed out that Roger professed to be an ardent admirer of the PM's & at the same time supported a motion that if successful would hurl him from power. Roger maundered on – it was almost embarrassing – it was so bad. Eva [Keyes] was sitting about two places away – passing a running commentary on the speech, which was rather aggravating. I smiled (rather nervously) at her as I went out but she stared through me. She was in deep mourning [their son Geoffrey Keyes had been killed in action and awarded a posthumous VC] & I feel so sorry for her and poor Roger . . .

Aneurin Bevan* made a poisonous speech. Point by point one could destroy his argument – but I should think the effect as a whole was very damaging. He speaks – pointing his phrases with little gestures – with a tone of wheedling spite. He at once attacked the govt on inferiority and quantity of weapons & also urged the importance of a second front.

Went to see Judy off to Breccles on her leave. I was so delighted to see her again – & she seemed in terribly good form. Prepared to go out with Sarah, Paul† etc. Paul came and collected me – and we sat and talked till about 9. At Manetta's in Clarges St we met a fellow journalist – & we sat and waited for Sarah and Malcolm Sargent till 10. Time passed pleasantly & finally they turned up.

EXQUISITE DINNER
Prawn cocktail
Chateaubriand steaks!
Strawberries & ice

Everyone very gay. We then saw Dr Sargent off on the train to Manchester from Euston. How mysterious and sinister a

---

* Aneurin, or Nye, Bevan, 1897–1960, Labour MP for Ebbw Vale and vocal critic of Churchill and the coalition government. Mary later notes that this speech was actually given on the following day, 2 July
† Another member of Mary's wide social circle, unknown

big station at night is. It reminded me of Papa's journeys up North when he was at the Admiralty.

Then Sarah and Paul and I and editor friend bundled back to Paul's flat – which we toured – viewing a rather wet and sickly looking puppy. We then drank iced milk & played records. Then Joe Evans (who I met once before when out with Red Mueller and found him fascinating) and Ed Parsons arrived. We talked about debate – & shortly afterwards Sarah & I went home escorted by Paul & the 'editor friend'.

Thursday 2 July

Very long and delicious lie. Read papers thoroughly. Dressed in a hurry – Mummie and I went to the House. I made a mistake – Aneurin Bevan spoke today – yesterday Bob Boothby made a competent & most helpful speech.

As I sat in the gallery & listened to all these carping voices – I watched the unhappy set of Papa's shoulders – & my heart went out to him in his anxiety & grief. I know his mind is more with the battle in Egypt than here – in the House. Sometimes I could scarcely control myself for rage at these little men – who have only jibes and criticisms to offer – For every one of these critics are little men – & failures. The only able one is Horeb* – and he's crooked.

Nana, Mummie & I alone for lunch. Put on sterner hat for afternoon instead of hyacinth creation. Felt terribly tensed up. Mummie obviously feeling the strain. Horeb made a despicable speech – slimy – clever – opportunist – ugh. The House was terribly crowded – Members standing at all the doorways. In the galleries – Mr Winant and Mrs W, M &

---

* Leslie Hore-Belisha 1893–1957, former Secretary of State for War, who was dismissed in Jan 1940

Mme Maisky, Averell, Kathleen, Quentin Reynolds, Nancy Tree.

Papa rose to speak at 3.30. His speech was a remarkable performance. Measured – exact – reasoned – dignified – & throughout an undertone of unalterable determination & sober hopefulness. I think my love and admiration of Papa is almost a religion to me – I sometimes feel I cannot hold the emotions I have for him. The House listened in rapt attention. Except for some of the critics – Eddie Winterton shrugging his shoulders & cracking his long fingers & smirking at Horeb. But Aneurin Bevan listening carefully & liking Papa's points & jokes – but maintaining his Opposition standpoint.

And then the division 475 to 25. And not as many abstentions as had been expected. Felt dazed & elated – Mme Maisky congratulated us warmly. On way out saw Wuthering Heights – Squadron Leader Grant-Ferris*. Went to Papa's room – he was pleased. Mummie & Sarah went on home. I stayed and had 10 mins all alone with Papa. A crowd had gathered outside the House & Papa was greeted by happy smiles & encouraging waves. One man shouted 'You stick it Sir.' Papa very much moved. Mummie very exhausted.

Wore my stripey dress.

<u>Dinner party</u>
Sarah. Ally
Nana. Paul
Self. M André Labarthe[†]

M Labarthe is charming but shy & has a somewhat tortured look. Discussed Free France, General de Gaulle etc. The Free

---

* Robert Grant-Ferris 1907–97, later Lord Harvington
† André Labarthe , 1902–1967, French physicist who had been director-general of French Armament and Scientific Research for de Gaulle and was founder and editor of the monthly review *La France Libre*

French evening at the Dorchester which we went to afterwards – was a hideous failure. Badly organised & not in good taste. Maggie Teyte sang passionate French love songs – with an indifferent accent – & it was laughable because she [is] stout & middle aged & has peroxided hair. Bea Lillie as usual v̲ witty. M Labarthe & I agreed over the awfulness of it & carried on an enjoyable conversation. He left after the show. Ally & I & Paul & Sarah went on to 400 – lovely evening. Just as we were going home we went to Jack Profumo's table & talked. I found him gay & charming. Invited Sarah & Vic & me to lunch tomorrow. Whoopee. Ally took me home. End of a lovely evening.

Monday 6 July

Manning. In evening Nat Gonella & his Stars in Battle Dress arrived & gave v high standard show, plenty of swing and quite good sketches etc – but my God were the Stars in Battle Dress trying – or were they? They kept on complaining about being in the army. I didn't enjoy the dance afterwards. It was so crowded & once or twice I thought I was just going to pass out. Then indigestion added itself to fatigue. (I wonder why I've been feeling so dead tired lately – perhaps my hectic and heavenly leave?!). I retired defeated to CP – & got hardest and awfullest bed – O God!

Friday 10 July

O/Sgt. Chilly & pouring with rain. Getting & keeping quarters clean in this weather – a hellish job. Rushed madly around. Mrs Dewar's inspection drove me mad. She's got such an unnecessarily brisk tone for the girls & she blusters & is awful.

V̲ realistic gas exercises in pm. Still pouring. Pip section behaved maddeningly . . . & everybody was rather cross and unco-operative – & I was absolutely at my wits end. Finally spider* <u>did</u> look all right for Mrs Knox's inspection.

She gave us all plus officers and girls from other sites – a wonderful 'pep' talk & question time. I asked (with shaky knees) about ATS wearing RA buttons and forage cap – got a straight answer. Girls thought she was the 'tops'.

Mrs Dewar got tight & we all stayed up late talking. Passionate arguments about commission question that has blown up to head. I was asked about it several days ago by Miss T – as soon as Judy came back we conferred. Regretfully we have decided to go – if we pass the Board. Probably we would go in September. It means leaving behind me so many things I truly value: Battery life, the girls and the men, the <u>real</u> people one meets – & the life that has made me feel a real person myself. It means losing the 'glamour' of being

> A sergeant
> A gunner girl.

But I have a feeling that now I should take a commission – that if I do not I shall be clinging too much to what <u>I</u> like & find interesting & exciting. Also, am I playing to the gallery a bit? I do find it so hard to made decisions. I find it hard to decide what I really OUGHT to do – & not to turn in my own soul the things I <u>WANT</u> to do into my duty. I have felt perplexed and fussed about it the last few days.

Monday 13 July

24 hours upset by Sgt Hooper's muddles and some of my own. Felt <u>v</u> miserable because I did so want to go home & I

---

* A block of barracks laid out in the shape of a spider

was feeling awfully depleted. Then gloom about OCTU descended on me. And finally I dissolved into tears to Mr Green – who, as usual – was sweet & kind & said he'd miss me when I went – then went off to spend afternoon and evening at home.

Mummie & Papa & Pamela at lunch – Randolph is on his way home – invalided out of the army. That makes me feel anxious. I hope to God he won't make things difficult for Papa.

Did a little shopping. Got a bottle [of] Coty & hand lotion – wow! Hair & nails done & then with Mummie to see *The Young Mr Pitt*. Excellent. I simply loved it. But it moved me very much – & made me wish more strongly than ever that I may always be connected with politics. To me it is not knavery but life & bread & the pursuit of happiness. I wish there was a fascinating young Mr P trotting around now. I wish young men were more fascinating & sparkling, witty & intelligent – but then of course they might not like me – ah well – *la vie*.

Sunday 19 July

Manning. Was just going to retreat for siesta when Papa RANG ME UP himself & suggested he & Harry Hopkins should come down to battery. I was in a twitter & so excited. The Major was sweet. The site was wrapt in sunny Sunday afternoonishness & Papa and Harry & Tommy all rolled up about 5.30. Papa was in his sunniest mood – & wearing a pale grey suit. Harry charming & debonair as always. It was a lovely visit & much more fun than when all the brass hats came traipsing round behind. The alarms were rung & we did a short show, which went very well. Then a quick tour of the camp which ended up in drinks in Sgts Mess.

I felt so proud & happy that Papa should have thought to visit me. It gave me such great pleasure.

Instead of marching drill I talked to Pte. Young for about ¾ hour – and tried to make her understand a little more about the point of army life & the Battery etc. I hope I succeeded.

Friday 24 July

Orderly sergeant. Doubtful whether I can go out tomorrow. I want [to] go SO much. Felt cross, spoilt, miserable.

Had a 'think' in the evening – as I was feeling generally rather low and depressed. Regard my behaviour lately with great distaste. Felt helpless and began to think about God and say my prayers. It suddenly occurred to me that when everything is going fine & people say what a success I am, and I am busy and happy I give God the go by & yet here I was tonight praying for his forgiveness, help and comfort because my own glorious faith in wonderful me had just been shaken a bit – and Mary wasn't feeling so good & had had a few knocks & was floundering – & so quite naturally & undoubtingly she goes to God as if he were a tap to turn on & off & asks for his help. And that made me feel how vain and arrogant & foolish I am – and I felt something approximating my true stature – which is mighty small.

Saturday 25 July

Definitely can't go out with Hugh. So sent telegram cancelling acceptance & had a good cry. (Not spoilt or cross this time – just disappointed.)

Worked hard all day. Lots to do. Mr Green is so kind & patient with me that it makes me marvel. I am more grateful to him than I shall ever be able to say for all he has done for me.

Am rather tired. Stayed up to check last people in. Hugh hadn't got my cancelling telegram so rang up in a rage and I felt embarrassed. Oh dear.

Tuesday 28 July

[WRITTEN IN RETROSPECT 20/8/42]

469 H(M) AA Battery RA WENT INTO ACTION AT 0136 hrs 29/7/42 and PIP section manning. Terribly thrilling. Rather breathless and not too frightened – just a little pang of agonising uncertainty and then a tearing roar & shaking & a vivid sheet of flamc & hot air rushing past one & then just the smell & taste of cordite.

And the girls were wonderful – but chattered rather a lot. But then as I was a little uncertain of myself I didn't quite take charge of them as I should have done. Rocket batteries were firing – lovely like fireworks and there were bangs & flashes all around. I can't really remember balancing my rate – tho' I suppose I did. But it's all been worth it & I'm so glad I've been into action with the section before leaving the battery.

I'VE BEEN INTO ACTION and I do thank God I didn't panic – I prayed so hurriedly just over & over again – please God let it be all right. This is the moment to which I have been called – please make me all right – & all the while balancing the needle & taking furtive peeps at the sky. Never has cocoa tasted quite so delicious – what a pity Mr Green & the Major weren't there.

Thursday 30 July

Long lie as normal when on 24 hours. Back to camp. Decontamination job thrust on me. Spent afternoon crossly trying to swot it up.

Gathered squad & retired to snooze on gas store shelves for a while. Flapdoodle – bloody silly exercise. Lights in ablutions which are decontamination centre fused. O hell. Flapped around. Finally gas alarms went – 2 pathetic gas bombs fired off. Smoke drifted thickly over Enfield – wind in wrong direction ha ha. Finally took off attractive & comfortable – I don't think – a[nti]/gas clothing.

Retired to bed. 10 mins later alarms. Tore to gun park. Plotted – & fired. Somehow much more frightening in CP where blackouts come in with terrific WHAM. No. 4 misfired – round stuck in breech and likely to explode. Went up & talked to girls. Felt shaky but thank [God] everything OK – girls calm but I think we all felt a trifle sick!!!

O section fired. Judy and I carried cocoa to CP – hurrying down hill & all 4 guns went off <u>WOW</u>. Judy and I got the giggles & sang alternatively 'Land of Hope [and Glory]' . . . and Dvorak's Humoresque (popular version!)

Friday 31 July and Saturday 1 August

To Reading for OCTU board. Not too bad. Both passed. Stood all the way back to London – hell – & hot.

Toozled ourselves up & in very pressed & brushed uniforms went to Cumberland to party given by charming Polish airmen – Judy went on ahead – I stayed to say goodbye to Papa. He & Mummie arrived back from lightning visit to Chartwell – & he took me into his room & told me 'I am going to Egypt to try & win this battle & then I'm going on to meet Stalin.' There was so much I wanted to say – how much I loved him & feared for him – how much I <u>longed </u>for his journeyings to be victorious – & much more – instead I could only find a rather choky voice to say: 'I'm so glad you're going – you must go. God bless you darling.' Drove round to No. 10 with him & Mummie. Kissed him goodbye with a heavy heart.

Dashed on to Cumberland where found Judy floundering with 2 charming airmen but looking a little embarrassed. The reason transpired – party at NORTHOLT in officers mess & us in uniform & having to be back at 12!!! Sensation then ACTION. Tore to annexe, changed in 5 minutes. Tore to Northolt, hysterical party for an hour. Tore ourselves away, tore back to London, tore to Enfield. Judy practically having hysterics on station as we were late. She changed in road into uniform – caught a hitch hike. Arrived 10 mins late – hot, giggling & exhausted. I had to waltz in in civilian clothes.

On Sat bloody awful cricket match prevented me going home for few hours to see Papa and was I furious or was I?

Sunday 2 August

Spent in paroxysms of tears & fears about Papa & flapdoodle about a story in USA press – here included as cabled – but until I actually saw it, was represented as a 'drunken brawl episode'. I was in hysteria about [it] – & Mr G v helpful & kind – I was frantic – Papa away – oh dear, oh dear.

Monday 3 August

Girls divine & furious about it. Dashed to Chequers, explained situation to Mummie who was simply wonderful & so calming & kind. I felt a rag & so vexed at silly cheap story but relieved it is not worse. 4 – 5 – 6 & so on & then days of gloom pressed in.

It's over ten days since I wrote anything in this diary. So much has happened and is happening. We have fired and it is just a year since I enlisted and Judy & I have been accepted for OCTU. And I haven't written anything partly because I've been so busy – but more because I've been in such a muddled and bloody frame of mind . . . nothing is. But all things seem.

Last night at home I tried on my pale blue crepe dress. When I bought it a year ago it suited me perfectly, but looking at myself in the looking glass last night I realised that it doesn't suit me any more. The dress hasn't changed – so I suppose I must have. And now, suddenly, I realise I am a different person.

I am so perplexed & lost I don't find the will or the ability to write it down. Before I joined up I may have been inexperienced & ingénue but I had a faith and shining hopes. I believed in 'God the Father Almighty' etc unquestioningly. I had burning ideals and an acceptance of events & people. And now after a year of army life which has taught me so much – I find myself 'a foiled, circuitous wanderer'*. I have learnt much but I seem to know even less. Do I still believe? Where is my undoubting burning faith? And my hopes have lost their shine. I feel so wound up & muddled. I am bloody awful – cross, dictatorial, tough, noisy, fat and much more.

Wednesday 19 August

This is about a week later – O hell – I haven't been able to write anything. It's out in the papers now about Papa – it's a wonderful relief just to be able to talk about it – it's been like a suffocating secret.† The last fortnight I've been in an unbelievably confused and miserable state of mind. Last night I behaved most shamingly & all but had hysteria in the Command Post. Judy was sweet & calm & smacked my face. Mr Green was patient & very gentle at the end & I felt in such depths of muddle & misery that I longed for an enormous black velvet curtain to come down over me – over everything outside & even more in my mind & for everything to be a wonderful still velvety blackness – I longed to faint & just black out – but couldn't.

Thursday 20 August

Today I feel a little flat & very much ashamed. I was so uncontrolled & awful – I know I'm making myself miserable & am being bloody entirely through my own fault. Papa being away (I wish to God he'd come back), Andy [Drummond-Hay]

---

* From 'Sohrab and Rustum' by Matthew Arnold
† Churchill had flown to the Soviet Union (via Egypt) on 1 August for the Second Moscow Conference with Stalin

being killed.* Terrible muddle & hopelessness inside me & then many vexations in the Battery have all combined & I have weakly succumbed.

Battery vexations are mainly due to new AT officers – v nice personally – but so far maddening to work with.

I grieve so much about Andy – his brother wrote me a charming letter – it's just a case of 'the loveliest & the best' – & I mind so much more than I have a right, or necessity to – but he was a dear and I shall always be so proud & glad I knew him.

Monday 24 August

On 9 o'clock news – Papa is home. THANK GOD. Felt hysterically relieved. Raspberry from Mr Green – gloom – ended happily by reading poetry & gossiping till 1am.

Monday 31 August

Changed sites. Marched 5 miles in pouring rain. Felt flattened – so did the girls!! Hectic day. Think I have got nettle-rash – come up in awful sort of bumps & I itch & itch & itch. Slept uncomfortably in the Command Post.

Tuesday 1 September

Am feeling so scratchy and irritable – <u>must</u> take a pull.† I'm sure I never used to be so bad-tempered & it worries me. A bad-tempered shrewish woman is <u>so</u> awful. But I really am finding this life a strain just lately. I <u>love</u> it – & I wouldn't give

---

* Andy Drummond-Hay, whom Mary had met at Chequers, was killed at El Alamein in July 1942
† Family slang – as in 'pull up my socks'

it up if I had a 100 opportunities. But the uncertainty of when & where & whether I go to OCTU or not adds to the trying-ness of everything. But I am determined to hold on very, very tight – I will not go into hysterics again. I WILL NOT.

Thursday 3 September

Slept till 11. Went with Mummie & Papa to National Day of Prayer service at Westminster Abbey. It was rather solemn & moving. Third anniversary of the war – 'and take to arm you for the fight the panoply of God.' Thank God – I've found my faith again – & I'm clinging to it. I am frightened of the depths I sink into if I don't hold on to it. Lord I believe – help thou mine unbelief.

Saturday 12 September

Peeled potatoes. Finished *Candide*. Dusty, Rene and I went out early to see *Gone with the Wind*. I do think it's a good film. Oh dear, I <u>wish</u> I looked like Vivien Leigh – I wish I could hope to captivate a Rhett Butler – I wish I had a 20 inch waist – I wish life was more romantic – I wish, I wish, I wish.

I sometimes wish that I could be <u>thoroughly</u> femininely silly and wear a scarlet or/and white crinoline – & long earrings – & long shining hair – & many beaux – all of them fascinating & amusing & <u>madly</u> attracted to me! Instead of being rather plump & red in the face & in khaki & feeling thoroughly vocational & competent. Oh hell – & I wish I had beautiful <u>small</u> hands. Bought fish and chips on way back. Ate them & went to bed.

Tuesday 15 September

My 20th birthday. And it <u>was</u> a happy one too. I was O/Sgt & very busy: rather squalid and tiresome case of Pte. Woolley – who has pinched somebody else's things.

<u>Telegrams from:</u>

Mummie & Papa, Nana (Paddy & Sukie), Margot Beville, Sheila & Mrs Nicholson, secretaries in Papa's office, ditto Mummie's, Sarah, Monty and a letter from Michael* asking me to marry him. Felt so well and happy all day and went to bed contented & 20.

It was the 2nd birthday of the Battle of Britain as well today – I'm glad I and the 'so few' celebrate together.

Wednesday 16 September

Manning. The Russian news is terrifying. Stalingrad fights on.

Thursday 17 September

My cake arrived & was scrumptious. I am longing for my 24 hours tomorrow. I answered Michael's letter and said 'no'. Although I always knew the answer would be no – yet I have considered marriage generally very much the last 2 days – and I know I am turning down a very sincere and sweet person – *mais ça ne marcherait pas*†. Fixed with Mr Green for the Mayfair at 7 tomorrow.

---

* Mary describes Michael as 'a charming young officer I had known slightly in Chartwell days.' Sadly no more is known about him
† 'But it wouldn't work'

Thursday 24 September

Slept till 12. Lunch with Judy. Went to see *This Above All*. It is the most shamingly bad film I think I've ever seen. I hated it so passionately I longed to jump up & protest. It was phoney, phoney, phoney from beginning to end. Tyrone Power with his weak womanish face trying to act a tense & tortured part. Joan Fontaine with condescending grace dillying about in WAAF uniform. O awful. And worst of all her long speech about England – yes & do you know they had the nerve to have the white cliffs of Dover in the background! If you want to make a speech about England, why be complicated? Why all this balderdash about new mown hay and London fog and thatched cottages and whatnot. Why not just say 'England is the island I have been born and bred in and I would proudly die to defend it'?

Saw Katharine Stanley for a moment. Talked for a long while to Mummie about Randolph and Pamela after Judy & I had put Cousin Venetia on train to Bognor. Mummie I think tends to make out that Pam is heartbroken & her life shattered. I do not think so – thank God it is not so. Somehow I cannot shed many tears over the break-up of this marriage. Randolph wanted a son, Pam wanted glitter & fun and a new milieu – both have got what they wanted & now there is an end.

I am sorry that it has failed – because of all women, I do believe Pam is most able to help Randolph & make him happy. I think he will be a loser on the bargain – but I think & hope she will be all right. It was not a very fine romance & I personally regret its breaking up but can in all sincerity find no tears to shed. Now Sarah and Vic – ah that is very different.

Thursday 1 October

Still no news [about OCTU] – feeling desperate so rang up Mummie who found out that we could either go on Oct 6th to Windsor or Nov 5th to Edinburgh. We chose Oct 6th – all this hanging about has made us unwilling to wait longer – but I feel we shall regret missing firing camp.

Saturday 3 October

Not a very busy morning. I don't know why but I can't see Mr Green without beginning to moan about something or other or behave badly or be cross. O Mary, Mary – where are you going to – are you going to be a querulous bad-tempered woman. I feel dissatisfied & unsettled somehow. And with this uncertainty it is so difficult to take a real interest in the work. Besides now, I do want to be an officer – NOT because I can't take it – but because suddenly I feel I can do it. In all humility that with many mistakes I yet can do it – & that I am capable of more. Dear God – help me & do not desert me for all my weakness & evil behaviour.

Ed came to camp in the evening & I felt all upside down. J divine & calming. Spoke to him a little. J & I then sat in canteen drinking cocoa & planning our wedding to mythical & fascinating Americans! Early bed – wrote up diary.

Sunday 4 October

Behaved quite foolishly whole day – felt remorseful & miserable. Tried to pull myself together & it seemed to make things worse. In evening after violent explosion of temper suddenly dashed off to gun park. Dusk was falling fast & no one could see my tears & I felt I could not bear the lights & camp – &

also I hoped Greeny might find time to talk to me – I wanted to tell him I was sorry I had been & was so utterly hopeless & childish. But he was busy & indifferent – I don't blame him, I expect he was fed up – I'd been like a fiend all day.

And so then I wandered out over the fields at the back of the gun park crying hopelessly & uncontrollably – I wanted to be alone – the hell of not having anywhere to be alone & people staring at one & wanting to comfort one – And then when I got nearly to the fence I suddenly felt frightened – & had to go a little nearer camp – & I wandered like a silly sheep aimlessly until I just sat down on the road & howled & howled. And I hated this army life so much – & I wanted someone to come – no one in particular – but just someone infinitely kind & comforting who would have a handkerchief & would just understand – But no one came & I just cried on.

There is something awfully ridiculous about a large woman of 20 sitting in the road crying for home!! It makes me smile a little now – because I felt so unutterably homesick & I longed for a natural life – not idle – but a busy life against a background of the people I love – & who love me for all my faults & foolishness. Not this strained, queer existence, where relationships are made so unnecessarily difficult.

And I came back to camp & Judy was sweet & gave me butterscotch & we talked till lights out. After I took roll call I checked in at guard tent – Greeny was there & I just longed to say O please forgive me & try to understand. I like him & respect him so much – & I should hate to leave this camp forfeiting his good opinion – But I just said 'Goodnight sir' – O hell. After all my tears & bemoanings & wailings I said my prayers – & tried to find something to hold on to. Went to sleep fairly happy & very warm.

Think this limerick in *New Statesman* rather funny:

There was once a flock of wild geese
Whose numbers were on the increase.
Remarked Peter Scott*
'I must paint the whole lot.'
Which he did – & still does – without cease.

Monday 5 October

Took a definite pull at myself – Mr Green a bit grim – don't blame him either. Created about food & flapped about Pte. Adey [sic] have a baby.

Sudden summons – 'will Sgt Churchill & Cpl. Montagu pack their kit & go to BHQ at once.' Fled to Command Post & said goodbye to best part of section. Had so much I wanted to say & couldn't. Wrung their hands chokily – everyone very sweet. Greeny charming & me tearful – clutched his hand said goodbye sir – & just ran as tears ran down my cheeks.

Because despite the fact that I want to go now – I hate leaving 469 and the girls & the instruments & a life that has taught me so much & given me so many opportunities. I have been through these goodbyes so many, many times in my own mind – p'rhaps that's why I wanted to get them over. Finally departed on lorry & Pip section waved us goodbye – and I felt determined but sad as I lost sight of their gay smiling faces.

No – I'm glad to go & sad to go. But I do want to be an officer now. I want to try terribly hard to make this strange army life as happy as possible for the girls – I feel so much how terribly important they are – & how much there is an officer can do. But as the lorry drove us over to BHQ I knew this is an end of a chapter of my life.

---

* Peter Scott, 1909–89, ornithologist and artist, specialising in bird-painting

And of course – I would have regrets – O damn. I just wish I had been my best self instead of my worst self for the last few days.

Spent afternoon at BHQ tearing around after kit. Home in evening. Mummie tired & rather cross. The Winants, Diana (who's going to have another baby – hooray) & Mr Myron Taylor (USA envoy to Vatican). It was v interesting. Messages from Mr Taylor to Pope & vice versa read. Most beautiful language & very encouraging.

Feeling a little dead.

Tuesday 6 October, Windsor

Finished packing – said goodbye. Dashed to London – shopped frantically – lunch at Fortnums. Caught train. Arrived at Imperial Service College at about 3.30. A very good modern building – Everyone looking terrifying tied up in white tape. Judy & I in same co[mpan]y: C, but different platoons & rooms. Dreary girl (vicar's daughter) & <u>charming</u> FANY in my room. Pleasant & busy afternoon & evening.

Before I went to bed – but last thing I took down my sergeant's stripes & golden guns. I minded that terribly. I am so proud of them & they mean such a lot to me. They were mine of my own getting – & winning & keeping. So I went to sleep not Sergeant Churchill – but Cadet Churchill. 'Tomorrow to fresh woods & pastures new.'

Wednesday 7 October

Breakfast 8. Wrote essay 'How far does the platoon officer influence the happiness & efficiency of her platoon.' After break there was Kit Inspection. After lunch a very good inaugural lecture by the Commandant. Made me feel very

inadequate & vocational. Medical Inspection. Awfully nice
MO (woman). Judy & I went out & after finding Cockpit closed
had good tea at Fuller's. Rang up Mummie – Papa is not very
well – oh dear.

Thursday 8 October

Settling down love it – Lectures very interesting.

Friday 9 October

Judy & I I think came top in Gen Knowledge. Some answers
were really rather frightening – M. Maisky is – ballet dancer!

Wednesday 14 October

Guest night. Major Dwight Whitney – Judy was Cadet Officer
& sat next to him – lucky girl. He gave a very good talk. A
little long – but plenty of meat. I was maddened at question
time by the idiocy of some of the questions! 'Why do
Am[erican] sgts wear their stripes a different way from ours!!!!'
& so on. He was very patient.

Thursday 15 October

Thought constantly about Ed – damn. Oh I forgot – in morning Sen Cmdr James (ex Charity Loveday) lectured us on the
AEC. EXCELLENT. So cultured & civilised & common-
sense. She referred to some of the General Knowledge
answers. I must say when someone says M. Maisky is a ballet
dancer – & many howlers akin – one feels depressed. For
these girls are, I suppose, the pick of Eng[land]'s women – &
yet dear God – some of them seem singularly inert.

I am feeling all afire with crusading feelings!! How <u>awful.</u> Oh dear God – I do want to be able to do something real & worth while & worthy of the girls I have had the honour to live & work with in the ranks – they indeed are the salt of the earth. I only ask to serve them well.

Sunday 18 October

Woke up quite early with a feeling of excitement. Delicious not having to get up early. Snoozed – read *Soong Sisters*. Wrote diary & letter to Mummie. Cleaned brass & shoes. Got up about 11. Served in bar 12–1.

Judy & I both caught 2.25 & met Sandy in Paddington Booking Hall – feeling terribly excited – giving Ed up for lost – he turned up – I felt a little breathless & tried to be very casual. Made an unsuccessful attempt to get into Officers' Sunday Club – but 'only commissioned ranks miss' so feeling rather mortified we went slumming down Park Lane to the Dorch[ester]. Ate tea & Judy & I behaved atrociously & I felt quite light headed. Walked through Hyde Park & listened to tub-thumpers – none v amusing.

All went to very funny film – *They All Kissed the Bride* – Melvyn Douglas & Joan Crawford. Walked back through dimly moonlit streets to Vanity Fair in Stratton Street, Ed & I holding hands & laughing – & I felt I was walking on air. <u>American custom</u>: If two people walking hand in hand are parted by something – eg a lamp post – they must hook little fingers & say 'Bread & Butter' & once it was 'Sugar & Jam'!

Vanity Fair is heaven – very quiet & gay. Had 2 iced Pimm's & felt WONDERFUL. Good dinner. Then we all started walking to Hyde Park Corner to put Ed on his train – Judy & Sandy with consummate tact seemed to disappear. I became foolishly dumb as we walked so happily hand in hand & people surged past us & the noise of Piccadilly traffic waxed & waned & yet we seemed isolated together – & suddenly – right near the Federation Club (!) – ED KISSED ME.

And then we remembered when we'd first seen each other – & how I'd thought he & Miss Barker were having a walk-out – & how he'd seen me in the concert – & I felt deliriously happy & he said 'I'm crazy about you, Mary.' And then at Hyde Park gates he kissed me again – & to be in his arms seemed all this & heaven too to me. And then we discovered Judy & Sandy & went into the tube – & Ed had lipstick on his face & we all shrieked. And then he kissed me goodbye – & was gone.

But I felt so elated & ever since then I've thought about him constantly – & remembered the things he said. I can't remember feeling quite like this before – am I in love? And how will it all end? Or is it just a beginning? O darling Ed – Judy was too kind & patient & tactful.

Wednesday 21 October

. . . My thoughts have turned constantly on marriage during the last few days – I think because I am so bemused with Ed – I want it & yet I own I fear it in so many ways. And as this week wore on I began to have doubts as to whether I want to get married now – not to Ed particularly – for one thing I hardly know him – nor has he asked me – but the whole problem has been in my mind.

At moments I feel – how romantic & nice to be married young & have a fascinating husband & bouncing babies – & at other times I think I don't want to marry yet – give me a few years to be with Mummie & Papa again – & that thrilling interesting world they move in. A world which I feel is real &

matters because it is built on ideas & dreams & conceptions & affects life the world over so profoundly. I should hate to marry someone who didn't love that world – who couldn't or wouldn't fit in. Judy thinks I love my family too overpoweringly – I think in a way she's right – but I don't see what I can – nor would I could I – do about it. They are my life. I see I would have to love someone unbelievably much to leave them.

Ed sent sweet letters & then towards the end of the week they cooled off – & I cooled too – & then I went home to Chequers for the weekend – & I didn't want anyone else any more. And joy of joy I felt they needed me & that I could be useful to them & I felt so much beloved & wanted. But first I must finish the week.

Thursday 22 – Saturday 24 October

On Thursday night I was Fire Picquet. Cleaned & pressed & mended & read etc. On Friday night Judy & went to see *Torn Banner* at the Theatre Royal – it was very moving. On Saturday the whole OCTU got a terrifying raspberry from Mrs V – about blackouts – disciplinary measures threatened. Long CO's parade – but successful. Spent afternoon getting cheque cashed & odd shopping etc. Went to see v good film *Dangerously They Live* – had supper at Hell's Kitchen.

Too awful – Chequers is so full tomorrow Judy can't come. Felt awful about it & she was awfully disappointed. Poor sweet I fear she is awfully unhappy these days – she seems to have a lonely life – wish I could do something.

Sunday 25 October

Woke up with happy feeling – 'I'm going home today.' Long rather sick making C[hurch] parade. Caught train to Slough by 5 mins dashing all the way. At Slough was Sawyers to drive me to Chequers. It was lovely driving through the autumnal countryside on this chilly day – pale gleams & shadows of light flickered every now & then across the woods & fields.

Arrived at Chequers about 12.15 dashed into hall & found blazing log fire & Mr Winant – who seemed most pleased to see me – & I was certainly pleased to see him. Mummie & Papa were glad too – & I was overjoyed. Party for lunch was:

Mrs Roosevelt

Miss Thompson*

Anthony & Beatrice Eden

Robert Hopkins (weedy & has a family look)

Elliott Roosevelt

Flags, Mr Martin – Mr Winant, self, Mummie, Papa, Sir Charles & Lady Portal, Miss Brookes.†

M & P & I were at door to welcome Mrs R – she is so natural & kindly & exudes energy & life.

Lunch went off very well. Scrumptious food – had double helpings! After lunch all the 'girls' except Mrs Eden & me went off to Fulmer Chase. Sat & talked with the men & listened for a while – then Papa – who was in terrific form – went to sleep & sent us all out for a walk. Pouring rain & very cold – but quite fun. Goodness how charming everyone was to me. It made me glow with happiness. Had tea in White Parlour – wonderful fire – & I suddenly was acutely aware of

---

* Malvina Thompson, private secretary to Eleanor Roosevelt

† L. M. Brookes, hon. secretary of Fulmer Chase Maternity Hospital for officers' wives, where Clementine Churchill was the chairman

the gleaming lights of the silver tea set & the soft glow of the fire & a feeling of warmth & protection & cosiness – and being 'chez soi'.

They all came back from hospital – I gather visit was a great success. I am glad – Mummie & Lady Portal & Miss Brookes have all striven so unendingly to make it the TOPS. Had luscious bath – talked to Mummie & had short talk with Monty (who alas – through ill-health is leaving – she will be a great loss).

Dinner great fun – Sarah arrived looking very beautiful but very ill. After dinner Papa v sweet & tender – & I left about 10.15 feeling strong & loved & so proud of them. And somehow this day banished all thoughts or feelings for Ed – so strong is the charm of being chez soi for me.

Beautiful moonlight. Chilly. Had puncture on way – took long time changing wheel . . . Rolled into bed – happy.

Saturday 31 October

Went to London in afternoon & met Ed alone for first time. Felt so happy in his company & he is good-looking.

Found Mummie resting at annexe – in state of exhaustion after her week with Mrs Roosevelt. Ed & I went to Haymarket Club – joined later by Sandy. Co-opted both boys for Belinda's party. Returned to flat & found Judy. Had bath – made boys clean our shoes & buttons & made lightning appearance in one of Mummie's fetching housecoats (pink one with lavender sash) – had desired effect. Dashed to Dawsons' party – conglomeration of dimmish girls & guardees. Dined at Savoy. Packed with tarts & actresses getting contracts – business men & queer girl friends – Americans & blondes. Had to leave early – Ed & Sandy put us in train – Ed kissed me goodbye. Am feeling very much head over heels with love???

Monday 2 November

Find that I await Ed's letters with wild excitement. Have invited him for next weekend. Am in flutter.

Wednesday 4 November

Blanket fog descended & cast cold gloom over passing out parade – which however was a great success – Gen Paget took the salute and it was all most military and impressive.

I spend most of my time now thinking & writing 'Mary Conklin'. Drive Judy mad by continual maunderings – do you think he'll propose – if so when & where – what should I say. Could I bear to live so far from Mummie & Papa. As week goes on I feel more and more that I would rather like to be Mrs Edwin B. Conklin Jun.

Thursday 5 November

Poured with rain all day. Cold & gloomy. Longing for weekend's leave. Had hair done at Louis in 'leave' style!

And O of course most important of all – the 7 o'clock news. I woke & heard 5 strike & for 2 hrs lay in the dark warmth & thought & thought – & imagined how lovely it would be to be married to Ed. Outside the rain fell steadily. Dewar woke up & said that on the midnight news it had said Rommel's army was in 'full retreat'.* The seven o'clock news confirmed this – I felt stunned with excitement & dashed down & told Judy. Can it be that the tide is on the turn at last? Felt a warm, excited glow all day.

Series of ribald telegrams passing between me & Ally all

---

* Towards the end of the Second Battle of El Alamein

this week. In reply to his first one I wired 'Like some of our elder statesmen my lips are sealed.' And got back an Allyish reply.

Friday 6 November

Morning seemed to drag. Caught 1.05 by skin of teeth. Thought of Ed all way up . . .

Ed (looking fascinating), Sandy & a charming WAAF called Nan Smith arrived for drinks. Then walked to Lansdowne – delicious dinner – hors d'oeuvre – Homard Thermidor & ice CHAMPAGNE. Ed fascinating & sweet & said the NICEST things. About 11.30 we went on to the Embassy [Club] – it was a starless, moonless night – dry & very still – the trees in Berkeley Square were dark velvety forms against deep gloom. There he kissed me – & said 'Mary I love you so.'

And then as we walked along Bruton St just in front of Sandy & Nan – he said – 'I want to ask you something I have no right to – Mary, will you marry me?' Sandy began talking to us then – & we only evaded them in Bond St. Ed said – 'I don't want your answer now – but think about [it] – I don't want to rush you' – and I felt so so happy in his arms. And we told each other just how seriously we regarded marriage.

And then we joined the others in the Embassy – which was very crowded. Went home around 2. Said my prayers very earnestly – I felt I needed guidance so much.

Saturday 7 November

Breakfast in Mummie's room. Nana a shade discouraging about Ed . . .

. . . Went to pay visit to Sarah – she had gone. Met Mr Winant in hall – he was sweet. Mummie said Miss

Hamblin rang up embassy the other day & Mr W himself answered! I expect he'd sent all the staff out for a holiday – as Mummie says he's 'Jesus Christ in trousers'. Walked home. Was wearing the new Molyncux dress – it's too lovely really. V simple & tailored. After scrumptious lunch – pheasant – queer mushrooms & goffies & honey – Ed arrived & Mummie & he & I drove to Chequers.

I told Nana in the morning that he'd proposed – she said yes she knew 'cos of the look in my eyes – balderdash. I told her which was quite true I hadn't at all made up my mind. America's an awful long way. Decided to tell Mummie after weekend. It was a lovely drive   Ed & Mummie seemed to get on very well. I think he is a bit deliberate & lengthy.

Writing all this up in retrospect I see really that it was during the car ride that I first became conscious of feeling irritation at his sweet, minute & leisurely way of recounting the most trifling details of his life 'when I was a youngster' . . .

The woods are most beautiful just now round Chequers. Papa greeted us on the doorstep – & Tommy & Uncle Jack were there & Monty, who joined us all for tea. After tea Ed & I went for a walk to the top of Coombe Hill. It was a lovely walk – I love the closing in of a fine autumn afternoon – and it was quiet & clear. But there didn't seem much to talk about. But I felt very proud to be walking along with such a fine & good-looking person – & he does look rather fascinating – in his US uniform & that wonderful gold eagle.

We came in & toasted in front of a huge log fire. He had brought me down a tin of peanuts, p[ai]r of silk stockings, packets of hairpins, lipstick, too lovely. Sarah arrived looking ill & lovely. I was feeling a bit irritable about Ed by now & defensive. Before dinner Papa told Sarah & I that the American & English forces were to attack at 1 o'clock the North African coast. We all felt a little breathless all evening I think. Sarah it now appears has been doing the intelligence work for it under lock & key for the last 2 months! Sensation!!

I sat next to Papa at dinner – Ed next to Sarah. We got nearly to the end of dinner when Papa asked Ed which way he voted – 'Wal* – both ways' said Ed. And something shut in my heart – for he had told me he voted Republican. Oh Ed – on such small phrases does emotion hang! Then he embarked on 2 stories – I SWEATED & prayed (literally) for the end – Papa was too sweet & patient. After dinner we saw a bloody film called *Across the Pacific*. I went away soon afterwards with Sarah & Mummie – feeling no stomach to face Ed alone. I stayed & talked to Sarah for ages – I felt strained & a little wild – just a CRUSH dying – & I had so believed it was the real thing! Sarah was sweet. Long, fascinating gossip. I made up my mind irrevocably then – the answer is NO.

Sunday 8 November

Sarah had to leave early. Ed & I breakfasted in sunlit dining room in an empty silence that fidgeted me – I think I commented on the lovely, beautiful, nice, fine DAY a thousand times. After breakfast left him to read papers – went & saw Mummie & Papa. Papa, Mummie told me, was in a flap & said she was mad to let Ed come to Chequers because then I'd marry him & go to America & she'd be miserable & I'd be miserable too. Mummie quite calm & very sweet. I told her he'd proposed – & said I'd decided 'No'. When I went to see Papa he was so sweet & did his duty as a father! 'Now don't you go marrying that young man – he's very nice – but you wouldn't like American life . . .' etc.

Papa left to entertain General de Gaulle at No. 10. G de G

---

* Mary's attempt at American drawl

wasn't told of attack because of security! This was to be a soothing down luncheon. The news broke too wonderfully – Mummie & I listened to the radio messages & instructions to the people of North Africa. Dear God – what wonderful news. When I think of the sad & disappointing news we have all waited on at Chequers – & now. It is like breathing again – great breaths of strong sea air – or coming suddenly round a corner & gazing on the lighted glory of snow covered peaks. Victory – we are all so happy & excited.

Mummie & Miss Lamont & I all went for a long, lovely, Sunday morningish walk. At lunch were Monty & I & Ed & Mummie. I nearly went <u>mad</u> at Ed's narrative – & hustled him off to catch a train. I was rather glad when he was gone.

Wednesday 11 November

Poppy Day. Short service. Thought of Tom & Andy. 'They shall not grow old as we . . .'. In the evening famous brouhaha with a ridiculous old brig called Firebrace. He gave us monstrously patronising lecture on the Red Army. Judy & I <u>shaking</u> with rage. Afterwards I asked him as boldly & as icily as I dared about what <u>he</u> called 'inefficiency of R/Army'. The way he spread himself pompously in front of this audience of admiring women gave me the sick [sic]. I was almost in tears with rage – had several rows & went to bed SEETHING.

Friday 13 November

Had 2 most <u>devoted</u> letters from Ed. Felt irritated by them. Wrote & said 'no' as simply & unwoundingly as possible. I <u>am</u> fond of Ed – & I do value his love – for I know he loves me deeply & truly & I also know he is good & sweet. He is just one of the nicest people. I feel a little guilty as I did lead him on – But I thought I was madly in love with him. It's all this seeing of one's friends constantly in restaurants & at parties – & never calmly & quietly & normally.

I said in my letter 'I don't know much about love – I have not had much experience of it. I do not know how it lives or why it dies & leaves one treading the earth again & seeing the world in focus once more – but I do know marriage without it can be hell.' And I mean that – I am perplexed. I loved him – & now I do not. Why? Or how?

Sunday 15 November

Church parade. As we paraded the chimes from Windsor began – victory bells – Our own college bell clanged discordantly but still the <u>thought</u> was there!! We sang 'Onward Christian Soldiers' – 'At the shout of triumph, Satan's forces flee' – O it's too wonderful. Apart from good hymns the service was dreary. Got lift in taxi – caught train. Sawyers met me at Slough. Drove to Chequers – where big conference in progress. Mummie had gone to London. Lady Portal there. Felt inefficient & overwhelmed by lunch party of 17, with which I had to grapple – But WHAT a party.

I sat between 'Glamour Pants' & Sir Charles Portal – great fun & very hilarious. The rest of the party was:

General Smuts (who so gay & v kind to me & full of life & vigour)
CIGS
Pug
Tommy

Mr Peck*
Brig Hollis
Gen Smith (Gen Eisenhower's 'shadow' here)
Gen Gale
Sir Dudley Pound
Papa
Lady Portal

It was an enjoyable & exciting lunch. Afterwards talked to Lady Portal till second session of conference ended around 4.30, '16th Front' now having been planned.

Everyone left. Felt depleted. Tea. Prof arrived – & Mummie came back <u>v</u> tired & fell asleep straight away. Bathed – then wrote 'duty' letters till dinner. Very quiet & pleasant – Papa in good form. Afterwards saw heart-rending excellent film *The Old Maid*. Entertained the RA & CG officers to drinks – Papa came in in his dragon dressing gown & gave us the news – 13 subs sunk in Med. Left about 12.30 – feeling warm & loved & happy.

Saturday 21 November

CO's parade. Spent whole afternoon preparing for dance – Moyra Garvie & I are responsible for buffet. Dewar was WONDERFUL & constituted herself sandwich queen all pm – all evening organised coffee etc etc. Felt happy having something real to do. Enjoyable gossip with Judy (in her bath) (I mean Judy was) about the young men we know – p.a.† Charles Rutland – ugh – Hugh F – mad – Ronnie – soaking wet, OH HOW GLOOMY.

---

* Sir John Howard Peck, 1913–1995; Assistant Private Secretary to Churchill, 1940–45
† Presumably Mary means 'par exemple'

Dance – after all nerves & fears – was a <u>roaring</u> success. In the end more men than girls. Fascinatingly gay Americans, solid Guardsmen, Sandhurst cadets, F[ree] French, RAs, some civilians. Band of Lifeguards the TOPS – food lasted out & was success – oh heaven – great fun. Bed exhausted but happy.

During week had Ed's letter in answer to mine. It was sweet & kind. He really is THE nicest person. But it devastates me if people put SWAK on envelopes[*] – I shall retaliate one day with a SWAKUA – (sealed with a kick up the arse). And also he wrote me a 'POEM' – O DEAR. But anyway he & Sandy were coming to the dance   but never came. Sorry. Telegram arrived later – saying he couldn't make it.

Sunday 22 November

Lovely frosty morning. Judy and I left early for home. I love driving – & it is a beautiful route from Slough to Chequers. What lovely names the Buckinghamshire villages have – Great Missenden, Amersham, Aylesbury, Chalfont St Giles, Beaconsfield. Judy & I think Meriton[†] must have been like Beaconsfield. And how gay, with all the militia!

Talked to Mummie. Am so thrilled for the Queen has included me in her invitation to Mummie & Papa to a 'Thanksgiving' day party for American officers at Buckingham Palace. Wow & woof!

Judy & I set out at 12 to have drinks with the RA officers at Coombe House. Mummie walked a little of the way with us. It was great fun – but I blush to confess Judy & I both got 'Tiddly'. It wasn't altogether our fault – we only had 2 gins &

---

[*] 'Sealed with a kiss'
[†] Meryton, from *Pride and Prejudice*

limes & masses of soda. I fear they must have been <u>terribly</u> strong. Luckily I don't think they noticed – as we knew we were a bit tight & took wild control. Dreary AT officers. Arrived home we decided empty stomachs accounted for this light headedness. Felt terribly vague & unreal – control a great effort. By the end of lunch I was awash with iced water! Didn't feel properly sobered up till halfway through afternoon.

Mr Morrison* arrived for lunch – also Brendan. Judy & I took Mr M for walk afterwards. Lovely frosty air. Sir Stafford Cripps had meanwhile arrived. Mummie left for London, she is going to have slight leg operation tomorrow. She told me about the cabinet changes. After tea (oh I forgot Mr Law, who is to be V-R of India, was here too). Judy & I went & had drinks (this time plain water for me & v controlled booze for J!) with Coldstream. Riotous 1½ hrs. Great fun.

On 9 o'clock news cabinet changes announced. Sir Stafford & Mr Morrison were sitting on either side of Papa & we toasted them. I can't express how much I admire & like Sir Stafford. He is so deeply sincere – & one really does feel he <u>only</u> cares about winning the war & not his own career. Papa is indeed well-served, and I do honour people who have ideals & keep them & follow them. I sometimes wonder how many of my shining ideals which I had when I was 17 will remain when I am 40 – I sometimes feel sort of lost & dead – & then sometimes again I suddenly feel sure & strong. And then too I wonder what being not young will be like. I dread it.

I am wondering so many things just now – what my life is going to be – whether I will marry – I want to marry – but not now. And although I know that the things I seek in life & can

---

* Herbert Morrison 1888–1965, Home Secretary and Minister of Home Security

give to life will come from a happy marriage – I can't visualise the person I would fall in love with. I've never really been in love. I <u>thought</u> I was with Ed – but it passed as suddenly as it came – and now he irritates me – his admiration & his eyes IRRITATE – & yet, God knows I'm vain enough & anxious enough to be desired – and perhaps that's it – I want to be desired & not possessed, either physically or spiritually or mentally. I felt irritated the moment Eric had a right to be in my company, to claim my affection & kisses – and although Ed was never my fiancé – yet the minute the closer intimacy & right to probe into my heart & mind – which seems to belong to someone who has proposed – appeared, suddenly, I see, of course only in retrospect, I felt irritated & a little hostile. I wish I understood it – to Laurence or Ally my mind & heart are an open book & I don't feel hostile, just safe & restful. Laurence has no <u>right</u> – nor can ever have. Ally has no right – save the one he has created through long years of friendship.

And yet I believe in marriage as laid down in the Prayer Book, I would want to defer to my husband – I could not bear to be a bossy, over-bearing wife. And I would not want to lead an independent 'I go my way' marriage – or rather try to – I think it would crash in 5 mins. 'My true love hath my heart And I have his.' That is how I would like my marriage to be. But how or where to find my true love – & then – he might not want me.

Oh I couldn't bear to make a mess of my marriage – And I want to put <u>everything</u> into it – my heart & mind & will. But what haunts me is that my husband would weary of me – & look to other people for pleasure & gaiety & comfort. It would drive me mad – & miserable. And then too – I am very ingénue & hopeful, I dream of a man:

as good-looking as Glamour Pants
as charming as Sir Charles Portal/Pug
as witty, intelligent, entertaining as Ally/Hugh/Laurence
and who would love me dearly, truly & only. Ah me –
    where is this beeootiful young man and of course he
    must be well-up in current events, politics etc, love
    poetry, reading, plays, be an exquisite dancer, have
    good taste & ambition.

And so I fear I'm a bachelor girl – for a while anyway and just now I feel <u>no</u> desire for marriage yet. There is so much to do & see & think about – so many people and then of course my family. I belong to them – & I love them so much. As soon as I get out of the army I want to enjoy their company to the full – and live the exciting, thrilling, interesting life they can give me. And I want to help Mummie and take the strain off her – & be with both Mummie & Papa – I love them so much. And then again, I don't think I really like <u>young</u> young men very much – oh dear, la vie, la vie. And yet I think I could take very much to heart Polonius' 'This above all – to thine own self be true, And it will follow as the night the day, Thou canst not then be false to any one.'

Thursday 26 November

Thanksgiving Day and I'm <u>thrilled</u> at the thought of the party at Buckingham Palace. Caught 1.05 train & had picnic lunch. Found Mummie still in bed – but quite well & very gay. Tidied up frantically. Car took me to No. 10 at 3. Found Papa talking to Adml Noble who is off to Washington on a mission. We set off about 3.10.

    I felt <u>so</u> excited – couldn't have been more thrilled if I'd been in white satin & feathers (tho' of course that <u>would</u> have been rather gay). And I felt so proud going with Papa. When we arrived we were shown into a drawing room by Sir Alexander Hardinge. Here we waited – there was Mr Winant, the Mountbattens, Ladies in Waiting, Admiral Stark & so on. The other guests were being shown into the next door room. Then another door opened & the Queen followed by the King & the 2 Princesses came in.

Papa unnerved me by saying in a hoarse whisper as Patricia Mountb. kissed the Queen's hand & then her cheek – 'You don't do that' – I was feeling <u>VERY</u> nervous by this time & I do hope I curtseyed ok. The King asked me about the OCTU – which was rather nice of him I thought. Then we stood behind the R[oyal] F[amily] as they received the guests. Papa had the King's permission to leave soon afterwards & left me under the friendly wing of Mr Winant – who was looking more like Abe Lincoln than ever. Sir Charles Portal also adopted me & introduced me to S[quadron] Leader Nettleton VC (so good-looking AND married – tant pis) & S Leader Scott Malden who's just made a tour of the USA.

Then I suddenly got caught up in a whirl of American army – cols, gens, majors etc – <u>Very</u> kind & gay & charming. Also some charming marines, Admiral Stark's ADC. Stood for about 2½ hrs. King & Queen talked constantly to the Americans. They (the Americans) were very much impressed – & I felt so proud that they are <u>our</u> King & Queen. She is so beautiful & fresh & gracious – she was wearing lavender & pearls & was quite perfect. Then they played 'God Save the King' & Mr Winant took me home.

I suppose I must still be very young because I was simply THRILLED by the party & felt stupidly shy & overcome & excited – & it was so full of colour – red & gold & beautifully lit & lots of uniforms & gold braid!

Sunday 29 November

Went to Communion. Found it a great strength & comfort. Teach me to worship Thee not as 'I think Thou art, but as what Thou knowest Thyself to be.' Spent gor* morning washing, tidying etc. Room looked as though hurricane had blown through it.

All OCTU & HQ Co[mpan]y paraded to Prisoners of War service in St George's.[†] It is breathtakingly beautiful – so gay & light. Lovely service. Judy & I had tea at Miss Marsters'. Went to movies. Wonderful broadcast by Papa[‡] – how can I say any more – it was so, so great.

Wednesday 30 December

Can't think why, but just haven't written up my diary for a month. So I'll just have to give a 'short news summary'.

OCTU came to an end at last – passing out parade excellent. Mrs Knox spoke to me – she just stopped & said 'Well done Mary, I don't know where you'll be posted but I wish you the very best of luck' – & she said I'd got thinner!!

My leave was ALL and MORE than I could ever have hoped. At its end which, as it always does, comes with deadening & swift finality – Judy & I were posted to 205 Training Regt at Arborfield, where we have been now for over a fortnight, & I for one am feeling increasingly happy here.

---

* A later note reads 'gor = good & reliable'
† Assumed to be St George's Chapel at Windsor Castle
‡ 'The Bright Gleam of Victory'

1943

New Roles

---

*'I must go where I must & just try
to be courageous & calm.'*

Mary and Judy now spend ten weeks undertaking anti-aircraft training at Arborfield, just outside Reading. Clementine warns Mary about her father's health, something that becomes a serious worry when he falls ill in February with pneumonia. There is an amusing account of watching the Humphrey Bogart and Ingrid Bergman film *Casablanca* with her father, just after his return from the wartime conference at Casablanca in Morocco, and there is much introspection about Mary's 'inappropriate' dalliance with a battery sergeant.

Mary is now without the company of Judy and embarks on a quick succession of postings. She is assigned to 643 Battery, which spends a month at practice camp in Whitby, North Yorkshire, before taking up a position outside Newport in South Wales. But someone decides she is needed in London, nearer to her parents, and, not without misgivings about preferential treatment, she is transferred back to the capital and to 481 Battery defending Hyde Park.

This does mean that she is available to accompany her father on a rather special mission.

The first Quebec Conference is the result of Allied success. Sicily is about to be taken, Mussolini has fallen, the Russians have turned the tide on the Eastern Front and progress is being made against the Japanese in the Pacific. But big questions remain to be resolved with the Americans about future strategy including the timing and command of a Second Front in France. Churchill likes to be accompanied on these big trips by members of his family and Mary is to be his aide-de-camp. She later describes how although she was 'of course much excited by the prospect of this journey, I was genuinely concerned about the "rightness" of this arrangement; however, over the next weeks I would feel that I was able to make myself useful, as well as having a most thrilling and interesting time.' Her trip will last over six weeks and take her to Quebec, Hyde Park – Roosevelt's home in New York State – the Laurentian Mountains, Georgia, the White House in Washington DC, Harvard University in Boston and colonial Williamsburg.

Mary does not attend the formal sessions of the Quebec conference and her diary is discreet about any issues of strategy or policy that may have been discussed by the president and her father at their more private meetings. Yet her account does give some real insights into the atmosphere in which these discussions take place: the danger, anticipation and claustrophobia of the sea voyage; the ceremony of the public sessions, and the wonderful informality of Roosevelt's personal diplomacy at Hyde Park and in the White House. She captures her father's happiness at his temporary escape from London and the cares of high office. It finds its reflection in her own obvious enjoyment and excitement, and contrasts with Clementine's nerves; hinting perhaps at why Mary's presence was so important. She has grown into her role and is now more relaxed about speaking in public and helping oil the diplomatic wheels.

Mary returns to the routine of battery life, and again sees action, though her guns also seem to serve as a showcase for impressing visiting dignitaries. *Journey into Fear* is a thriller that Mary watches on 4 December, but the title captures something of her own emotion at the end of the year, after learning that her father has fallen gravely ill with pneumonia in Tunisia. Churchill had stopped at General Eisenhower's headquarters on his way back from the 'big three' conference with Roosevelt and Stalin in Tehran. Mary's sister Sarah is with him and Clementine also flies out, leaving Mary on her own for Christmas.

Sunday 3 January

Slept till 11 – what utter heaven. Gen Browning (he commands the airborne division) came to lunch. <u>V</u> good-looking – blimpish – & we afterwards discovered is husband of Daphne du Maurier – sensation.

Went for long & lovely walk alone with Mummie after lunch. We talked entirely of the family – & specially of Papa. It appears that he MIGHT get coronary thrombosis – & it might be brought on by anything like a long or high flight. The question is whether he should be warned or not. Mummie thinks he should not – I agree with her. It is not possible for me to write all I think & feel about it – it is frightening & yet I feel perfectly calm. Funny how I fuss & fret about comparatively small things & yet this shadow & menace to someone I love so much, much more than life itself – doesn't throw me out of gear – I just feel numb – & calm. And yet how desperately, longingly hopeful that it will be all right.

Also talked of Randolph & Spam. I used to kid myself I loved R – I don't anymore. I am rather shocked at myself. I cannot forgive him for the disappointments – sorrows & troubles he has caused Papa & Mummie. Papa loves him <u>so</u> much – and R could make him so proud & happy – & would be beloved by everyone for his own & Papa's sake. But he's missed all that. He says he loves Papa – but he never seems not to say or do something because of any harm it might do to Papa.

I wish I loved R – I am such a sentimental old thing & long to be able to be madly admiring & proud of my big brother – and also my family is very precious to me. I can't even really think of R as family any more. I used to write him an occasional duty letter – trying to rouse in him & me an affection & interest. I grieve there is none. I do not REALLY <u>like</u> Diana

193

– but I do have a deep affection for her. Somehow both liking & affection have died within me for R.

And I feel bitter sometimes – because nothing Diana, Sarah or I can do, could ever make up to Papa or please him as much as R's success – for after all he <u>is</u> the eldest & only son – & our constitution is built on the 'prime importance of being a man'.

Tuesday 5 January

232 Sgts Mess dance in gym. Went determined to have a dance with Sgt Sloman. Judy & I heaving with giggles. Had NO success in early part of the evening. Danced with Maj Edward Jones of 232 – absolutely charming – but both of us felt we couldn't cope with the party – so sat in bar for ¾ hr & talked. Then finally got my dance aim & got on quite well. He's a dream of insolent swarthy good looks & I should imagine his nature is damnable. However he asked to walk me home – so I said er – yes. And then I made the grade in a big way! This was followed by an invitation to go out – which with questionable wisdom I accepted – rather from inability to say NO than otherwise. However – bed pretty late.

Saturday 9 January

Had tea at the Dorchester with Ed – good-looking, good-mannered, good. WOOF – *l'ennui*. He took me home – waited while I packed – took me to Baker St & put me on train. We said goodbye – because he goes back to America next week.

Sunday 10 January

Slept till 12. Gen Catroux to lunch – which was not altogether a success as Papa was faintly cross & spoilt. However Mummie went down like treacle with 'le général'. Saw film, Fred Astaire & Rita Hayworth – *You Were Never Lovelier*, which might well have been called *You Were Never Sillier*. It was gay & stank of opulence & triviality. Went off at about 6 with Tommy who we dropped at Henley. Foggy.

Thursday 14 January

Still hating G/L course – & terrific speculation & chi-chi going on about postings. Maj B in bed with cold deluges me with long letters about the posting – & puts me in unholy flapdoodle. Judy I think is fixed up on staff of C B[atter]y eventually to be an instructress. She is delighted & I am happy for her. As for myself I am NOT in demand at all. Ah well.

Friday 15 January

G/L course drags on. Chi-chi/chi-chis on. Feel <u>v</u> anti-social. However home in the evening for 24 [hours leave]. Cousin V & Diana Duff to dinner. Wore my tartan housecoat. Delicious woodcock for dinner & amusing gossip etc. Talked to darling Mummie for long time. She really is my favourite gal.

Sunday 17 January

Long G/L day. I like the Captain who takes us so much – he has plenty of quiet charm & plenty of sense. Judy gave me faint rocket – about being man-mad – she said. Feel completely bored, depressed & restless – & at loose end. Read quite a lot from the anthology of the Bible Nana sent me. Goodness how beautiful & grand the language of the Bible is. It is so far from second-rate that it somehow raises me from the rather second-rate level I am conducting myself on at the moment. It made me feel calm & yet terribly near to tears.

I don't think I'm man-mad a bit – & she said later when we talked it over quietly that she didn't think I was exactly – but that I was being sort of absorbed terribly by the little trivial flirtations. I know what she means.

I have lost interest at the moment in my job. I hope it'll be better when I'm posted & can begin to have responsibility again.

Letter from Tony Hogg (senior instructing officer at Arborfield) to his wife, 27 January:

I've had a most interesting talk with Mary C this evening, who's been behaving rather loudly and badly lately and who I'm afraid is going to get a wigging from the S.C. tomorrow. She's really a very nice and charming child who can state her case as well as any barrister. She says she's tried all ways of behaviour, but every one of them seems to be wrong as people will put interpretations on them. If she's quiet and unassuming they say she's smug and stuck-up, on the other hand if she's noisy and matey with all and sundry they say she does it to draw attention to herself. I can so well understand how she feels about it and how difficult it must be for her.

Sunday 31 January

I've just spent a heavenly day at Chartwell with Mummie, Nana & Uncle Jack. I slept till quarter to ten – & Judy & I ate a scrumptious breakfast. Then I put on my brown tweeds, blue jumper & Cousin V's lovely bauble & we all (minus Judy) drove down to Nana's cottage at Chartwell . . . Nana's cottage is furnished now & all the pictures hung. It is charming & very warm & comfortable.

We sat down to an ENORMOUS & scrumptious lunch brought from London. Horatia joined us afterwards & we spent an afternoon doing <u>nothing</u> – what heaven! All the strain and miserableness of the last fortnight seemed suddenly to fall away – & become unreal & insignificant. We left Chartwell at about 4.45 – with a pang of homesickness & longing to be 'chez soi' – not boarded out as paid guests.

I don't think I've ever before been consciously, consecutively and calmly – unhappy. It is a stupid unhappiness – because it is an arrogant, pusillanimous self taking arms against things-as-they-are. I have missed out writing in my diary a very hectic, eventful fortnight. I have been more disillusioned & shaken by people than ever before. And I've got so tied up – I hardly know what to do. But it is a strange feeling this for me – always before so <u>positive</u> & now I just know I am <u>not</u> happy.

Monday & Tuesday 1–2 February

Gloomy & sad days trying to make up my mind what to do about Joe* [. . .] Up to now I felt bitter – muddled, but confident that in Joe I had found a very, very worthwhile friend – and that he said he loved me [. . .] But now – it seems I shall never know whether he is genuine or not. I've never in my life felt so utterly lost & knocked about.

---

* Probably Sergeant Major Joe Sloman, from Mary's battery. The main issue seems to have been that officers and other ranks were discouraged from going out together. Mary also finds out later that he only went out with her for a bet!

I feel I've made a fool of myself – laid myself open to gossip which might harm Papa [. . .] That I have made a fool of myself – that is not important. At cost of a slight heart break & many tears & some disillusion I hope I may have gained some badly needed worldly wisdom. It's hurt awfully – but if I've learnt something worth while & necessary to me – then that's OK. But the gossip side – there again I've learnt that there's nothing people won't say – that the people one <u>least</u> expected derogatory criticism from will change – I swear before God that if I had considered it would have caused harmful comment which might reflect on Papa – I would NEVER have gone out with Joe.

But sincerely I thought – innocently, foolishly & wrongly – that had all the press hounds & movie cameras of the world been there – nothing detrimental could have been thought or said. But I was wrong – & I shouldn't have been. I thought at first of writing to Joe & saying never again, & then as this week wore on & I became calmer, I saw I was magnifying it all too much – & that it is better not to make a sort of dramatic incident out of it. I did tell him however I would never again see him as long as I was here. I hope it'll die down – Hope above all he was sincere – there is more than hurt pride in that.

Friday 5 February

On Friday night Judy had her 20th birthday party. We had a riotous time getting ready – rushing & screaming in & out of poor Mummie's room. Shall I wear this – Can I borrow – may I have – How do I look! Etc de suite. Finally we were ready, me in my blue jersey & Mummie's diamond clips – Judy in black tailleur & Mummie looking as usual like Beauty triumphant. Ally came & collected us & we all went to the

Jardin des Gourmets. Cousin V, Brendan, Victor, John Sparrow, Stuart Preston (American sgt) & a G man were there already. Dinner was noisy (chiefly us I suppose) and greatest fun. Victor was simply charming to me. John & I talked army & ABCA of which latter he is one of the chief parents.

Brendan departed early to nurse the MoI [Ministry of Information]. Dinner v good. Mummie, the G man, Victor & Cousin V went home – Ally & the Sgt & JS went to 400 – where lolling in dim comfort we sipped ginger ale & whisky & talked. After a shortish interlude with the Sgt – <u>very</u> nice & the first American I've met who's ever heard of Elizabeth Bennet – I poured my sorrows about l'affaire Joe into Cacadone's [Ally Forbes] sympathetic & lovable ear. He made comforting, calming & understanding noises – and said anyway he was sure it hadn't harmed Papa – felt better. Thought often of Papa – now on his way home.

We went home about 1.30. Judy poor lamb terribly tired, as previous night she was sent to Reading to collect two drunken ATSs as they were paralytic, she was up with them till 4.

Saturday 6 February

Woke 8.15 – dashed in feeling excited to Mummie – oh great disappointment – Papa's flight postponed 24 hrs because of engine trouble – wow & wow! Mummie anxious about the flight – me too.

ORANGE JUICE for breakfast – <u>Boiled egg</u>, tea & preserves. Talked for long time to M then put on brown Molyneux, tied my head up in yellow & scarlet turban & went out shopping – chiefly at Bumpus. Bought for J's birthday present *Admiral's Wife* and *Admiral's Widow* – the life of Fanny Boscawen told in her letters – charming & interesting. Lunch at No. 10 – Cousin V, Judy, Ally & M & Uncle Jack.

Argument waxed <u>v</u> hot over Gen de Gaulle. Ally had brought a written account of the Gen's speech made to some F[ree] F[rench] parachutists. Saying – we must pretend to like Eng now – that is diplomatic – but we really are her enemies & must never forget that – etc etc.

It turned one's blood cold to realise just how much he hates us – & how he abuses the hospitality we have sincerely shown him. But for us the F French cause would be discredited – unknown maybe without funds or means of any kind. Blow, blow thou winter wind. Mummie who looked a dream in a petunia velvet hat got ferocious – rather unreasonably with Cousin V. Then leaving M & Uncle Jack behind we all went to see *The House of Jeffrey's*. Improbable – slightly unreal in atmosphere but quite good. Returned to tea & found Lord Lamington. Wrote letter – changed. M went to bed.

The awful 'cafard' which usually descends before going back to camp enveloped me. After supper caught 9.24 & travelled down with Blanco & a friend – Noisy, gay journey. Returned to camp in 'Provost' – dropping in for drinks at Provost mess.

Sunday 7 February

Cold day. Church parade. Dreary – stagnating. Thought all morning of Papa returning & <u>longed</u> for news. One o'clock brought it – & an account of the review of the Desert Army in Tripoli. Got permission to sleep out – rushed up to London by 6.10. Rather enjoyable journey up, fat & pleasant civilian, v talkative & obviously intelligent sergeant & 3 sweet little ATS. We all discussed woman suffrage etc & the woman's place. Rather tiresome faux beau RAMC Capt snatched into conversation – & escorted me home – said we'd met at a specified dance – & would I dine one night – me 'Yes I'd love to' – LIAR.

Just in time to change – Papa came in – WOW.

Diana, Sarah, Mummie, Papa, Brendan & for coffee Uncle Jack. Oh how heavenly – Papa in excellent form. Sang 'Poultry' & 'Half a Woman & Half a Tree'*. Then we went & saw *Casablanca* at the MoI. There were Oliver Lyttelton, Anthony E[den], Kenneth Post (now a colonel), Duncan, Noel Coward. Papa & Anthony talked incessantly throughout the film – one or other of them occasionally saying 'What's he doing – who's this – oh' – Noel & I got helpless giggles. Apart from slight interference *Casablanca* was excellent & very moving & I long to see <u>& hear</u> it again. It suddenly made me wish foolishly & childishly that fighting for ideals & high causes was for me mixed up with a passionate & glamorous love affair – conducted in a glamorous night club in Casablanca – & involving excitement & tense but clear cut situations – & not a Mon, Tues, Wed business involving head inspections, pay books, boot lists & sausage rolls. Feeling utterly dead & depressed about my military career. But before I went to bed I got down on my knees – and thanked God from the bottom of my heart for bringing Papa safely home.

Saturday 13 February

The other day while Papa was away Mummie & Nana went to see *Dubarry Was a Lady*. In the audience was a whole submarine crew & their girl friends. Their Petty Officer introduced the men to Mummie – she said they were charming & at the end the Petty Officer said 'Will you tell your husband that we dive for him.'

---

* Old music hall songs

Wednesday 17 February

This last week was very difficult – from military point of view I shall be glad to be out of Arborfield – but parting from Judy looms uncompromisingly black. All these days we've been snapping & irritating each other – & that close intimacy and understanding seem to have been lost. Judy went to wash hair – I stayed – rather naughtily (& 2 days later how bitterly I regretted it) and talked for ages to Tony – kind – penetrating & charming as always.

Thursday 18 February

Papa, Mummie tells me, is in bed with feverish cold.

Have had inoculation – arm pretty stiff. Paid out. Night shoot – felt v nervous. Everyone <u>v</u> sweet & said I did all right. Phyllis v forthcoming about plotting – G/L etc. to an audience containing the I/G, C[hief] Instructor 232 & several P8ls. Blushed for her. Fools rush in . . . or perhaps I'm just jealous because I <u>certainly</u> couldn't have held forth so bravely or clearly about technicalities. But – God – she irritates me beyond everything – & yet I am far from not appreciating her virtues, charms & gaiety.

Friday 19 February

Tension still makes a strained atmosphere between Judy & myself – she was cross because of my dates tonight – I felt irritated & rather truculent about it . . . Cold crystal moonlight night – at 9.30 met Joe. <u>V</u> glad to see him. Passed 2 pleasant hours with him. I wonder if I ever will find anyone else I find so physically attractive. I think I know now how strong temptation can be.

Came in much later than intended – Judy in bed & <u>very</u> cross. Felt sad.

Saturday 20 February

Very busy – felt little happier. But burst out to Tony in evening about Judy & me. Tony wonderful, as ever. Pointed out to me how much of it was my fault – & how necessary it is for one to give & give & go on giving. He said he thought I took more than I gave. As I was feeling upset & martyred, this remark went home.

On reflection I felt he was right   anyhow as regards this week. Went straight up to Judy who was in bath – and tried terribly hard to put it right with her – & said how sorry I was about Wednesday (& I meant it). Both of us collapsed in unhappy floods of tears on each other's shoulder – a privilege we will both miss. Mopping up ourselves we then embarked on farewell celebrations – starting with v long drinking party – then feeling rather tight to a long dinner – which ended with quite ENDLESS series of speeches – Brig, Col etc spreading themselves. Maj Johnson – as might be expected was well worth listening to – then the Col called on me to make a speech – unwarned, unnecessary, ridiculous . . . Felt quite sick & hot & helpless. Rose to my feet & saw nothing. Sat down after 1 minute. Hope it was all right. Everyone seemed sympathetic to me & furious with Col. I despise that man.

The dance was fun – the cabaret excellent. Danced a lot with Joe. It was a relief to be quite open & natural for a change. Also talked a lot to Sgt Vian who J & I both agree is très sympathique. Bed reasonable hour.

Sunday 21 February

Up to early service expecting some of our girls to make their first communion. None of them turned up. So the padre and I were à deux. I was unprepared – & have been so neglectful – and yet found as always – a calm restfulness I find so rarely & want so much.

Got taxi – Eric, Roly, J & I & my extraneous luggage went to London. In train – reading the official bulletin about Papa, I got into a sudden panic. Might this then be the beginning of the end?

Arrived home M was ready for church. In her lovely dark cloth coat trimmed with beaver & the flame-coloured scarf bursting out – beaver muff & hat. To me Mummie has all the lovely graces of life – tempered with a steel-like integrity. We two went to service at the R[oyal] Military Chapel. It was rather lovely & comforting. M is not seriously worried about Papa – but he is pretty ill. I was shocked when I saw him. He looked so old & tired – lying back in bed. What beautiful hands he has.

I found the house frightening – nurses' caps – kidney bowls & bed pans – in the office slips of paper with bulletins – messages, fond enquiries. All the panoply of illness. Diana came to see Papa before lunch. Anthony & Simon Eden to lunch also Uncle Jack. Simon – 18 – Eton – good manners. Then all afternoon a perfectly frightful & dreary Russian demonstration. A monument of dreary poor taste. Except for 2 quite moving moments. But how supreme the Russians are – & how we have undervalued them & misunderstood them. But people who suddenly have become wild Russomanes irritate me – and how Russians must despise our more fulsome overflowings.

Back to annexe just in time to have an egg & tongue for our tea – finish packing & catch 6.24. Enjoyable, rowdy party at Barcombe Bull. Joe was ill & so not there. Missed him.

Monday 22 February

Cold. Busy day. Packed – flapped around. On ringing up M am told Papa is really better – so will leave for Whitby with easier mind. Began embussing girls at 8.15 pm. At Wokingham was chiefly occupied with Pte. Slater trying to make up her mind whether she would be sick or no – No – thank God. Brief glimpses of Judy looking unhappy & strained. Masses of everyone in Railway Hotel. Finally troops entrain – quick goodbyes – Judy weeping – me quite dried but not unfeeling – just whirled & dazed – train goes out. Another phase of my military career is over. And now for the first time I am miles from home & with no Judy. I only hope I shall be as gaily gutful about it as so many people have been for three or 4 years of separation & loneliness.

Good journey – arrived Whitby about 9. Frenzied day settling into our billets which are boarding houses (à la 3rd floor back) & cheap hotels on sea front. The girls in uproarious form – never still or findable or quiet. Phyllis bossy, irritating & I thought, quite useless. I am sharing a small bare room with her – How good for me – I wonder who'll be most tried. She is the soul of kindness & gaiety & natters ceaselessly, lends me everything & tucks me in at night.

The sea is comforting. By 9 pm I was unconscious with grubbiness, fatigue & weariness. O sleep – the death of each day's life. Have left lipstick behind. DAMN.

Friday 26 February

Kay went on leave at cock crow – her husband is on the verge of going abroad. Sweet letter from Judy. I am enjoying the work here so much – the weather is lovely & I feel so well & glowing – but I have moments of deep loneliness – thrown into sharp relief by the barrenness of Phyllis's company. And yet she has great qualities of good temper, kindness & gaiety. Evelyn has taken over as J/Comdr.

I have, shamefacedly to confess, felt a pang of jealousy – simultaneously with an adulation of how just & right that she should be. And finally – aftcr mental spanking & pulling together – a feeling of pleasure and contentment at being able to work under someone so well fitted to do the job – & some-one so likeable too. But, quite apart from this, I am disap-pointed in myself. For I feel submerged by my job. I seem to muddle along – putting right things that go wrong, but never seeming to be able to avert muddles or arrive on the scene 2 minutes before trouble begins. And always feeling, wisely after the event, how much better I could have done it. When I was a sergeant – I knew I could get things done. Now I feel shackled, inefficient – with a faulty unwieldy instrument in my hands.

Saturday 28 February

½ day off. Frightful shambles & muddle about 10.30 parade. I was O/Officer & rose at 6.30 – not funny. Girls hopeless at coming out on parade – gave my first real rocket to them – Longed not to – & play to gallery – but screwed myself up & was icy & furious & CBd them for tonight. Poor sweets. I do honour & love them so much – & long for their affection – can hardly hope to command their respect. But I will not pander – God helping me, I will not.

In afternoon our section fired . . . not v good results. I was safety officer & felt panicked between the prediction of the first fuze & fire – but afterwards enjoyed it & got a kick out of it. I suppose because I felt important. HOW ignoble & like me.

Mary to Clementine, 1 March:

. . . I am afraid I have some long homesick months ahead of me – it is almost certain that our battery is going to <u>South Wales</u>*. O, wow and wurrup! I hate to think of it; I shall miss being able to come home so much more than I can say. It is bad enough here with the prospect of leave in a few weeks – But 3 months – I just won't think of it now. But I do feel I have been* <u>very</u> *lucky – so many people have been too far from their homes even to get home on 48 hrs leave. But I can't pretend I'm feeling brave or gay about it. For darling Mummie, you've no idea how much I rely on you and Papa. Sometimes when I've had a pretty bloody week I've come home, feeling deprimée and upset, and once I've got home it's all seemed all right again; and I used to go back to Enfield feeling so strong & calm & re-established.*

Friday 5 March

Busy. Went to dance at St James' Rooms in evening – Quite fun. Danced with I.G. – smashin' dancer, [and danced with] fascinating sergeant who was very serious & charming & said 'I just want to say before I go – that well I know your father saved this country.' How proud & happy people make me feel. And how full of pride & gratitude it makes me when people praise Papa – & show me kindness because of their love for him.

When we got back from dance I.G. got beer after hours – (well, I mean, what's the use of a red hat ribbon . . .). Suddenly realised I was having a slight 'succés'. Courage wilted badly when I was left alone – & when I saw things were blowing up to something – I ratted <u>v</u> quickly. He seems quite fun – & gay.

It is now **the 23rd** – I am on LEAVE & Home again. God be praised.

When I came into tea yesterday (Monday) afternoon, after a bath – feeling utterly exhausted from long train journey – I very nearly wept. No one was in the sitting room – but tea was laid – lovely food – & pale afternoon sunshine was falling in shafts across the comfortable & yet rather elegant furniture – and the pictures & warmth & calm pale light & the spring flowers from Chartwell – daffodils, jasmine, narcissi & some sprays of small budding magnolia – combined to give me a feeling & thoughts lying too deep for tears.

And so Whitby which I shall remember very pleasantly has come to an end. What shall I remember about it – feeling <u>v</u> well – steps & more steps – sun drenched fresh spring days – convoys moving slowly & fatefully out at sea – enjoying my work & it troubling me – enjoying increasingly John's company – the Golden Lion – & that <u>awful</u> plush sofa & ghastly mantelpiece in the ante room which made us laugh so much. And the guns firing & crashing – & me never really getting used to them – & endless professional jokes – battery gossip – battery problems – battery life. Moments of homesickness – long letters from Mummie & Judy – bracing myself to go to S. Wales & feeling strong & brave!

And now I hear I am destined w/e/f [with effect from] Apr 2nd for 481 in Hyde Park – tumult of conflicting feelings – great pleasure at being near home – & <u>so</u> near – for chance of action. BUT – the tactlessness of the posting – pray God it won't do harm – the misery of leaving my beloved girls, just when I am beginning to be a little less inadequate & know them – regret, deep regret at leaving 643 where I am indeed most happily placed. Fright & jitters at going to a long established b[at]t[er]y – & once again to start to try & break down a hostile expectant & you-wait-&-see atmosphere – & once again to feel terribly new & an outsider. Everyone of course will think it's string pulling. It isn't – I suppose the W[ar] O[ffice] have done it because of Papa having been ill – but as usual they've managed to do it in the most clumsy way possible.

I don't think one ought to intervene – I must go where I must & just try to be courageous & calm. But I confess I am deeply upset about it – in fact it kept me awake for ages last night & woke me this morning.

Thursday 25 March

Dentists made me late for lunch. Mummie Papa & Nana had started when I arrived. Mummie blew off steam at great length & with great violence about Randolph. I sympathised with her so much – although I thought it a little unnecessary. But she has had a lot to put up with from R – and it must be so terribly mortifying for her that her only son should be such a trouble & grief. Papa adores him – and yet R hurts him dreadfully. Papa believes in R's abilities – our belief in them is dimmed by his dreadful conduct – which is so utterly regardless of the harm it does Papa.

I said my little piece about Pamela. It does irritate me when people try to make out she's a poor pathetic little lily – heart-broken & maltreated by R – that is not true & not fair. Pamela has many gracious & civilised qualities – & she is a good business woman. I do not like her very much. I think I am jealous – Papa loved her so much – & I remember at Chequers sometimes feeling an unworthy – but very real stab of jealousy.

Friday 26 March

Shopped in morning. Very G & R*. Judy's departure for Os[westry] delayed by the holding of uniform by cleaners – emotions, alarums & excursions.

The 'Randolph' scenario occurred today & not yesterday as I have put it. Mummie & Papa made it up & so I think it was OK. I <u>wish</u> I loved R – I used to – but somehow he is most unlovable. And I find his treatment of & vis-à-vis Papa difficult to forgive. I see his ability – I think I even understand something of his difficulties – and they say 'tout comprendre c'est tout pardonner' – I'm afraid I can't 'tout pardonner'.

As for Pamela – I am a little ashamed of my hostility to her – but I resent her in a lot of ways. And I resent especially being treated as if I'd just been discovered as a rather new member of our family. But R is a fool. He has lost or thrown away one of his greatest assets – someone who could & would have helped him loyally & ably.

Down to Chequers. Tommy & John Peck made the drive pleasant. Chequers is now AT run. Papa took me with him to dine with officers of the US 8th Air Force Bomber HQ at High Wycombe. Quite fun. Papa made quite a good speech – it went down very well. Everyone short snorted wildly.[†] They were all terribly kind to me. Several of them were decorated. Felt exhausted on my return – bed 11 & slept till 10.30 the next morning.

---

* Good and Reliable

† A banknote signed by people who had flown together. If you signed one and the short snorter could not be produced later, you were then owed a dollar or a drink – 'a short snort'

Sunday 28 March

Breakfast in Mummie's room. Poor darling she is far from well – I think Papa's illness was a great strain on her. Down very late. Reading some of my old diaries – they made me laugh so much. What a horrifying little prig I was at 16. I find it interesting to compare the diaries I wrote immediately after the outbreak of war & up to the time when I joined up with my 'ATS' journals. Then the war & world events dominated the pages – now removed from so vital & intense a contact – AT events & chi-chi & unbelievably trivial happenings hold the majority of comment. Not to mention long introvertial scrawls – But when I'm in a frightful muddle – I find if I write it all down – it suddenly becomes much easier & clearer. How fascinating that year at Chequers was – I sometimes feel now, that although I am personally much more in the war – yet I find myself not so acutely & passionately conscious of it.

Partly of course it's because I'm removed from the source of information and can only follow events in the press & on the radio. I miss so much knowing what's going on – & hearing all or at any rate some of the difficulties & problems. Press news & radio news seem rather flat always – after sudden & breathtaking telegrams & code messages.

News of the capture of the Mareth Line [Tunisia] came at lunch. Papa vexed – because his news was from Gen Montgomery & nothing can be released till it comes officially through Gens Alex[ander] & Eisenhower. Slight scenario going on about Randolph – <u>what</u> a change. Decide I am very ignorant ill-informed girl – spend afternoon making sporadic attempts to read *Tribune, Time & Tide, Tablet, Spectator* – Don't feel much better.

Wednesday 30 March

Up early. Finished packing. Caught 8.50 for Newport with large gathering of battery. Nana & Sukie saw me off. This time 20 months ago Judy & I were waved off by a small family clan as we left for Aldermaston. One thing I feel sure about in a welter of uncertainties & that is – How glad I am I joined up. And nothing will ever make me regret it. Told Eric & Pat the 'Hyde Park' scenario – they were sweet & understanding about it.

At Newport evaded the *S. Wales Argus* sleuth by a whisker.* Hid behind some daffodils in the utility. Our new site is bloody awful. It is 5 feet below sea level – vision is bounded by brushery more or less all round with some unimpressive hills in the distance – & some docks derricks & so forth & a sea wall. Sanitation is negligible – accommodation nothing to shout about. Buses – distant & erratic. Newport – almost unreachable tho' 7 miles away. No public telephone – PO 1¾ up road. Command Post is a wind shaken shack.

Thursday 1 April

This site almost might be a bad April Fool's Day joke. More & more amazed & angry at living conditions imposed on girls – Place filthy. <u>V</u> busy morning – Paid out. Am reading quite a lot of *W&P* [*War and Peace*] while relieving at CP. No papers. Perhaps the war is over? However we proceed on the basis that it isn't.

---

* Mary was hiding from a local journalist

Friday 2 April

. . . Kay & Phil both having gone onto other site – I was OC the ATS for a day.

<u>My morning</u>
Relieved Eric at CP 7.30
Relieved & then breakfasted 8.45
<u>Went into action</u> (I did) 9.30
Inspected 'lats' [latrines] – gloomy view taken.
10.00 Began conversation – (to be carried on at intervals during morning, sometimes à deux & sometimes à trois with the CSM) with the foreman in charge of the new drainage system. SUBJECTS – lavatories – flushing (practical demonstration), drain blockages (causes thereof) – Pump ('The pump only pumps water Mum – so the solids – well they have to be dissolved – Then (triumphantly) the pump pumps them').

Cookhouse looking filthy – but contented myself (already a little exhausted with drainage) with going into action over unwashed & unscraped cast-a-way tins. Also got duckboards in ablutions scrubbed clean. Relieved for lunch. Spent hot & harassed afternoon plotting & dealing with fads of this GOR. Row by RA officers about AT fatigues – after preliminary & trial eruption, I subsided. Dealt with NCOs at 7.

Went to bed early hoping for bath. However had to indulge in that acute form of misery called a 'real good wash'. Wrote to Mummie. Read more of *W&P* which enthrals me so much.

Saturday 3 April

Terrific battles in Tunisia – it looks as tho' it's pretty hard fighting. Papa has been given his wings – what a great compliment.

Friday 30 April, Hyde Park

Papa & Mummie (returned from Weymouth) visited the Battery* in the evening. Great success. Was shocked to see Papa looking tired & old.

Friday 7 May

GOC brought Lord Wigram to see battery in afternoon. Everything teed up. Lord W obviously regarded G/L as a blatant manifestation of black magic – & on being told about the tubes getting 'cluttered up' looked thoughtful & said – 'Oh I see, like too many pheasants coming over.' He then asked me what 'hours you spend here' – I said – 'I LIVE here sir.' He said – 'Oh good gracious me.'

Sunday 9 May

Very busy. Preparations for camp & advance party of which I am one. Wet & cold. Rang up Diana. Bicycled to have tea with her. Poor lamb she is very full of baby. Lovely tea & gossip, stayed to supper. Helped her get it ready – Duncan came home. Both of them SO sweet to me.

Joined wild dance & party in NAAFI – Americans – strange majors & MTC parts – faked up party spirit – & had to do all my packing at 1.30. Mr Bond & friend had to be installed for night owing to transport difficulties – in ante room.

---

* From the middle of April, Mary was posted to 481 Battery, based at Hyde Park in London

Monday 10 May

Started on advance party expedition in pouring rain with plenty of good advice. Long journey – young & moderately fascinating sailor, joined by another naval officer – who on removal of mackintosh proved to be a VC and DSO. My eyes filled with romantic and admiring tears & I went into a coma of hero-worship-cum-wishful-thinking in which I attended investiture on arm of dreamlike hero in navy blue & gold (the d-l-hero I mean) & me in scarlet trimmed with fur – I think with sparkling aquamarine on my third finger & a proud possessive tiresome look in my eye. These roseate reflections overcame successfully the cold, length & wetness of the journey.

Arrived Bude camp about 7 – settled girls & got to our own quarters about 8.

Wednesday 12 May

Got up 4. Worked thereafter till 7. Battery safely installed. On 8 o'clock news – Papa's arrival in Washington announced. Thank God. Triumphant news.

Wednesday 19 May

The Mohne & Eder dams busted – Bravo the RAF.[*] Diana has had a daughter.[†] Papa's address to Congress broadcast. I felt so, so proud and thankful. I see Sir John Wardlaw-Milne has praised Papa – How many friends one has in good fortune.

---

[*] The 'Dambusters' raid, carried out by 617 Squadron
[†] Celia Sandys

Friday 4 June

Busy. Went home about 5 for 24hrs – O whoopeeeeeee. Nana & Mummie at tea when I arrived – Papa due to leave Algiers at 12 – flying home. M & I & Sarah all going to travel to meet him. However first to see *Brighton Rock* (v good & exciting) with Mummie & Nana, Cousin Venetia & Judy.

Ally at supper – rather tiresome about French. Suddenly saw with sick making clarity the connection between the attack of the passenger plane the other day & Papa.* But just lately I have a sort of faith that a divine providence is watching over him. God grant that this is so. We <u>all</u> need him so much.

So many thoughts occur to me continually about life. How interesting & thrilling it all is – How <u>can</u> people be bored – and yet I've been bored myself sometimes. But just recently I have felt as tho' life or something was pulsing through my veins – I've felt elated, vigorous, vital, alive. It is strange to compare my mood now with the awful black 'cafard' of Arborfield.

Saturday 5 June

Woken at quarter to six by Lena – PAPA IS ARRIVING IN ½ HR. 06.15 Papa's plane touched down – 06.45 Papa HOME. Well and in wonderful spirits. I lay in a sleepy haze in Mummie's bed & he padded up & down in his blue rompers & told us the news.

---

* Presumably a passenger plane had recently been attacked, and Mary is drawing a parallel between this and the dangers of Churchill flying home from Algiers

Sunday 4 July

Hot & heavenly. Wore white dress – no stockings (save à la peinture!) – feeling relaxed and happy. Party going well – Robin S recovered – Robin M clearly not recovered from desert warfare. Drinks at mess – <u>Noel Coward</u> arrived for lunch – very charming . . . Papa a little tedious about basic English. Felt rebellious – rebelled – rebellion quelled.

. . . After dinner Noel sang again his new song 'Don't Let's Be Beastly to the Germans' – & then many more old ones. Lovely.

Saturday 31 July

Prelude to Adventure
Drove to Chequers with Archie [Sinclair] and Marigold in time for lunch . . . King Peter of Yugoslavia came to lunch accompanied by most charming ADC . . . Played croquet 'à quatre' after lunch – the King stayed to tea & left (after one false start owing to flat tyre).

Mummie arrived after tea. Conversation at dinner became rather strained about the French – Archie's manner more than his matter clearly irritated Papa. A film was the happy solution! *The Man in Grey* – Papa loved it & so did I – very 18th century & 'gadzooks' & I thought most romantic & pleasing.

Sunday 1 August

. . . This evening after dinner (Mummie was in bed – Papa, Tommy, Mr Peck, Uncle Jack & Prof & Self were dining) we all sat round the table in the dimming light – and the candles shed a soft glow on the table and added to the colour of the red roses – and Papa was in wonderful spirits. He read us bits of Rudyard Kipling's unpublished works & then started remember[ing] & he told us of Mrs Everest [Churchill's nanny] & her 2 sisters & his visits to them. It was so pleasant and quiet and intimate. I am always preoccupied (almost morbidly) with the thought of life without Papa – it will be a less colourful & vital thing – he is such a <u>life-giver</u>.

For me, never again will there be anything so wonderful or so invigorating as Papa. It makes me furious when I catch people like Archie & Marigold giving each other sly little I-told-you-so-Winston's-very-good-at-the-war-but-needs-humouring sort of looks. Bloody fools.

Wednesday 4 August

Departure

I am writing on the train speeding North. The adventure has begun.

Brig Wingate 'the Clive of Burma' [Orde Wingate] came almost straight from the plane. He is a triple DSO. Looks like Lawrence & is a <u>Tiger</u> of a man. We were all greatly impressed – I can see Papa has great things in mind for him. He is to come on the trip. Mrs Wingate was snatched off from the train from Scotland southbound and instructed to wait at Edinburgh. Very dramatic & exciting. He looks terribly strained & ill & I do hope the sea voyage will do him good.

All set. 11.30 we left. Dark starless night – Sarah came to station. On train: 1st Sea Lord, Brig Wingate, Averell, John Martin, Leslie Rowan, Tommy, Miss Layton. I am <u>so</u> excited I can hardly believe it's all true. Pause to remember – this is the anniversary of the outbreak of the *last* war: 'I GO AWAY THIS VERY DAY TO GO ACROSS THE SEA, MATILDA'.

Thursday 5 August

Breakfasted with Pug, Averell, John M & Tommy. It is cold & wet & we are speeding along the coast Northwards. The sea looks pretty rough. We picked Mrs Wingate up at Edinburgh – of her more later. Arrived at Faslane 14.30. Went aboard the *Maid of Orleans* & went down the Gareloch & there was the *Q.M.* [RMS *Queen Mary*] in the tail of the Bank, opposite Greenock. (At Faslane came the news – CATANIA IS OURS.) Nearly two years ago it was here I went aboard the Prince of Wales, a lance corporal, & said goodbye & godspeed to Papa, setting out on the first of his many heroic & fateful journeys.

Dutch notices are plastered all over the ship to kid everyone it was Queen Wilhelmina coming aboard. (Their figures at any rate are not dissimilar). Our suites are luxurious & most comfortable – I am in a little green room next to Mummie. I have no sense of direction & feel I will inevitably get lost in the vastness of the complications of the *Q.M.* The 'special' party is over 200 strong – among Cs of Staff & their staffs are also Kathy H [Kathleen Harriman] & the Dam Buster [Wing Commander Guy Gibson] – who I met this evening & who seems delightful.

To dinner: Averell & Kathy, CIGS, Lord Leathers, Tommy. The food is UNBELIEVABLE. White rolls & masses of butter.

Friday–Saturday 6–7 August

At 8 o'clock we were 300 miles west of Point Malin. Dirty weather & a fairly heavy sea which grew worse. Our escort could be at times very clearly seen wallowing in heavy seas 'coming over green'. Breakfasted in Mummie's room – ORANGE JUICE! Scrambled up at 10.00 (!) for boat drill which was then cancelled. Found Kathy & the D/B [Dam Buster] & went for an extremely wet & windy walk. Sat idly & happily gossiping till lunch. D/B, Glamour Pants, CAS, Mr Rowan, Lord Moran. Papa in a benign & sunny mood.

Had tea with John Martin & CAS. For dinner: Brig & Mrs Wingate, Sir Dudley Pound, CAS, Sir Pug. Mrs Wingate is I think 26 & beautiful, and she has a low, clear, melodious voice. She has opinions. She is clearly intelligent & well informed – & CLEARLY she knows she 1. Has a melodious voice 2. Is intelligent & well informed, and firmly, & kindly she is determined that one shall be improved mentally & spiritually by contact with her . . . I sat next to Brig W at dinner. He is extremely interesting but very intense. God – what a menage with Mrs W. But he is not so tiresome – I wonder if he will be a great new figure.

Saturday 7 August

. . . I had a long talk with Guy D/B. He is truly charming, good & brave, a chevalier 'sans peur et sans reproche' & gay & good company as well. This evening I quite forgot all desire for personal success & was absorbed naturally & completely in truthful & calm conversation. I am having a WHALE of a time.

Monday 9 August

Canadian Adventure
Went up on bridge. Visited the engine rooms. After lunch finished packing – saw ship's radio. Land sighted at about quarter to 4. Went up on bridge with Dam Buster & watched Canada appear. Saw 2 whales! It was lovely & most impressive steaming into Halifax harbour with our U.S.N. escort

'line astern'. Mounties in scarlet & blue patrolled the quay-side. Papa was met by Malcolm MacDonald [British High Commissioner in Canada], Mr Angus Macdonald (Secretary for the Navy) & Admiral Nelles (C of the Canadian Naval Staff) and Edwardes (Deputy Minister of Transport).

At 8.30 in the evening we started our 700 mile – 22 hrs journey to Quebec.

Tuesday 10 August

During the night we passed through New Brunswick & in the early morning we picked up the line of the St Lawrence.

If I started to describe everything I saw I would never get down the sequence of events of this thrilling adventure. I am going to record the bare facts – & I trust to my memory to recreate for me the interest & beauty and atmosphere of the scenes. On our journey to Quebec we were passing through French Canada. We arrived at Charny at 4.45 & Papa was met by Mr Mackenzie King* & the Lt Gov of Quebec – Sir Eugène Fiset – with whom Mummie & I drove over the Quebec bridge & to the Citadel. He seems an old horror.

The Citadel & the part we are to occupy exceeded my expectations. Mr Mackenzie King dined with us. Note for an A.D.C.! I see it is important to distinguish between Federal officials & Provincial officials. Went to bed very tired but very happy.

Wednesday 11 August

Pressed & petted my uniform. At 11 Mummie received Lady Fiset – who brought under her wing Mrs Power (wife of the

---

* William Mackenzie King 1874–1950, Prime Minister of Canada

Canadian Minister for Air – & <u>VERY</u> Federal) and Mrs Mathewson (wife of the Quebec Minister of Finance – absolutely charming). Papa met with the Canadian cabinet & did not come into lunch until 2. We were all ravening!

<u>Lunch</u>: PM of Canada, Sir John Anderson, Guy Gibson, Tommy, High Commissioner, Lord Moran, Lord Leathers, Col Connor (A.D.C. to the Governor General & very nice – an old poppet). After lunch Papa went off to visit the Quebec Government with Mr M-K (who afterwards told me Papa made them a speech in French which had gone very well & they were delighted).

Mummie decided to 'rat' on the expedition to Niagara – she is feeling <u>so</u> tired & has missed too much sleep. Papa <u>terribly</u> disappointed poor sweet – he was longing to show her Niagara & the Hyde Park. But he understood. She was sweet & said 'certainly I was to go with him', so we left her in the care of Lord Moran, Hambone[*], Col Connor & Mr M-K.

Pouring rain – we left Wolfe's Cove about 6.

<u>Star Spangled Weekend</u>
As we left Quebec we left the rain, and soon were running through rich fertile country, with little white wooden farms & some livestock. It was very touching for out in the country little groups of people gathered at the side of the track to wave at Papa. <u>That</u> is Papa's strength & his greatness – people who know & love & trust him. It was a really lovely evening, calm & warm & quiet & this rich gracious land slipping past. And such lovely names, Champlain, Trois Rivières, Louiseville. And the houses! But I could rhapsodise forever – for me I only know it is all inexpressibly thrilling, beautiful & moving.

---

[*] Grace Hamblin, Clementine's secretary

And this journey especially – just me & Papa à deux is a real treat for me.

He is being so sweet & kind – calling on me at 8 on Thursday morning (12 August) to see if I was getting ready & had eaten breakfast. At Victoria Park at 8.30 we left the train to be met by Gen Constantine, the Mayor of Niagara and a battery of press hounds. I was bunched, Papa too with gladioli & then we saw the Falls – O they are <u>wonderful</u>. We then drove on & saw the rapids from various viewpoints & then went to Brock's Monument & looked down on the River Niagara – broad & peaceful after all its convulsions & swirlings flowing into Lake Ontario.

We drove across the bridge & left Canada (for a short while only) & entered the USA – me for the first time. We left our beautiful Mounties & we were joined by the Pres. S.S. men [Presidential Secret Service] – who look so criminal & tough they scare me to death.

Back in the train & travelled through the state of N.Y. – Albany – Syracuse – and then followed the Hudson to Hyde Park. The Pres. & Mrs Roosevelt & Harry Hopkins met us & FDR drove us to the house. Cocktails were at 7.30, we dined at 8. Other guests were Mr & Mrs Edward Grey (U.S. Ambassador to Eire), Mrs Delano Roosevelt (a cousin, aunt or whatever?) and Adml Brown the Pres.'s P/A. I sat next to the Pres. He was <u>most</u> kind, charming & entertaining.

Saturday 14 August

Very hot but clear & sunny after thunderstorms yesterday. Rode – FDR showed us his lovely library . . . Picnic lunch at the Pres's pavilion . . . Hamburgers, corn & water melon.

The Pres. & Mrs R, Papa & self all drove through beautiful country, with lovely original 'colonial' style churches to the

Morgenthaus' for tea, or rather mint juleps. Back just in time to change & pack. Dinner. Departed at 10.30 wishing Mrs R Godspeed & good fortune on the brink of her voyage.*

Canada Again

I loved these last few days – they were so wonderful – & what an enthralling personality the President is – & what a great & noble character Mrs Roosevelt is. It is truly a privilege & an education – as well as a pleasure to have known such people. How pompously that reads – but I don't know how else to put it.

Sunday 15 August

Arrived Quebec in downpour at 11. Mummie & Mr M-K came to meet Papa. Mummie is looking better – but it appears she's had a pretty strenuous time. Chiefs of Staff to lunch. I entertained Dr Coleman (Under Sec. of State) to tea . . . Gen Marshall dined.

Papa told Mummie he had liked having me with him alone at H. Park. O darling it has always been enough to feel you loved me – but to know you enjoy having me with you makes me very, very happy.

Tuesday 17 August

Listened to M[ummie] do her Aid to Russia broadcast. Rushed out on extensive, expensive shopping. Papa & Mummie went off to visit the Gov Gen [1st Lord Athlone] & Princess Alice in their train. I gossiped with Mr Rowan – he is so agreeable. Gov Gen & Princess Alice entertained us to

---

* To New Zealand and Australia for the Red Cross

lunch. She is one of the loveliest women I've ever seen & so beautifully dressed . . . Papa was naughty & wouldn't come & say 'goodbye' till ferreted out from conference with Pug by Mummie.

Felt exhausted – M & I both had 60 winks. Titivated like mad – the men went off to meet the President, the girls remained behind. Suddenly the sun came out & shone warmly & mistily down – on the Citadel walls 3 flags were flying, the Gov Gen's, the Canadian flag & the Union Jack, and as the President's car drove up the Stars & Stripes were hoisted & fluttered out over Quebec. The band played 'O say can you see, by the dawn's early light.' And this balmy after-noon one could not but be moved by this momentous meet-ing at such a critical moment in the world's history – and how much the romantic loveliness of the setting adds to the atmos-phere & significance. Papa has on several occasions remarked 'People say "why do we meet so often?" But what I say is "How is it we manage to be away from each other so much?"'

After the Pres's arrival there was a frightfully badly organ-ised sherry party – it was unbelievable. It was largely for the Chiefs of Staff etc. Gen Marshall was most charming to me – so was Gen Arnold & Adm. King. Everyone is SO kind – CAS is a pet & asked me to join their fishing party next Sunday. Wore my pale blue crèpe for dinner with M's gloves & diamond clips & felt <u>NO</u>how! Quite amusing dinner – sat next to Dickie M-B who is such fun & makes me laugh. After dinner the Pres talked to me for quite a time – I find him <u>so</u> stimulating & gay. O <u>what</u> a wonderful time I'm having – I can hardly believe it's true.

I feel my diary is rather ignoble – & certainly useless to any would-be biographer of Papa. Here am I the daughter of one of the greatest men & on reading my diary I find it is an account of <u>ME</u>! And my ridiculous emotions & doings – but

I don't think it would be much good me trying to be madly objective & Boswellian – so egotist to the end. I will continue (sticking my tongue out at frustrated researchers) to record – My day, my dear.

Wednesday 18 August

Sun. Drove in a 'calèche' around Quebec. Pursued by an unattractive press hound with a movie camera . . . Mummie & I paid a visit to the President who was on the terrace. Then we went off to lunch at Spencer Wood with Lady Fiset. It was a delightful lunch – 40 women, all of them the wives of officials, generals & what have you or else 'fait accompli' in themselves. The food was HEAVENLY . . . Sensation caused after lunch by A.E's [Anthony Eden] & Brendan's clipper arriving.

Thursday 19 August

Capt Paul called for me at 11. We went to the Frontenac & did some 'voice' recordings in preparation for my broadcast on Sunday night. Then drove to the Blood Clinic & was shown round in great detail by Dr Girard who is charming & I found it all very interesting. Then we drove to Kent House, which is about 10 miles outside Quebec near the Montmorency Falls – to lunch with the CWAC officers of the Quebec company & depot. Lunch would have been very enjoyable – but the PRESS was there in its full force. Poor hounds, they've had a pretty bad time out of the Conference – a few V signs from Papa, a mere glimpse of the President – even Fala [Roosevelt's dog] has not had a conference – so failing all else they set on me. They were intolerable about photographs & I lacked the courage to control.

Lunch was slow & rather laboured & I felt a little anxious. Then in a rush I held a conference 'en miniature' with the p. hounds & dashed off to Capt Paul's office to discuss broadcast with a M. Savard. Then torn away to a party given for children of Canadians serving overseas – it was in a kind of 'White City' & looked to me <u>intensely</u> gloomy & ill organised – but perhaps it wasn't. After a brief appearance in stumbling French & hysterical Eng in an <u>appalling</u> 'mike' I <u>dashed</u> to the Citadel – made 3 telephone calls – reorganised myself & fled with Mummie & Lady Fiset to a tea party – all hen *comme d'habitude* – at the Garrison Club – screamed & yelled for an hour and ate quantities of delicious food & returned to Citadel <u>flattened</u>.

Friday 20 August

<u>Flying Commission I</u>
5.00 Got up.
6.00 Left Citadel with Capt Paul, Mr Heeney & Mr Galdwin.
7.00 Left Ancien[ne] Lorette Airport
9.30 Ottawa – breakfast – changed planes
10.00 Left Ottawa
11.30 Arrived Brantford [Ontario]
12.00 Lunched in Mess – Group Capt Richards v charming
1.30 Left Brantford by car
2.30 Arrived Kitchener [Ontario]
Saw BWI recruits. Posed for P/H (press hounds), saw all over centre. Conference with P/H. Addressed recruits. Tea fight in Officers Mess.
4.45 Left Kitchener
5.30 Arrive Brantford
6.00 Leave Brantford

8.30 Arrive Ottawa
9.00 Leave Ottawa
10.30 Arrive Ancien[ne] Lorette
More P/H
11.00 Chez nous again. EXHAUSTED – but happy.

Saturday 21 August

The Conference Ends

Slept rather late – manicure. Shopping – bought 'foundation garments' & a lovely housecoat. Drove out to Pointe Platon with Mummie & Col O'Connor to lunch with M & Mme de Lautimère. Lovely day. On return, struggled – assisted by Capt P & M. Savard with broadcast. Dinner with Papa, FDR, Admls Brown & Ross Macintyre & Harry [Hopkins] & [Mummie]

Sunday 22 August

CWAC 2nd anniversary.
10.00 Church parade – very hot.
11.00 Parade – hotter still (took salute for CWAC)
11.30 Drinks in HMCS Montcalm. Less hot.
12.00 Struggled with broadcast.
1.15 At Frontenac listened to M's Aid to Russia radio
Lunched with FDR, Papa, Mr Stimson, Admls Brown & Ross Macintyre, Col O'Connor, Brendan & Mummie. Struggled with broadcast.
8.00 Filming etc at Chateau Frontenac. Most intimidating.
8.45 My first broadcast
9.00 Joined the Pres, Papa, Mummie, Harry, Anthony [Eden]. Washed hair.

Monday 23 August

Got up late – feeling v flat. Shopped expensively in morning . . .

June Blais (who is a real pain in the neck), Miss Gordon & Miss Gowling – both work in High Commissioner's office & have helped me with my letters – to tea. Operation Lobster – large dinner in the Mess. After which we went to see *This Is the Army* which was I thought <u>unbelievably</u> bad & hot making. Returned to Mess afterwards & had delightful sing songs – Saul Rae & Mr Baldwin produced among some v witty songs this – & unashamedly – blatantly I confess I am DELIGHTED.

'Her name was Mary, Mary, Sweet as any name can be'.

1. I am now forever reconciled to being called Mary
2. Things like this <u>always</u> happen to other girls – but not to me
3. I am complimented
4. I <u>LIKE</u> IT
5. I shall jolly well see my grandchildren see it!

Tuesday 24 August

Went out early & shopped with Harry. At 11 went out with Capt Paul to see the CWAC Company's headquarters. Then went on to Blood Clinic – & feeling that it's all very well to encourage people to give their 'life's blood' – hanging firmly on to one's own – so was 'bled' – felt a heroine & was much cosseted. Felt a little 'frail' in the afternoon but otherwise no effects.

Lunched with M & P & FDR, Harry, Anthony. Papa & FDR had held a press conference – evening papers' reactions so far satisfactory. Lady Fiset et filles to tea plus Mrs Mathewson (who brought 3 pairs of nylon[s]!) & D/Buster.

Mummie getting her broadcast for YWCA ready – at 9 she broadcast – <u>frightfully</u> good. We all listened at dinner – P & FDR, Harry, Miss Tully, Averell, Admls Leahy & Brown, Tommy. Brouhaha going on about Uncle Joe [Stalin] – who is a cross old bastard which ever way one likes to look at it. FDR leaves tonight for Ottawa.

Thursday 26 August

<u>Fishing Weekend (fish only)</u>
Chilly grey day. Drove up early to Lac des Neiges with JM to join Papa. Mummie & Lord Moran stayed at La Cabane. Spent cold day's fishing – but it was fun & I adored being incredibly 'backwoods' & wearing slacks & sweaters & kerchiefs. Caught 4 fish. We all came down again to La Cabane in time for 10 o'clock dinner.

Sunday 29 August

Mummie is clearly in a very nervous state – the slightest things seem to perplex & worry her & fuss her. It is so difficult to know how to deal with it. I'm afraid I got a little cross & cold because really she does fuss almost unbelievably over entirely trivial points & it makes life so exhausting.

We left at 7 for Lac des Neiges – lovely day. Fished unsuccessfully. However at end of day I'd caught 1 fish, 1 sardine, the same guide 4 times, 3 logs. Had headache in afternoon, fished in evening. After dinner returned to La Cabane with Tommy and Mummie, & the others remaining at Lac des Neiges. Excitement of the day was Boris of Bulgaria's death.

Papa has broken the back of his broadcast* – it really is a joy to see him having a good time. He is loving it up here & is really relaxing. He was in terrific form today. He looked a delightful figure in bluc sircn suit with an exceedingly tight fitting tweed overcoat, buttoned (with difficulty) on & his old hat – sitting bolt upright in a boat & tearing off down the lake to fish far into the evening.

Monday 30 August

<u>Flying Commission II</u>
Left La Cabane early for Citadel. Organiscd myself & nails, packing etc. Maj Newsome of the WAC turned up in time for lunch. Malcolm MacDonald then appeared suddenly to say 'goodbye' – he was more kind to me than I deserve & said I'd done very well & in fact – this suddenness & his apparent sincerity quite overcame me. After a hurried lunch Maj N plus Lt Newman (who I was galvanised & flattered to find was in charge of my safety) & myself set off for the airport. Gen Marshall's plane was waiting – two kind & delightful pilots, Col Munsen & Capt Barron. During this & succeeding flights they were charming – & spoiled & petted me beyond everything. I LOVED it.

We dropped some trout for the Pres at Washington (where I worked a Coca-Cola slot machine – for the first time in my life). We arrived at Chattanooga airport about nine thirty & were met by Col Browne <u>and</u> the press. Fort Oglethorpe is situated about 12 miles from Chattanooga (Tennessee) & is in Georgia. The camp area adjoins & in parts includes the battlefields of Chickamauga & Missionary Ridge. We arrived, had supper & wcnt to bcd. It was hot – <u>vcry</u> hot, in fact I didn't know it <u>could</u> be so hot!

---

* Broadcast to the Canadian people, 31 August

Tuesday 31 August

3 Press 'bitches' (one of them very nice) invaded breakfast –
so I pecked ethereally at some toast & sipped coffee & fruit
juice – at the same time trying to give enlightened opinions
on English life, habits etc etc. Then we toured the camp &
ended at 11 with a wonderful review. Then lunch in the
Officers' Mess & away to Daytona Beach – arriving there
about 6 in the evening. I endeavoured to keep cool by auto-
suggestion – there seemed no other way.

After a rapid shower & change we proceeded to the
Officers' Club where we dined. It was lovely & not too hot on
the screened veranda in the dusk. The centrepiece was red,
white & blue – so were the candles. The enormous 3 tiered
iced cake for the reception after supper had the Stars &
Stripes linked with the Union Jack. Such kindness & friendliness as I met with on this tour, & in Quebec & wherever we
go is so difficult to describe, all because of Papa – himself &
all he has come to represent. I find I'm incapable of recording at all adequately the scenes & impressions I see & receive
– but indeed I do not believe I shall ever forget them. All this
tour I felt so terribly responsible – my name & my uniform – I
so longed to do both credit. It is exhilarating & yet awfully
frightening to feel so many eyes on one. But because of the
kindness & naturalness of the people I met I enjoyed it all
tremendously & found so much that was thrilling & interesting in the WAC training etc.

After the supper there was a reception & I shook hands
with about 500 people – and then spent a long time talking to
some of the officers.

Wednesday I September

The programme was hot & delightful & included a huge review & ended with a ride in a jeep which I drove to my delight & everyone's danger. After lunch we left – regretfully – it <u>was</u> such fun. Most of the flight back I had a heart to heart talk with a dreamlike Maj Stillman (<u>not</u> a WAC) who is 2nd in command at Fort Oglethorpe. We discussed the whole field of the women's services – then I retreated to the cockpit where I interfered with the controls – got in the way – ate ice cream & iced cake – asked fool questions & had a heavenly time.

Mummie met me at the airport – which I thought was sweet of her. Also Ruth Elliott Roosevelt, Miss Suckley & S/Cmdr Hannick. At the White House Papa & the Pres & Elliott were on the porch. Col Hobby came to dinner & was charming.

Thursday 2 September

Ruth, Mummie, Miss Suckley & I all visited this morning the Lincoln Memorial, Jefferson Memorial and the Mellon Art Gallery.

We wrote & rested during the afternoon & in the evening Mummie laid a wreath on the tomb of the Unknown Warrior at Arlington & saw also the Confederate monument (sorrowful & beautiful) & Robert E. Lee's lovely house . . . We were accompanied by Col Chester Hammond – intelligent – beau – amiable & a little too well fed looking (who am I to talk?). Ruth & Elliott took me out – with Harry Eidson – great fun – and Mr & Mrs Boyd – very nice indeed. We dined at the Shoreham outside (& later inside, owing to violent thunderstorm). I had a <u>lovely</u> evening.

Friday 3 September

<u>4th Anniversary of War</u>

Shopped with Ruth in the morning. Mummie & I lunched with Gen Marshall at the Pentagon – Maj Newsome was there & a dream like Col – Frank McCarthy with a Southern drawl & exquisite profile. After lunch we saw a wonderful film sponsored by Gen M about the British. It has all the distinction, delicacy & goodwill one has learnt to expect from anything he touches. Thank God for Gen Marshall – one feels he is truly 'great'.

The President collected us from the Pentagon & (in pouring rain) we drove out to see Mount Vernon. I fell heavily & immediately for the house – but who wouldn't. We could only stay a comparatively short time, but it was an enchanting glimpse.

Mr & Mrs Butler's press party. I still find the Pres magnetic & full of charm – his sweetness to me is something I shall always remember. But he is a 'raconteur' – & it can be tedious. But at other times it is interesting & fun. I wonder if recounting anecdotes etc is an American trait? Ed had it badly – without the Pres's greatness or wide scope of subject, which completely defeated me. But what a cultivated animal FDR is – I now understand the article out of *Profiles* (the N York series) comparing Wilkie & the Pres, & saying the Pres is 'sophisticated' – he certainly is – and a cute, cunning old bird if ever there was one. But I still know who gets <u>my</u> vote.

Every evening FDR makes extremely violent cocktails before dinner in his study. Fala attends – & it is all very agreeable & warm. At dinner Mummie is on his right & several nights no other outside guests being there I've been on his left. I'm devoted to him & admire him tremendously. He seems to have fearless courage & an art of selecting the warmest moment of the iron – Papa & he are an interesting contrast.

Sunday 5 September

Mummie, Miss Suckley, Chester Hammond & I walked across the square to St John's. It was Sung Eucharist – one of the most lovely, gay & alive services I've ever attended – the church was packed – & nearly everyone took communion. I felt very strongly then the 'anchorage' of our religion – 'on this rock'.

The news is thrilling these days – but I find the American papers defy anything except a determined & long onslaught, to extort from them any news or sense, they are <u>so</u> thick & enormous – & as Tommy says they are most misleading, the 'Leaders' nestling between sporting articles & the weather forecast. Not to mention the Social page, where I notice the[re] are at least 57 varieties of ways & means of announcing marriages & engagements.

Monday 6 September

Arrived Boston at 11 – the degree conferring ceremony* was colourful & moving. The hall (hideous & Victorian & unlike the lovely Georgian style so many of the college buildings follow) was packed. The faculty of the University – bright colours contrasting with dark – naval & army officers – the women in gay dresses & hats – & then lovely singing & a moving ceremony & Papa resplendent in crimson & petunia robes with a black velvet 'mob' cap perched on his head.

---

* Churchill was being awarded an honorary degree by Harvard University

Papa hailed – the champion against the dark forces of tyranny. Papa speaking – warming to his subject – England & America – United we stand – divided, all is lost – 'I am the child of both worlds' and then launching out on his idea of the full military alliance.

I am happy beyond all words I was there to see him so greeted and honoured. Pride and gratitude surged up in me, and a feeling of inspiration & hope – that indeed here is the corner stone to build on. Always I have been pro-American – always I have admired certain Americans – but since my even short & fleeting visit I have learned a little bit of what being an 'American' means. I have felt a passionate admiration for their broad conception of life & liberty – their tolerance. The pride & glory of their institutions and the beauty & splendour of some of their buildings & monuments – the triumph of their Union & constitution.

We lunched scrumptiously in the Art Gallery. I sat between Governor Saltonstall & Mr Calfin (the University treasurer) & was greatly entertained. Then away again to Washington.

Tuesday 7 September

Shopped with Mummie & then visited the Mellon Art Gallery again. Enjoyed it <u>very</u> much.

Just before lunch Papa showed Mummie (& then allowed me to see) news which tomorrow will shake the world [the surrender of Italy]. Praise God. At lunch Gen Watson (the Pres's military adviser) & Mr O'Connor, the head of the Warm Springs Infantile Foundation*. Rather a dreary lunch

---

* Finding that swimming in the thermal springs in west Georgia had helped with his own polio, Roosevelt funded an institute there for the treatment of the disease in 1927.

– the Pres is not <u>really</u> a good conversationalist – I do not find him nearly as entertaining as Papa. After lunch spent afternoon with Chester Hammond visiting the Capitol & then the Supreme Court building – very interesting. Wrote letters till dinner.

Now Papa says there has been a hitch about Italy.* <u>Oh dear</u>.

Wednesday 8 September

Mummie, Leslie R, self, Lord Moran, Chester Hammond all flew off in Gen Marshall's plane to Williamsburg in Virginia. We arrived about 11.30 & started our tour. It was when we were in the Capitol (I think)† that suddenly a strange man looked into the room – 'It's just been announced on the radio that Italy has surrendered unconditionally.' O thank God.

Friday 10 September

Up at 8. Left . . . at 9.30 for Baltimore. Arrived 11, was greeted by Bendix Radio workers & to my horror had to say 'a few words' to 2000 men & women. I don't know <u>how</u> I did it – I only pray it was all right – I felt quite sick with nerves – then round the shops immediately before press conference. Sticky questions about women's conscription, then lunch in cafeteria – delicious – then more shops. Then at 3.15 went to other half of works in Baltimore. Here there were fewer & the work is heavier. Nor was there quite the same atmosphere of friendliness – I felt nervous & unhappy & sought to overcome it. I

---

* Churchill was anxiously awaiting both the Italian surrender, which was finally announced on 8 September, and the Allied landings on the Italian mainland at Salerno, which followed on the 9th
† Later note says no, it was the Raleigh Tavern

spoke & fear it was not as good as the last – tho' I said more & meant it <u>just</u> as sincerely. However it went a bit better later & I hope it was OK . . . I shall never forget it – I feel so strongly how important we are to each other & how <u>utterly</u> trivial the differences are.

They seem to have an enthusiasm for life & a vitality which is amazing – and the welcome they gave Papa through me today especially at the first & biggest plant & then after a while at the second. It was more than heart warming – it made one feel humble & strong. Driving home I felt exhausted.

Sunday 12 September

Arrived H[yde] Park. Sun was deceptive – chilly day. Spent morning going round with FDR, Fala, M[ummie] & Leslie. M is so astute – I am so easily taken in by people – but she has the faculty of discrimination. She sets a frighteningly high standard – but how often I see how right she is. I wish I could analyse all I feel & think about FDR – not that it matters – but I am so intrigued. To me he seems at once idealistic, cynical, warm-hearted & generous, worldly-wise, naïve, courageous, tough, thoughtful, charming, tedious, vain, sophisticated, civilised. All these and more for 'by their works shall ye know them'. And what a stout-hearted champion has he been for the unfortunate & the battling – and what a monument he will always have in the minds of men. And yet while I admire him intensely and could not but be devoted to him after his great personal kindness to me – yet I must confess he makes me laugh & he rather bores me.

We lunched (in arctic chill) at his own cottage. It would be a heavenly view of the Catskills but FDR has a phobia about cutting down trees – I would understand it if they were ancestral oaks & beeches – but they are the scruffiest little sycamores I've seen in years. Papa presented a charming sight after lunch – flat on his back in a patch of sun (shade is v cold – sun deliciously warm here) warming his tummy after the chilling atmosphere of the veranda. I lay near him and we gazed up at the very blue sky & the green leaves dancing against it – flecked with sun. He described to me the colours he would use were he painting – & commented on the wisdom of God in having made the sky blue & the trees green – 'it wouldn't have been nearly so good the other way round.' And he told me how Alexander the Great stood one day before Diogenes & said 'what can I give you' – and D replied from his tub 'Get out of my sun.' To me these moments with Papa are the golden peaks of my life.

Back to the house – where after a pause FDR, self, Tommy, Lord Moran & John piled into a car & drove off to have tea with Col & Mrs Hull. I may be ingénue & inexperienced – indeed I know I am & I tried NOT to seem surprised when I discovered that the charming family weekend party gathered in this brand new house (semicircular – not altogether unpleasing & designed by John Churchill, son of the other Winston Churchill) consisted (hors of Col & Mrs Hull themselves & her father & uncle) of Mrs Hull's former husband Vincent Astor & his present wife Minnie C. Astor. Gee – how confusing bedtime might be – force of habit is so strong in some people.

So at dinner FDR proposed M & P's health, for it is the 35th anniversary of their wedding – Mummie told me Papa's told her he loved her more & more every year. How well I believe it – what those two mean to each other is something even I can only guess at.

FDR drove us down to the train & off we went with the

lights twinkling on the Poughkeepsie bridge & the moon shining down on the broad Hudson.

Monday 13 September

All day in the train – passing through lovely country. Canada again & then Maine & then New B[runswick]. At Danforth in the evening Pug & I & a few others got out to stretch our legs – the train started without us & Subaltern first, Gen next & Min of Information last we doubled along the platform & collapsed safely into the train again. News from Italy continues to be most serious – Salerno must be grim.

Tuesday 14 September

Homeward Bound

Am in Halifax at 11. Until v last moment Papa was uncertain whether he would not have to fly owing to the Battle news from Italy being so disquieting. However – in the end I am relieved to say the original plans were carried out. Capt Parry (formerly of the Achilles) and his officers and Adml Murray [C-in-C Halifax] met Papa at the station & we went straight on board the *Renown*. The Marines were paraded on the quarter deck & after a general salute (Rule Britannia) Papa inspected them.

Our quarters are <u>most</u> comfortable. After lunch Adml Murray collected us & we drove a little round & about Halifax to pass the time. Then we went on board again. Earlier we had watched our escort steam out – HMS *Kent*, HMS *Obdurate* & *Opportune* – with all hands lining the decks. At 3 o'clock we sailed. The band played 'You Fair Spanish Ladies' – 'O Canada' – & as we took up position in midstream heading for the open sea – the band struck up 'Should Old

Acquaintance Be Forgot'*. It was a lovely afternoon. Clear skies, bright sunshine, a soft breeze – shipyard hands & workers (men & women) waving & cheering. Papa went onto the bridge & I went too. What a wonderful land we were leaving – the shores looked so lovely as they receded very gradually – and then the ship was working up speed.

I was changing for dinner & Papa sent for me to walk with him on the quarter deck – I dashed up – & we walked up & down & watched the sun set together. For me that was one of the moments of my life I cherish. It would seem so utterly natural to me had Papa <u>not</u> sent for me – so many things to occupy his mind – so many other people to talk to – and that he remembered me & wished for my company & that we walked together so companionably & happily – watching the sun go down & the thrash of the screw – pacing the deck for 20 mins or so – that was one of the bigger moments of my life.

During the voyage our party always met for meals – we three – John & Leslie – Pug – Lord Moran – Tommy & Brendan. Tonight & every night Papa proposed 'The King' – sitting down according to the naval traditions. And then we started on the Duke of Wellington's Peninsular toasts: Our men, Our swords, Our religion, Ourselves, Our women, Absent friends – and drank a different one every night.

After dinner Papa, Pug, John & I (in a duffle coat!) paced the quarter deck doing cavalry drill! Papa was in highest spirits & when we returned to the Admiral's cabin he showed us the basic principles of cavalry drill in matches – & afterwards the layout of the Battle of Omdurman. Tomorrow I am 21 – Papa told me he was under fire for the first time on his 21st birthday – Hooray I beat him by just over a year!

---

* Auld Lang Syne

Wednesday 15 September

I am 21 – quite a remarkable 21st birthday all things considered.

1. I am a woman at sea in a British warship.
2. It is wartime.
3. We are homeward bound after a very memorable trip.

Sweet letters from M & P – 100 gns from Papa towards a hunter – and M telling me that exquisite aquamarine set is mine. A golden key from the wardroom officers – a small, damp & v sweet kitten (christened Quadrant) from the ship's company & lovely cards from all the Messes – I certainly never expected such kindness & everyone was absolutely <u>charming</u> to me.

Friday 17 September

Papa & party (girls firmly excluded) have taken to poker – which they played with match sticks to all hours. Went to prayers at 9 – went for'ard in the morning – got wet – climbed around ship. About 5 o'clock I was standing on the quarter deck with one of the officers – the sea was grey & heaving – and a brilliant light gleamed on the waves – & the wake of the ship was white & aquamarine. It was fresh and lovely. We talked of this & that & threw cents overboard for luck. And then with no premonition – but mild interest I said 'Oh look' & we watched for a split second the huge green white-lipped wave. Part of it washed the quarter deck further down than we were – 'We'll get wet' I thought – & suddenly we both of us simultaneously gripped the top wire – & then all thought was interrupted & the world was just an irresistible weight of warm wetness – green – my hands were torn from the rail – it might have been a bit of cotton I was holding – & I was swept

along – completely conscious & certain I was going over &
suddenly I felt a wire & held on – the force subsided – &
suddenly I could get up – soaked & feeling hilarious & light
headed. We walked in – & the risk & gravity only impressed
itself on me as I saw the face of the Cmdr & a WREN officer
– white & terrified the latter, grim & rather frightening the
former & then everyone took charge & I was led in – protest-
ing – & bathed & given brandy & then drinks (Scotch) in the
wardroom. P & M were NOT told – and on reflection I think
I bought my luck pretty cheap.

And then as the event receded so I began to go over it again
& again and lights seemed very bright & warm & the throb &
rush of the sea as I lay in bed meant something new to me.
The Cmdr had said 'now you know a little of what "preserve
us from the perils of the sea" means.' My prayers this night
were not long or complicated – but I meant them.

Saturday 18 September

Touring ship continues great fun – feeling <u>very</u> respectful
towards the sea. Still visiting parts of ship – dined in the
wardroom & had to answer toast of 'Wives & sweethearts'.
Talked a lot to the Cmdr who I think is brave – a bounder &
very flirtable & amusing & rather nice too. Dance & frivolity
in W/Rm afterwards.

Sunday 19 September

Misty & wettish – sailing up the Clyde. Dropped anchor
opposite Greenock about 9.30. All hands on the quarter deck
– Papa, Mummie, all of us. Papa spoke to them – then 'Off
caps' & we sang 'Eternal Father, Strong to Save' and then we
gave thanks for our safe arrival. It was lovely – warm in the

sun coming thinly through the mist & ships passing by in this land locked bay and then standing beneath those tremendous guns we sang 'Onward Christian Soldiers' – & 'God Save The King' – 'Send him victorious, happy & glorious' & then we left – & 3 cheers for Papa & the decks crowded with the ship's company waving & cheering. And so we left HMS *Renown* – may God bless her & all who sail in her.

We arrived in London at 9.30 – all day I felt a sort of mild depression – and felt suddenly ashamed & faithless as the sunset shone across the dim fields & trees & hedgerows so familiar & beautiful – I had forgotten. And so it <u>was</u> nice to be home & Sarah & Diana & tout le monde was there at Euston & Nana & Sukie at No. 10 – and I opened Mummie's present – gleaming lovely aquamarines – & Nana's – Granny Airlie's diamond brooch – Oh <u>how</u> lovely. And then bed – & talked to Nana for ages.

Monday 20 September

Unpacked – scrimmaged around – saw Sarah – long talk with her. Aunt Nellie, Ally, Pam (who I suddenly got on with wildly – hooray) for lunch. Ally detached, sweet & entertaining as always. The Winants came to dinner.

Tuesday 21 September

Sir Kingsley Wood died very suddenly. Mummie, Diana & Pamela off to hear Papa's speech. I sat with Papa while he dressed – & then said 'Goodbye' & signed off as ADC. He was so sweet & said I'd done all right – if I've pleased him – then that's OK by me.

Returned to 481. Everyone v sweet. Have got a cold.

Wednesday 6 October

Am utterly horrified by development of Ringworm caught from that B— cat.

Monday 11 October

Dined with Ally at Ritz. Had tea at home first with Mummie & then walk in the park.

John Winant is missing. O dear God – why are the most vulnerable people always <u>so</u> hurt.

As usual – 'the loveliest and the best'. Poor, poor Mr & Mrs Winant.

Mary to Nana from Chequers, 8 November:

I came down here yesterday morning and have had a very agreeable 24 hours. Randolph was here. As you know there has been a distinct froi-deur between us since he was last here, as I wrote him rather a violent letter. We have had a reconciliation – I am glad to say. Poor creature, he is dreadfully unhappy about his life – and I think is feeling things very much. He is of course so much in the wrong – & nurses a violent sense of grievance. But he certainly does seem in a depressed & unhappy state. Anyway right or wrong, I'm glad I've made my peace with him, as divided families are rather sad & depressing.

Wednesday 10 November

Early reveille – girls worked at double speed. General Smuts and GOC in C, Brig & everyone came at 10.00. We did firing demonstrations –The General was absolutely terrific.

I disentangled myself from the press who began 'hound-ing' and then in mess I proceeded to be loud voiced

– truculent – opinionated & generally loathsome. Afternoon was free for all. Hockey league match. I felt exhausted and ashamed and retreated between blankets till tea.

Thursday 11 November

Poppy Day – and so unlike all Poppy Days I can remember – before the war. It is strange it should have such atmosphere for someone for whom the last war was only a recounted memory. And yet looking back, I see how much 'the war' was impressed on one's mind – by countless little things – Poppy Day and people's relations 'killed in the last war'. I remember as a child those years having a strong fascination for me. They seemed unbearingly [sic] & romantically tragic – and gallant and full of Red Cross nurses looked strained and pained but beautiful. I remember how I read with voluptuous grief *A Farewell to Arms* and *Testament of Youth*. And trying desperately hard to imagine what heavy casualties meant. And above all Poppy Day was special. I suppose I rather loved it – grey November day – and buying poppies in break at school – then the broadcast service from the Cenotaph – the sorrow and pride of the music and then 11 o'clock and the solemn stillness, and trying to say a coherent prayer and a dog barking in the distance – and some of the older mistresses' faces looking strained.

And one Poppy Day I remember so well I must have been very small and Nana took me to St James's Park and we stood inside the park watching the guns on the Parade. And trying not to mind the guns and trying hard to say the prayer Nana had taught me.

And always wanting to know 'what <u>was</u> it like in the last war' and feeling there was something the grownups shared on that Poppy Day at the Silence and in the evening when on the radio the Albert Hall gathering was broadcast and 1 million poppy petals fell from the roof – one for every dead English soldier (for me an exquisitely sad and final gesture, that). A feeling they shared something we could never understand or capture – but nevertheless always Poppy Day seemed grey and solemn and sacred.

'O valiant hearts who to your glory came . . .' And a fresh poppy would be twisted on Cousin Mark's photograph in Nana's room – to stay getting rather limp and dusty till next year.

And since the war it's all been so different – and it seemed to me sacrilege the telephone should ring at 11 and as I ran up to the office I tried to say a prayer – but it got muddled.

I suppose there'll be a new Remembrance Day soon – and one's children will try to read in our faces what it is we remember. And I shall think of Andy and Seymour and countless saddened homes and so much courage and devotion shown in a million ways and how suddenly people became different – dumb rather dreary young men turned to 'our glorious dead' – and girls in pigtails one went to school with doing long responsible jobs – and service life – and discovering real people and unknown courage and patience and rupturing of home life – and England turn[ed] upside down and inside out – I shall remember in the years to come something that had form and light amid so much that lacked shape & was dark – but I don't know whether to call it the human spirit or the soul – or the dignity of life – but there it is.

R rang me, and asked me to go and see Pam on his behalf – O Hell – I did feel embarrassed – however I went at lunchtime. She was sweet and gave me some lunch – & I am glad I went. – R was terribly pleased and was sweet to me. I am so glad I made it up with him.

I am so glad about Sarah – it will be such fun for her and also a rest. Said goodbye to Papa – it always is a wrench.*

---

* Churchill, accompanied by Sarah, was about to travel to Tehran for his conference with Roosevelt and Stalin

Friday 12 November

The moonlight is so lovely these nights.

John Winant is safe.

Wednesday 15 December

Inspection on – then off. How typical.

Went to Eltham on battery business – dropped in at annexe on way – heard news from M – Papa ill. Eltham journey cold – tiring and dreary. Home in the evening. Further telegram – Papa has pneumonia. Evening of rather breathless flap – Mr Attlee and Air Force officers came and went. Mummie haggardly calm – Diana wonderfully practical and a little crisp – but me – suddenly finding myself on the verge of frightened tears – & finally had a good howl while I can in bath.

. . . Supper with M – who is feeling the strain terribly – but is wonderful.

. . . Thank God, Sarah is out there – I wish I were – & yet – I feel she is the one who will be the best comfort and help to him – I am so glad she is there.

Thursday 16 December

A marine brought the bulletin – not very good. Went home.

Mummie, Uncle Jack & I sat all ready to go sipping tea while the fog closed in – and Jock and Leslie and Mr Beaver arrived and went with new plans, counterplans and a more encouraging telegram.

At last we started at 4:15 and motored to Lyneham. We arrived there at 8:30. They were so kind to us there. After dinner M and Hambone got on their flying suits and we drove to the airfield. Saw both of them tucked in immense Liberator and then went on to control tower to watch take off – and as at last it heaved off the ground I could not but feel happy – long and hazardous though the journey was – I don't know why I just <u>knew</u> it would be all right – and as I stood a little desolate and heard the plain drone away, I felt happier than I had done all day. Bed at last – feeling rather part-worn.

Saturday 18 December

Leslie read me a message to me from Papa: 'Your mother is here.* All is joyful. No need to worry. Tender love. Papa.'

Sunday 19 December

Church parade. Tried not to dissolve so hard – but did melt a little – Spent afternoon covering chiefly myself and some holly with paint for concert. News of Papa is really much more cheerful. Molly [Oakey] v sweetly – and Phyllis urged & arranged for me to go to Regt. dance.

Dashed home – went to party which was really great fun. People so sweet and asking about Papa. The Brig was there looking unshaven and saturnine. I fed him as a sop to my slightly ruffled vanity – played about 3<u>RD</u> fiddle unashamedly. Enjoyed a mild flirtation – and my confidence took a deep breath and dusted itself down a bit. But *au fond* this pointless, banal success – so easy with 'that certain age' is no substitute.

Disturbed night on return by alarms and excursions.

---

* In Tehran

Friday, Christmas Eve

Last minute preparations – shopped for RA presents and prizes all morning – then rehearsal.

Afternoon decorating like mad – Christmas message from M and P made me a little choky.

After an evening spent in indecision and increasing sleepiness – Molly and I at 23.15 made a dash for St Martin's in the Fields – arrived (having been almost suffocated by pressure in the underground) late – church full to the doors – we stood right at the back. It was a lovely and moving service – I found myself swaying with sleep and weariness – and was thankful for a pew at last. I'm afraid I wasn't a very active participant – I just stood & let the simplicity of the service – its comfort and beauty – wash over me. Christians awake, salute the happy morn.

Thank God for even my wavering faith – during these last days I found my religion an unspeakable comfort – I am not brave enough to manage without it. Somehow this Christmas has seemed more full of meaning than any of the other far happier ones. In a way it has been the happiest – certainly the most thankful. Everything else seemed unimportant beside the joyful news that darling Papa is getting better – that he and Mummie are together and Sarah and Randolph in lovely sunshine.

And after all it was a gay Christmas really – different – but a good Christmas.

Christmas Day

0615 Got up
0630 Cookhouse
0730 Called girls and RA officers with tea. Helped cook
    breakfast.

0815 our breakfast.

0830 all officers, sergeants to cookhouse for fatigues. Had great fun making lots of noise

1130 Church – Padre very late. Communion.

1.30 Helped with lunch – which was enormous and delicious. Washed up.

Eric Baume* had descended on us earlier and returned with Lady Margaret Stuart apparently to get 'copy' for a story about A/A [Anti-aircraft defence] at Xmas. We couldn't have been more bored because we were longing to eat and were a little part-worn – I don't think they got much copy and went away after a bit. Christmas lunch at 4:30. Very filling and delicious.

Laurie and I then struggled rather spasmodically with the NAAFI. Dance from which I faded and then reappeared.

Monday 27 December

Eggs stolen out of mess in evening. As only visitors were Colonel and superintendent HP police – do not think enquiries would be profitable.

Friday 31 December

Living all day for the party and the prospect of wearing one of my ambitions – a crinoline. At last it was tea time and getting dressed was <u>such</u> fun. Pantalettes – hoops and the dress – water green taffeta – yards of it with white flounces – very pretty – mittens, cameo set and a hairdo which really <u>did</u> look quite Victorian. I LOVED dressing up and was unashamedly vain and conscious of my dress – it really did become me

---

* Eric Baume, 1900–1967, New Zealand-born writer and journalist

and I felt so excited. Molly wore Edwardian style – lovely. Phyllis looked magnificent in a cowboy outfit.

Nearly everyone at the party in f[ancy] dress and some lovely ones. Scrumptious food – very gay. Enjoyed swirling around in my voluminous skirts. The General dropped me home – which was sweet of him – he is an old honey.

Farewell romance – she said, clambering out of her crinoline into green flannel pyjamas and yellow bedsocks. Romance farewell she sighed – smearing Ponds Cold Cream all over her face.

1944

Taking the Fight to the Enemy

'How easily I've fallen into the lazy habit of thinking to the end of the war and no further.'

M ary spends the first half of 1944 with her battery in London. As tensions build ahead of the liberation of France and German bombing intensifies, she spends more time in action. She sees the huge build-up of the Allied invasion forces for herself when she attends a course in Aldershot and waits nervously for the D-Day operation to start on 6 June (having been told by her mother that it would commence on the 5th). Her father's health remains a cause of anxiety and she plays a role in distracting him during this period of waiting prior to D-Day. She also commences an Anglo French liaison of her own with Jean-Louis de Ganay (J-L), a young Frenchman serving in the Free French army.

Hitler's response to the Allied landings in France is to unleash his secret weapon, the deadly V1 missile or 'Doodlebug'. Starting on 13 June and continuing until the autumn, when the launch sites are largely overrun, thousands of these unmanned flying bombs are fired at London and south-east England. Mary now finds herself part of the front line of defence, initially in London but then moving out of the capital to Kent and ultimately to the south coast at Hastings. The death of her friend Tony Coates comes as a real blow.

In November, newly promoted Captain Mary Churchill joins her father on another journey. It is one that is close to both their hearts; a triumphant return to their beloved France. They go first to Paris for an Armistice Day parade with General de Gaulle, then to eastern France for an inspection of the First French Army. Mary returns to Britain to find that her battery is to be deployed to Europe and moves to Weybridge in Surrey to help prepare for its departure. She is present at her father's seventieth birthday celebration, but the year ends on a note of anxiety with his sudden departure to Greece at Christmas (Churchill is attempting to broker a truce between the warring nationalist and communist factions).

In August 1943 Mary accompanies her parents to the first Quebec Conference and on to the United States. Here Mary and Clementine wave to the cheering crowds from a second-floor window in Quebec City Hall.

Mary and her father posing for a photo with Niagara Falls behind them.

Mary chatting with two American Women's Army Corps officers – Capt. Mary J Regan (left) and Lt. Marion Mitchel (right) – on the steps of a museum in Massachusetts.

Mary and Clementine at Williamsburg with General George C Marshall's pilots and others.

On 15 September 1943 Mary celebrated her twenty-first birthday aboard HMS *Renown* on the return journey from Canada. She is pictured cutting her cake with a midshipman's dirk. Below, her diary entry for that day.

Wed. 15th Sept. '43 Wed ③

I am 21 –

Quite a remarkable 21st birthday all things considered.

1) I am a woman at sea in a British Warship –

2) It is wartime

3) We are homeward bound after a very memorable trip

Back home after more than six weeks, '& 3 cheers for Papa & the decks crowded with the ship's company waving & cheering. And so we left HMS *Renown* – may God bless her & all who sail in her'.

In June 1944 Mary was back with 481 Battery just two miles from Chartwell. Her parents visited her on 30 June and watched a fighter tackling a flying bomb.

Mary writes on 3 July, 'The whole of the rest of the war seems eclipsed by the more immediate claims of our own rather unsuccessful but noisily impressive firing.'

On 21 April 1944 Mary travelled to Ridgewell, Essex to christen a B-17 Flying Fortress nicknamed 'Stage Door Canteen' with a bottle of Coca-Cola. She was accompanied that day by Hollywood stars Vivien Leigh (second from left) and Laurence Olivier.

Mary walking arm-in-arm with her parents, who had just arrived back at Euston Station in London from their second Quebec trip in September 1944.

Visiting her beloved Paris after the Liberation on Armistice Day 1944. Mary sits among the 'really enormous' crowds with (*left to right*) her mother, Mme de Gaulle, Beatrice Eden and Diana Cooper watching Winston and General de Gaulle walk down the Champs Elysées.

Embarking on a ship for Belgium on 25 January 1945 with other members of the 481 Battery. In her diary, Mary wrote, 'I could not help feeling proud to be there with them – and as we moved away from the quayside we sang "Auld Lang Syne".'

Amid a sea of baggage and fellow ATS members in Belgium.

7th May 1945. Monday.
Lovely day.
Every news bulletin told us. the announcement of Victory would come at any minute.
At about half past six it was announced that Germany had surrendered unconditionally to the Allies early this morning.
It is such a beautifully calm evening after the winds & rains of the last week.
I am feeling quite stunned.
The war is over.— I can't quite grasp it.

'I am feeling quite stunned'. Mary's diary entry for 7 May 1945 attempts to capture her feelings about the announcement of victory.

On Wednesday 9 May 1945, VE Day+1, Mary flew to England to be with her Papa. She wrote in her diary, 'How can I ever describe the crowds – or their welcome to Papa as he made his way through London.'

Winston and Mary at Potsdam on 16 July 1945. Mary acted as her father's aide-de-camp at the conference with FDR and Stalin.

PROGRAMME OF MUSIC

by

The String Orchestra of the Royal Air Force

Conductor - Wing-Commander R. P. O'Donnell, M.V.O.

I

"Ay-ay-ay" (Mexican Serenade)	Frière
"Carry me back to Green Pastures"	Pepper
"On Wings of Song"	Mendelssohn
"Sons of the Soviet"	Curzon

II

"Serenade"	Mozart

III

"Holberg Suite"	Grieg

IV

"Serenade Espagnole"	Chaminade
"Deep River"	arr. Coleridge-Taylor
"Irish Reels"	arr. Hartley
"Skye Boat Song"	arr. Moffat

Dinner

10, Downing Street,
Potsdam.
Monday, 23rd July 1945.

Signed seating plan for the dinner hosted by Churchill at Potsdam. In his history, *The Second World War*, Churchill describes how Stalin turned 'autograph-hunter' and took the plan round for other participants to sign.

Mary with her father and Anthony Eden in Berlin, viewing the ruins of Hitler's Chancellery during the Potsdam Conference.

Troops giving three cheers for Mary aboard the *Southend Belle* in July 1945. Mary performed the christening and is seen here drinking champagne with the officers to complete the ceremony.

Thursday 13 January

Some news I scarcely dare to believe.

Tuesday 18 January

Woke early with that <u>special</u> feeling. Left W5 at 08.15. Wet, warm, dark morning.

Found annexe in expectant confusion – Diana and Duncan and Uncle Jack all rolled up about quarter past 9 – we were first at Paddington. W/ Cabinet and etc soon arrived – and AT LAST the train rolled in. Dashed inside and was seized with mistiness and choking. A whirl – Mummie, Sarah, Jock and then Papa, Papa, who for one cold despairingly calm moment I'd thought never to see again. Papa – home. I'm so much more glad than I could ever write.

Back to battery. Lecture, tea and long girls gossip with Sarah. <u>What</u> a lovely/agonising time – but how glad I am she went – in <u>every</u> way. Dinner party at annexe with Christmas food & crackers and candlelight and champagne. M & P, Diana and Duncan, Sarah, Beatrice and Anthony and Nicholas, Uncle Jack, Nana, self, Brendan. Great fun – and oh they're home.

Brendan drove me home at midnight. Papa has given me <u>lovely</u> rug for my bed under which I write now (fascinating tassels) & M a beautiful red leather bag.

Friday 21 January

Busy and flew off for my naval rendezvous with Sir Bruce Fraser, his Flag Lt and his girl friend at the Savoy.

I had my doubts about the evening – they couldn't have been less well founded. From start to finish it was immense fun. We saw *Halfway to Heaven* then returned to the Savoy as the sirens wailed for dinner. Heavy barrage. We were all removed to downstairs ballroom. Here Evelyn Laye and her husband Frank Lawton joined the party. They seem <u>so</u> gay and charming.

We out-sat the band and finally all dashed back and visited the battery. A second stand to* was just finishing – the gun barrels were still warm from action. Drinks and so on in the mess. Molly and I retired to bed at 02.30 with visions of 5 hours heavy heavenly sleep. Not so. W5 in action with the rest of London in a big way at about 5. The noise was highly impressive and fireworks will seem tame to me after the slowly descending beauty of some of the flares.

It was by far the noisiest night I have ever experienced. At six we all went to bed rather weary but with a tremendous sense of duty done and something accomplished.

Thursday 3 February

Molly has gone on course and I am deputising. Home for tea. Mummie entertaining Monsieur Emmanuel d'Astier†. I listened absorbed and enchanted by an exchange of flowing intelligent French conversation.

Dinner *à quatre* with Papa & cousin Venetia – what could be nicer?

After dinner V played some bézique with Papa and then we both called on Max who was entertaining Lord and Lady Brownlow, Lord Winster. Max gave us his version of the Abraham/Hagar/Sarah set up. New light on the Old Testament! Very enjoyable.

---

* The second time the guns had been ready for action that night
† French journalist and poet, who was a key member of the French Resistance

Thursday 3 February

I have just come back from an evening with Papa. We went à deux to see *There Shall Be No Night*. The first scene was 1938 – back to Munich. In the interval I said 'It takes one back a bit – we've come such a long way since then.' Papa said 'I knew what would happen then –and I don't now – that is the difference.'

The last few times I've seen Papa I've been struck with his anxious preoccupation with the future – his uncertainty. I know he foresees so much more trouble and grief and struggling ahead of us than we can imagine. Even I, who flatter myself I am aware of current events etc, see how easily I've fallen into the lazy habit of thinking to the end of the war and no further.

Saturday 5 February

Busyish all day. *Mrs Miniver* shown in the evening. It simply couldn't be less like an English middle-class family – or an English 'Lady of the Manor' – most of the latter at least have well-bred manners if NOTHING else. But as entertainment value it was the tops. Actually, I perfectly see why the *Daily Mirror* wrote such a 'stinker' about it. I do admire Greer Garson. Her loveliness also bears the stamp of reality.

The film set me thinking and brought to the front of [my] mind something that has been haunting me for some time. I have a sort of feeling something might happen which would require courage and calmness. One cannot help but think on these things now that we are going into action more . . . my greatest fear is that if something really awful did happen that I wouldn't be able to cope – that I'd have hysterics and run away – and here on this site I mustn't do that – because I'd be necessary – and I am <u>so</u> frightened of disgracing Papa – I've never been really tested and I dread it. I dread not being able to live up to the many examples of calmness and bravery that we have seen in these years.

Sunday Septuagesima, 6 February

Alarms at six – one aircraft – engaged but not by us.

Went to St Paul's Knightsbridge – rather a lovely little chapel and a very lovely sufficing service. I prayed for courage   I may need it so desperately. And I could not bear to fail.

Busy morning. Idle afternoon. <u>How</u> nice. Ate at tea LARGE hunks of chocolate cake – an orgy in fact. Tomorrow I <u>must</u> take control so I am sylph-like (well more or less) for my leave (if I get it). In fact I'll start now – <u>no</u> supper.

Monday 7 February

Monday has come and gone and my second slimming front is still postponed. Busy – fairly.

Lovely 'soapy air' day. Judy's 21st birthday party. First I had tea and a long gossip/giggle with Judy at the Dorch – then I went home and bathed and titivated and felt depressed and M was DIVINE and sweet and <u>how</u> I love her.

When Papa came in very late he looked so worn and weary it set my heart beating. Jock and I went on ahead to join the party at the Savoy – Princess Ida room. Victor [Rothschild] our host, Venetia – Angy Laycock – Judy – 'Crinks' [the politician Harcourt Johnstone] and us and Brendan. Dinner was scrumptious and I overate and slightly 'bibbed' champagne & Chateau Yquem.

Papa was cheering up. Then a conjurer – and a really miraculous one – appeared and the whole party was gay and fun and scrumptious and Papa <u>loved</u> the conjurer and I was happy anyway but twice as happy to see him enjoying himself . . . After the party back with Judy to Victor's flat – where we drank gin and orange – gossiped and fried eggs and bacon – and so back to bed – about 3.30.

Wednesday 1 March

Alarms at 3:30 quite heavy gunfire but not from us. How strange it is in the dark dawn padding around the middle of Hyde Park heavily wrapped in mufflers – and overhead stars and constellations and beams and weird lights burst and flicker across the sky – and guns mutter and call and rumble and bark and planes drone. It always seems a little unreal and frightening. And the quiet of when it's over and people going back to bed and tepid cocoa – and how cold one's bed has got.

Friday 3 March

Date with Jean-Louis. Went to the Argentine embassy and in deliciously warm and de luxe room caught a fleeting, scented and lovely glimpse of some of the Carcanos* – Mme 'Baby' & Chiquita (who is INCREDIBLY glamorous).

Jean-Louis and I sat and drank <u>delicious</u> cocktails and talked – and then bussed to the Bagatelle – which was for once enjoyable and uncrowded. We had a corner table and champagne – and I enjoyed his company more than I can say. And as the evening wore on he claimed more and more

_____

* Miguel Angel Cárcano 1889–1978, Argentinian ambassador

admiration from me – for the first time in three years I felt convinced of a hope for France!

He is going off on a new job – I have an awful sort of premonition. What a silly wicked thing to write. How could I? We danced at the Astor till 2.30 and walked home across the park. Clear starlight. And what a nice evening. Dear Jean-Louis – if I were never to see you again, all my life I think I should remember you as very charming, very kind – clear cut and shining.

Allons enfants de la Patrie.

Friday 10 March

Day of exhaustion, anti-climax and faint gloom. Bull's-eye. But highlight – Papa paid me a flying visit.

Monday 13 March

Dined with Jean-Louis – he came to tea first with M and I at annexe – then a movie – etc. Fun – but I got <u>awfully</u> sleepy at one moment.

I have caught a cold – damn.

Tuesday 14 March

Manning – really quite a bad raid – with some lucky escapes for us. Felt very excited and tense. Tricky for firing.

Sunday 26 March

Tonight Papa is going to speak.* This last week has been busy and rather exciting. Three raids – we fired quite a lot – and I

---

* Broadcast, 'The hour of our greatest effort is approaching'

spent Sat morning helping to clean new ammunition – satis-fying and gave one a sort of 'feeling'.

On Sat night I went out with Graham.* What a contrast Jean-Louis and Graham make! I feel I know G much better than J-L – I am quite at ease with him and he brings out the scarlet woman in me! (or do I flatter myself – perhaps pale pink?) And with J-L – I feel all the time how much I would be a disappointment and a disillusionment to him if he knew me well. Somehow I wish he may never know how cheap and vulgar and awful I can be. Dear J-L – he is so 'chevaliesque' – so courteous and charitable. It touches me almost in tears that he admires me and likes me in uniform and I know he thinks at the moment I am shining and fine.

How can I keep the squalid truth from him?

'THE HOUR OF OUR GREATEST EFFORT IS APPROACHING'
Broadcast, 26 March

Saturday 1 April

Shattered by the news of Gen Wingate's death. Jock told me that Papa said of him – 'a man of genius who might have been a man of Destiny.' His first meeting with Papa – the dramatic journey to Quebec – Mrs W's 'kidnapping' off the train – all came back. I hope with my whole heart those short weeks in Quebec were happy. Poor Mrs W, we weren't very nice to her – I feel he was the mainspring of her life. What will she do without him – God help her.

Very busy morning. After lunch home, changed and

---

* Sadly we never find out who the interesting Graham may be

CHEQUERS by tea time. Mummie's 59th birthday. Looking beautiful and surrounded by flowers from friends and admirers. Sarah, Diana and Duncan all came for dinner and sleep. Jock and I walked to the top of the hill between tea and dinner.

Papa in a very good mood – wearing his lovely new dressing gown of peacock blue, gold and flame Egyptian brocade. Oh the peace and <u>adequacy</u> of home.

Tuesday 18 April

After a longish sunny day – had a delicious bath and walked homewards through the park. I am finding the spring as entertaining and poetic and beautiful as everyone has always found it since creation – only I wish I could express it as gracefully and movingly as some do.

At dinner Papa, Mummie, Duncan (just leaving on his travels) and Diana. At dinner conversation turned on post-war doings and plannings – then on army and discipline. Duff and de Gaulle and Diana D. Our Diana waxed long and vehement on p.w.p. [post-war planning]. She is so sincere and intense about it all, but difficult to argue with and she <u>does</u> run on. For once, I had little to say except 'wow' to Papa, next to whom I sat – and to whom I listened as usual with intense interest and joy.

Friday 21 April

Long exhausting day driving to Ridgewell and christening bomber *Stage Door Canteen*. Vivien Leigh, Laurence Olivier and Alfred Lunt there. After all alarms and excursions it was great fun.

Thursday 4 May

Spent most of the morning in panic about CA [Church Army] speech. Went off feeling 'sickish'. However it was interesting – rather inspiring and unlike anything I've ever been to before. There were six speakers of which I was the last, the youngest and an 'outsider'. Sidney Dark made a very good dissertation – a sermon really – moving, sincere & so well spoken. Hugh Redwood and Miss Carlile – very old and inspired and rhapsodical – rather wonderful.

I said my little piece – and they were very kind – I hope I did well – but I feel rather at a loss for words before such devotion to profession, such zeal and earnestness. I would have liked to have crept silently away. Indeed it seems to me their light shines very brightly before men.

Then went to Downing Street – Nana & Sarah there. Titivated and went to party given in honour of the Dominions P.M.s[*] etc. The rooms were really lovely – banked with hydrangeas, lilac, scarlet roses and tulips. And it was all arranged most wonderfully. Slight fracas with the band. The family were all there – plus secretaries – Nana – Monty etc to help with entertaining. Mummie looked lovely in her new spring ensemble – and dripping with jewels – she is so beautiful. It was a lovely party & I hope everyone enjoyed it.

Talked to lots of people . . . Exhausted after party – Sarah got splitting headache. Lovely family dinner party and then 'home' (!) to bed.

---

[*] Prime Ministers of the Dominions, the self-governing nations of the Empire. By 1944 this meant Australia, Canada, Ireland, New Zealand and South Africa

Saturday 3 June

Cleaned up and learned my 'speech'. Mummie and Judy arrived & Horatia came to lunch. In the afternoon 'Salute the Soldier' at Westerham. It was rather impressive in its utter lack of affectation & its sincere simplicity. Sunshine and flags and the town band and passing lorries and Brig. Currie being very direct and soldierly with a glorious row of decorations – and all around familiar faces.

After tea at Squerryes returned via Mrs Cosgrove to Chartwell – and walked all round old house and garden with Mama.

. . . Mummie told me the Second Front starts on Monday. I could not begin to describe my thoughts and feelings – but I sat as in a dream all the way to London.

Sunday 4 June, Aldershot

Tea at the officers' club. Everyone in khaki – pleasant, calm & yet above it all the sense of waiting.

Monday 5 June

Waited all day in vain for the great news. <u>What</u> has happened?

Dined with William Home and went to party in his battalion mess. Great fun . . . Got home . . . threeish. I don't think I could have been asleep very long – I suddenly awoke – rather chilly – and heard overhead a throbbing continuous roar and I knew D-Day was here.

Tuesday 6 June

Rumours were rife all morning till the official announcement. We lived from one news bulletin to the next.

In the evening we went to a special service of intercession in the huge, hideous and yet curiously impressive St George's church. We sang 'O God, Our Help in Ages Past' – and listened to that wonderful lesson 'Only be thou strong and very courageous' – and then we sang 'Eternal Father Strong to Save'.

How can one pray for those in battle? I do not pray for their <u>safety</u> – somehow that would seem a vain prayer. But I prayed that they might not feel forsaken or frightened – or uncertain.

Early that evening we watched more than 400 planes towing gliders lumber ponderously out. What strange and awe inspiring days.

Saturday 10 June

After the excitements & atmosphere of Aldershot Hyde Park is deadly dull – and I'm nearly driven <u>mad</u> by all this footling barrack room competition, 'What did you do on D-Day, Mummie? . . .' It is all quite reasonable really, but <u>I</u> am not and I must own I allowed myself to get terribly out of hand.

Thursday 15 June

Wednesday morning came the announcement that Papa had visited Normandy. Oh wow. The news is all-absorbing & tremendous – I cannot even begin to put down all my thoughts & feelings. But my God – how brave men are.

Dinner at the annexe – Papa, Mummie, Oliver L[yttelton], Max, John Stanley, Angy Laycock.

A raid started just after 11 – Hell! We were shown the map room by Papa – that was very thrilling. Back at the battery everyone still standing to.

Friday 16 and Saturday 17 June

The raid lasted till 9.30 Friday morning & was full of incidents altho' we didn't have the opportunity of firing very much. All day, on & off alarms & excursions persisted. The whole life of the site is of course upside down – we are all tired but in the wildest spirits. I suddenly feel completely elated & thrilled & so glad to be able to play some part however small just now.

Mummie & Uncle Jack looked in on me (in bed!) at tea time. The alarms started again at one or thereabouts & today, Saturday finds us all once more starting off with no sleep – we are going to make it up this afternoon. This does seem exciting – but how terribly little it is in comparison with what is going on everywhere.

Sunday 18 June

Diver attacks continue. Rushing up & down to the gun park – Molly & I boxing & coxing. People snatching meals & baths in intervals. At night the firing has been unbelievable – the whole sky a mass of lights & tracer tracks & the noise is like hell let loose.

Sunday – a lovely, warm, breezy day. Mummie drove all the way from Chequers to visit me – bringing roses & strawberries. Within 10 mins of her arrival we were in action and she watched a plane come down – alas we discovered it fell on the Wellington Barracks chapel – packed for morning service. O God.

In the early dawn this morning the Command Post had an escape – the brute actually came down in the Bayswater Rd – but while it was over us it seemed for us alone – I & Buster & 2 spotters fell flat! The whole site spent the afternoon sleeping – an official rest period. And in the evening came the blow – we are to fire no longer. But obviously that is right.*

I dined at home on Monday [19 June] night – Mummie, Papa, Duncan, Diana, Oliver Lyttelton & Max. Diana has been doing her warden work devotedly & was <u>very</u> tired. Scenario after dinner with Papa who tried to say the girls shouldn't go on the roof with him – eventually we won our point but NO ONE went up as the key to the door had been mislaid.

During this week work on the site has continued much as usual, to the frequent accompaniment of a purring sound of crashes – with tall plumes of smoke & dust rising from the incident. On the whole <u>morale</u> is excellent – but people <u>don't</u> like it – it <u>is</u> frightening <u>&</u> dangerous. I get very scared! At night it's worst – lying in bed listening & thinking & wondering & praying. It isn't <u>death</u> itself I fear – but pain & the crash & that <u>awful</u> and worst fear – can I rise to any occasion?

I think in these days so often of those words, 'Teach me to live that I may dread the grave as little as my bed.'

On Wed 21/6/44 came the wonderful news – we are to move south to help in the defence of London. The Major told us on a muster parade – everyone thrilled & proud . . . went home to dinner, [with] M & P, Sarah & Cousin Venetia. Lovely dinner party – M & P are thrilled about our move. " 'A soldier's life is <u>terrible</u> hard', says Alice".

---

* Because shooting the rockets down over the city actually caused damage to London, as otherwise they might overshoot and come down in open country

Monday 3 July

It is just five in the morning. This is really the very first opportunity I've had to write my diary since last Saturday week. So
much has happened since then to 481 & so to me.

We have left Hyde Park – full of enthusiasm & a sense of
pride & excitement to be going south to deal with doodlebugs
– which incidentally have been flopping all over the place – &
some quite near W5! I know I left with faint nostalgic regret
– W5 looked so trim & neat & loved – and indeed 481 has
made it from nothing. It has been wonderful to have been
even a small bit in such a success & achievement.

Since leaving Hyde Park we are plunged in the fields of
Kent – 2 miles from Chartwell!! It has been & is being fun,
interesting, exhausting & at times quite infuriating. But we
are for the moment more or less established. Firing very often
– tonight we've had more than 23 engagements. Papa &
Mummie visited the site the other day [Friday 30 June].
Lovely visit – they saw some firing.

The whole of the rest of the war seems eclipsed by the
more immediate claims of our own rather unsuccessful but
noisily impressive firing – the struggle to keep everything
from getting wet – organising – censoring – pacifying etc. It
seems so strange to be encamped in battle order in the fields
I remember so well from riding & walking and to lumber at
dead of night with a 3 tonner down lanes last seen on picnics
or school outings. I landed up at midnight at Old Surrey
Hall – shades of Patsy & Sam – and Mr Anderson appeared
in pyjamas & mackintosh – we confronted each other – last
time we were in hunting kit – this time, a sleepy HG
commander looked at a weary, ruffled AT subaltern in
battledress.

Came off all night session at 8. Bicycled home in pouring

rain and began my 24 hrs off – which was perfect – just eating & sleeping. Nana came home in the evening . . . Lovely supper. Slept in the shelter.

Tuesday 4 July

Brig Currie has been killed – today Nana goes to the funeral of all the people killed at Weald House. Graham is dead – everyone seems to be getting killed. It gives me a strange feeling – almost one is <u>used</u> to the idea of death. Of course it's all very well being detached & philosophical when no one very precious to one has gone.

Wednesday 5 July

. . . Noisy night. A diver crashed in the field immediately in front of the guns. Thank God, no one seriously injured – L/Bd. Sanderson was badly blasted & shocked tho'.

Friday 7 July

Night noisy in patches. We had our second narrow escape when about one o'clockish a diver crashed just behind the men's ablutions. I was asleep & was spared the agony of fright! Rushed out – Molly poor sweet – nursing her behind [as] she had been on the loo. Thank God – no one hurt. One cook shocked & hysterical. Took her to Hildenborough and had tea & chat with charming & rather glamorous MO.

I wonder how many more such narrow escapes we are going to have. Truly we have been saved from what might have been two really dangerous incidents.

Tuesday 11 July

Left very early for London with Sukie – who was covered with marmalade – in her attempt to eat 2 sandwiches very quickly. Felt excited. Arrived home about 10.30 – Mummie so welcoming. Papa sitting up in bed in his beautiful & brilliant bed jacket. He gave me a peach off his breakfast tray – O wow.

Papa lunched with the King [. . .] I stayed and talked a long time to Mummie. RANDOLPH – is, as usual, a bone of sorrow & contention. He has behaved it seems with such odious unkindness, rudeness and heartlessness to Papa & Mummie. How I hate divisions in a family – for my own small part, I've tried to love R for himself – that failed, I've tried to love him as part of the family only, a holy thing for me – that's failed. Now – I know I don't love him. Indeed I wouldn't mind if I never saw him again as long as I live.

One could forgive and condone so much – defend & uphold him, but I cannot forgive & forget his awful conduct to Mama – I know he dislikes her, but he is so rude – and then worst of all – he says he loves Papa – seems to claim it as his own particular right to love Papa deeply & yet he does nothing but grieve him & beat him up & treat him with <u>anything</u> but love & tenderness.

It makes me bitter – I know it should not, but he is the only one – to Papa he means more than any number of daughters – if we do well or love him – he is pleased or proud but it isn't the same. 'My son' – O God, what's wrong with daughters? I wish there was something we could do – it is <u>so</u> grieving. Papa of late has been aged & tired – Mummie says so – & I notice it more than I like to confess. O darling, darling Papa – how I love and honour you – and how I wish you had not this grief and disillusionment over your adored

Randolph – for Papa <u>is</u> disillusioned now – and my heart is full of fears for him.

Sunday 16 July

We left Four Elms & drove in convoy through the incredible loveliness of Kent & Sussex, on a clear, warm day. Our camp is perched right above Hastings – our control room is a converted ladies loo.

Wednesday 19 July

More settling. Feeling tired – very tired – but invitation arrived at last moment from HMS Haigh at Rye to a party – so I thought 'Blow it' – & went. I must confess I had visions of being ferried across starlit waters to a destroyer lying like a grey shadow in the bay – and was a <u>little</u> dashed when I discovered HMS Haigh is a shore establishment – O the bitterness of life! However it was quite fun really tho' a little dim – but everyone was very sweet. Hair raising drive home – gallant naval officer with bow tie either tight or accustomed to MTBs.

Saturday 22 July

... I'm so happy here – <u>really</u> happy in my work – & feeling very glad that altho' I was born too late for 1066 and all that – I'm not missing 1944 and all this.

Monday 24 July

Lovely day. The church we were to have paraded to – was, unhappily, destroyed, by shooting a doodlebug down on it. So we all paraded at Marine Court – niceish service. Very hot marching back. Koffy* came down in the afternoon – we went for a long walk in the evening – and it was very calming & pleasant – I find him very easy to talk to. Life has been going on here more or less as usual – firing & not firing – ups & downs. But this is a lovely place to be stationed.

Sunday 13–Monday 14 August

Went to Emmanuel – lovely hymns, hideous church. Sarah did come at tea time & stayed till Monday afternoon. It was heavenly to see her again. Lovely battery dance at the Queen's – Ian came†. Sarah went to bed earlyish. I rather forgot about bed – and came 'home' at 0600 hrs! Ian is so delightful – gay & amusing & companionable. And to have a bit of a 'walk-out' adds to all the fun of being here anyway. I suppose if I were 17, I would be eating my heart out for him.

I felt so sleepy all Monday – but it was well worth it. There is something rather special about talking the stars out and watching the grey, chilly dawn come.

Tuesday 15 August

Tony Coates has been killed in action. When I read the list – and came so suddenly on his name . . . I felt stunned.

It has been the most perfect day – warm, breezy, sunny, with a bright blue sea flecked with white horses – and all day I've been walking round, working, laughing – carrying on so much as usual – with a record inside me just saying 'Tony

---

* Another unidentified friend of Mary's
† Major Ian Cowper, commander of an anti-aircraft battery at Pevensey

Coates is dead, Tony Coates is dead.' I will not – I must not exaggerate. There was nothing between Tony and I – except, except something intensely young & gay. Something I shall always remember with so much happiness and gratitude, and perhaps just a little nostalgia. He's one of the few people who I liked when I was 17 – & who I still loved to go out with now.

Wednesday 16 August

I thought night duty would never come to an end – but at last it did & I went home to Chartwell. Nana met me in Westerham and I had coffee & cakes – my hair cut & visited Mrs Boreham & Mrs Cosgrove – they were all so sweet to me. Had bath & got into cotton dress. Mummie arrived looking lovely – & we went for a walk before lunch.

After a huge & scrumptious lunch – I collapsed into bed & snored till 6. It was such a lovely day & evening. The three of us went for a long quiet walk after supper – and it was so warm & calm & still. The whole evening had a luminous gentle quality.

Mummie & I drove to London about 9. Uncle Jack met us – & we looked at map room. Jock too – looking <u>very</u> ill & he has got eye trouble. I think too he is grieved about Tony – He told me how it happened. I must confess I gave way at bedtime to some easy, futile tears – & tried to write something adequate to his mother.

Sunday 20 August

Went to early service. Washed hair. Went to bed & slept dcliciously. Oh I quite forgot – at about 05.30 this morning Ian suddenly appeared. I was completely taken aback – and really sorry when he said 432 is off to Folkestone. We talked for a little while – and said 'goodbye' – but he said 'this is not the end' . . . no – I don't think it is . . .

Went to tea with Bishop & Mrs Alston. I was a little disconcerted when on my asking about C of E monastic orders he asked most gravely if I felt I <u>really</u> had a 'vocation for that'!! I do not think the nuns would like a novice quite like me!

Sarah and I talked about the Randolph situation. Of us all – except Papa – I think she only acts with true Christianity. Looking into my heart – awful thought – might I be wrong? Sarah says one cannot just cast off a member of one's family – that that bond must remain despite circumstance or conduct. That despite the hopelessness of it all – shouldn't we try to even now reconcile Papa & R.

Her words have been troubling me – because I feel that I am falling very, very short of all my ideals. That in turning my back I am being not only un-Christian – but weak and taking the easier way. But honestly he <u>is</u> a trial – and one hardly knows where to begin. I am shocked by my own lack of affection – ashamed I was not a bit upset by his accident. I was sorry – but only as one is sorry when one hears of anyone coming to grief. I do not think I would mind if he died – except that it would grieve Papa – and <u>that</u> would make me sad too. That is <u>not</u> an attractive thing to write – but I'm sorry to say it's true. But I am NOT proud of it.

Monday 21–Wednesday 30 August

Day dawned at last & I set off for London. Arrived in <u>very</u> good time. Bathed & beautified & wore my new brilliant red dress with white collar & cuffs & white gloves – & went off in a 'bit of a do' to lunch with Ian. We met at the Devonshire

Club & lunched at the Berkeley & then 'window shopped' and then I put him on a train. Great fun.

Dashed down to Chartwell & fell asleep all over M & Nana – who put me to bed after a tea of tea & peaches till supper – when I staggered up & ate heavily & plunged back into deep sleep. Next morning I caught train from Sevenoaks to Hastings.

Battery in turmoil of packing up to go to Fairlight Cove. Great chagrin at leaving Hastings. There is a heatwave in progress – well anyway it's fine, warm & sunny! Bathed several times during these last 2 days. I was 'rear party' so stayed till Sunday afternoon.

The new site is bloody – but the view is beautiful. It is dirty, isolated, muddy (clay), roadless, waterless & completely exposed. I shall now derive a certain amount of pleasure by making 'all rabbit's friends & relations' say 'poor little Mary – such hard conditions.' Actually the next few days (Mon, Tue, Wed) have flown by, with duty & work & flapping around. The papers tell me Papa is home. Thank God. One more safe homecoming.

On and off I think of Ian.

Telegram for Mary from Churchill, dated 25 August:
Following message from your father please telephone reply
as soon as possible to Private Office. Begins 'Please send me
a telegram through my Private Office telling me about your
affairs.' Stop. 'I follow the triumph of your guns with lively
pleasure. Papa'. Ends.
Mary has written below: I was <u>so</u> terribly
pleased when this arrived.

Thursday 31 August–Friday 1 September

Thursday and Friday – cataclysmic gloom & bad temper for
me. Feeling frazzled & don't give a damn – which is NOT a
good thing.

Sank thankfully into deep sleep on Friday morning & woke
at 3. Did not intend to go on 24. Got up & went into the mess
to get my letters. Long one from Mummie about Papa being

ill again. It was such a shock – everything seemed to reel & go black – also there was a telegram saying 'Ring me. Urgent'. With failing heart I rang up. Thank God – O thank God. M said he is all right but could I go up tomorrow   yes of course. Stan & Milly sweet about it. Started to take bath parade & suddenly I had such a sick at heart longing to be home & see him I thought 'I'll go tonight.'

So I went. I arrived home at 9. Sawyers told me they were having dinner together in Papa's room. I went in – just for a moment I wasn't noticed – Papa, looking well, sitting up in bed in his glorious many hued bed jacket, M sitting by his bed in a housecoat. And then they saw me & were so so sweet & loving & welcoming. And I was fed & cosseted & felt once again that all the people I love are secure.

Saturday 2 September

Slept till 9. Spent morning dawdling, greasing, hair washing & talking to M & P. Rang up Nana. Ian rang up.

Max came to lunch & brought <u>the</u> most delicious Rhine wine. M & P and Max all said they thought I ought to go into parliament. I got enthused – & visualised myself in distinguished black (with a soupçon of white) making a speech about drains. I took it all very seriously – & am still wondering. But somehow – I don't know. Caught 3.15 & Ian met me at Folkestone. We had a drink with Bill & a friend of his. Then started driving to Fairlight. Lovely drive with squally gleaming skies. Great fun – I like him so much. Back in camp everyone kind & fun. Manned till midnight.

Sunday 3 September

Five whole years of war. When it started I knew it would go on for a long time – but I could not visualise it. I said 3 or 5 years – and it seemed like saying 'eternity'. And yet here we are today   entering on the 6th year. I thought in 1939 – 'if the war lasts 5 years I shall be 22' – . . . It seemed impossible! And now I'm nearly 22, and the 5 years have passed – it seems now looking back – <u>so</u> fast. And yet they have been wearisome – God knows how weary they must seem to some. But they've been tremendous too. Perhaps there lies the secret. They've flown these 5 years to me – and yet – paradoxically they seem a whole lifetime.

It's a lovely day – rather chilly – but clear blue skies and brilliant sunshine. We're on duty – and in a minute there is going to be a service in front of the Control Room. The news is so wonderful* – I can hardly take it in – trained <u>never</u> to be downcast by failure, <u>always</u> to discount defeat, ever to perceive light and success in a distance which seemed to be overcast with darkness. This victorious rush – the tumultuous retreat of our vile enemies seems like a huge meal after privation.

This then is the reward of valiant and faithful service . . . of endurance and patience, and backslidings & disappointments and mistakes, and dogged determination and undying, unwavering faith that we are serving a good cause.

---

* It's uncertain exactly what 'news' Mary is referring to here. Possibly the liberation of Brussels, which took place on 3 September, but it may also relate to the sheer speed of the Allied advance at this time

Monday 4 September

Ian met me at the Cove at 11. With him was Ron Porter who is charming. We drove to Moor Hall and had a scrumptious lunch after a scrumptious Pim[m]s. And afterwards Ian & I went for a walk in the garden. Windy gusty day with grey clouds tangled all over the sky. Then we drove back to the site.

Ian came again in the evening and I joined him and Ron at the Cove hotel.

Thursday 7 September

Rain fell down all day without respite. Wind howled. The site was reduced to a sea of mud. We all got wet – some of the tents leaked. It was HELL. Everyone cold & miserable. After lunch we were given permission to issue rum. So everyone had hot tea laced with rum & felt better.

I paid out – rather damply. The AD ATS arrived & said 'Good show' & went away again, no doubt consoling herself with how 'cheerful all the splendid little women' looked. Molly & the Major went to a conference at RHQ – dropped me at Mrs Stone's where I fell thankfully into a bath – I joined them after the conference & we went to a movie, a drink & then home – camp.

On the way home discovered L/Cpl. Crowe had been reduced to a Pte. – hadn't been told. For some unknown reason this was a LAST STRAW. I leant my uncurled head against my tent pole, and added to the general dampness of the tent by howling unrestrainedly.

Tuesday 12 September

Titivated & Ian came for me at 4. He'd got everything lined up for a picnic – & we went to Beachy Head. It was perfect & very windswept. But we muffled up in rugs, & sat behind a gorse bush and ate egg sandwiches. Then he gave me a birthday present – a lovely gold link bracelet – with 'Mary from Ian 15.9.44' engraved inside the links. Oh I was <u>so</u> delighted & happy – somehow it's always like that in films – & now & now . . . I've never stopped wearing it since. Then we went to the White Friars & then to Moor Hall & then home. It was one of <u>the</u> nicest ways to spend a day.

Thursday 14–Friday 15 September

Manned & woke up on Friday to discover I was 22. Left the Command Post feeling un-birthdayish – & <u>very</u> old. Was relieved early & had bath & titivated – met Ian at the station.

When we arrived at the annexe Nana, Mary & Janet, Sukie & a birthday cake were waiting. Also an array of presents – flowers from Ed – the faithful Ed – a lovely inkpot from Nana – one of Grannie Airlie's – a cheque of <u>great</u> size from Mummie & Papa. After tea Nana and 'suite' had to go – I went & bathed & 'glamoured'. I wore my blue Molyneux print and black shoes & gloves. Diana and Aubrey Moody called for me & we went to Quaglino's where Ian joined us & later Sarah, Jan & 2 nice, dreary Americans.

Dinner was greatest fun – they played 'Happy Birthday' & there was a cake with candles. Oh <u>how</u> sweet of Diana. But it was rather dreadful of me – I suddenly 'flopped' and felt terribly tired – & longed for bed. Perhaps we are tireder than we think. We walked to the Astor – & I longed for bed

– I must say I slipped away with Ian pretty soon. The Astor is rather haunted for me by gay but wistful ghosts – Graham – Jean-Louis – where I don't know, but care a little – & Tony.

Tuesday 19 September

Back to London – the girls singing all the way – 'If I Had My Way' – 'She'll Be Coming Round the Mountains' – 'Wrong, would it be wrong' – 'Tipperary' – & 'We're Here Because We're Here'. And here we are back in H[yde] P[ark] which is ablaze with snapdragons & paint.

Saturday 23 September

Gloomy rather – rows with Sgts – melancholy – ah well.

Oh I've heard from Jean-Louis – after all this time a letter & some Lanvin scent. Oh I'm so glad he's all right – & I really do look forward to seeing him again. Meanwhile I 'stink most prettily'.

Tuesday 26 September

Rushed to annexe – drove to Euston with Brig H[arvie] W[att] & Uncle Jack. Masses of cabinet etc at Euston, Diana, Duncan & Julian. And at last they arrived. Couldn't hear or talk enough – felt breathless all morning. O thank God they're home.*

---

* Winston and Clementine had returned from the second Quebec Conference

Wednesday 27 September

Conference about Education in RHQ. Colonel had long talk to me about Bty etc – I may be going to be promoted. I'd quite given up all expectation of that – I wonder if it will happen.

Thursday 28 September

Gave blood at St George's – they told me it will be flown to Holland. I longed to say – take more – let me give something for them out there.

Back in a rush – dashed off to RHQ for pow-wow re future arrangements etc. Everyone very sweet about it. Will be going to 487 when Eve Brown goes.

Tuesday 3 October

Feel tired – inefficient & no good. Mummie sent me a very sweet & loving letter.

At last minute – having previously cancelled – I went out with Jean-Louis – at 49 – saw Chiquita, as glamorous & charming as ever, Ally & Jakie* Astor. Dincd Marietta's – went on to the Milroy. Saw Eve Gibson – alas, the sweet & gallant Dam Buster is missing. O God.

---

* Jakie (John Jacob) Astor, youngest son of Waldorf and Nancy Astor, married the glamorous Chiquita Carcano, daughter of the Argentine Ambassador (1942–1946) in 1944. They had three children and divorced in 1972

Friday 6 October

Busy as possible. Dined at home – en famille plus Jean-Louis. Sarah & Diana there. <u>Lovely</u>.*

Friday 3 November

And at last leave came, and was just as heavenly & as perfect as I'd hoped & planned. I saw *Scandal at Barchester, Richard III, Pink String & Sealing Wax* & *Last of Mrs Cheyney*. I had my face & hair done – I was WILDLY extravagant on books mainly.

I spent a long, lazy weekend at Chequers, Sarah, Diana, Uncle Jack, Ian [Cowper], Mr Winant. And somehow Ian seemed in the way. In the light of after events I see it more & more. It was perfect at Hastings – but somehow I don't care any more & he even bores me a little. But I am ashamed I let him feel it at Chequers – indeed I did not mean to.

I've been feeling so muddled, undecided and frustrated just lately. First I'm going to stand for the House – then I'm NOT – and then I am. Then I have a scenario with Ian & soul searchings & brow beatings – and then a scenario with Jean-Louis – and one day succeeds another & I find I'm so irritable and unsettled – not mistress of my emotions or my mind. Selfish – conceited & cross.

And now that both of them have gone away – I feel a bit more relaxed. But oh how I wish I could settle to one – I sometimes feel in despair in case I never <u>really</u> fall in love. Long sessions with Mummie about living abroad in the future

---

* Later notes, added in 2004: 'Ian Cowper came for week commencing 14th–15th. WSC in Moscow 9–19th October. My leave Oct 10th–20th. This account written retrospectively.'

285

& RCs & France – I don't think I could face it – and anyway I don't love him. I'm impatient too for my promotion now – and I feel that will never come.

Our Stan is now a colonel – there's lots to do on the site. And today [Sunday 5] – I'm going home on 24 hours leave – whoopee.

Monday 8 November

... Drove to London with Mummie. Inspection on – then cancelled & finally took place at 10 minutes notice for benefit of the Regent of Iraq. As he and his cortege approached the Command Post every light fused & the plotter etc. Gee what a life – so Fred bravely explained *toute la boutique* in gloomy darkness.

We have just fired 32 rounds – I was plotting.

Friday 10 November

Paris Revisited

Cold, clear day. Spent morning packing & preparing wildly. Uncle Jack for lunch. Molly rang up to say my third 'pip' has come through [i.e. Mary was promoted to Captain]. I am delighted, so are the family – which doubles my pleasure & satisfaction.

The party is: Papa, Mama, Anthony, Pug, CIGS, Tommy & John Martin. We embarked about 3.15 at Northolt with usual brouhaha. I was feeling almost uncontrollably excited. Strange lights, colours & shades from a cold November afternoon. And soon we left England behind, and then we were over France . . . two years ago easy tears would have come to my eyes – but today I just gazed at the unfolding countryside – the rivers & blue roofed villages & towns, and felt profoundly so many emotions which would sound so trite and banal if I wrote them down.

And then we arrived – the airfield apart from one main

runway was a sea of mud – pitted & marked with bomb craters. A mass of people were there to greet Papa, headed by Gen de Gaulle, Gen Koenig,* M Massigli[†], the Duff Coopers (& Eric Duncannon, now 2nd Secretary at Embassy!!) & Beatrice Eden. Great 'Bonjours' & 'Ow are you's' – and then the band of the Garde Républicaine resplendent with scarlet cockades played the King & 'Allons Enfants de la Patrie'[‡]. Mummie & I drove with the Président de la Chambre – M Jeanneney – 80 and battered by four years' oppression. Just after we started the car – which was also rather the worse for wear – broke down. However we transplanted into another one & then were driven at breakneck speed as the driver was determined we should maintain our rightful place in the procession. Crowds appeared from nowhere – mystified by the long line of cars. At the Quai d'Orsay, an even more impressive contingent of the Garde awaited. Lining, with drawn swords, the scarlet carpeted staircase.

The suite is sumptuous and ornate with gilt & 'lustres' & tapestries & Savonnerie carpets. Mummie & Papa's rooms are palatial with bathrooms like Roman Catholic cathedrals & beds à l'Empire. I am in a humbler room, and think it is the prettiest of the lot – cream & gilt & watered blue paper & sprigged blue taffeta curtains – and a huge bouquet of white lilac – in November!! Gabrielle, my femme de chambre, is charming and she cannot do enough to please me. She is so kind and we had a rather emotional meeting – and both became a little confused & damp.

---

* Marie-Pierre Koenig was military governor of Paris

† René Massigli (1888–1988) appears several times here, presumably in his role as French ambassador to Britain

‡ The British and French national anthems

Dinner this first evening was of course Anglo–French – English people & French food. Both were extremely agreeable. The party was us & the Duff Coopers & the Edens, CIGS & John & Tommy & Anthony's PPS – Nicholas Lawford. I sat between him & Anthony. Papa & everyone were in <u>excellent</u> spirits. See quite a lot of Eric on & off – I quite see why I fell for him when I was 18!

It's nearly one o'clock now – I'm so excited & feel so wakeful. But I must go to sleep. Pray God tomorrow passes with no mishap – one must not think of it. What a wonderful thing to happen to me, and how grateful I am, and <u>how</u> lucky.

Saturday 11 November

It was a lovely day, cold, clear and dry. The crowds were really enormous, and processions were forming from very early on in the morning till late that evening, awaiting their turn to lay wreaths and banners beneath the Arc de Triomphe. M Massigli came & collected Mummie & me at half past ten & drove us to our places on Mme de Gaulle's stand. Elisabeth [de Gaulle] was there – the Corps diplomatique (all the women that is). I sat between Beatrice Eden & Diana Cooper – who looked exotic & beautiful – but nearly died of cold. Mummie looked beautiful in her new black hat. Papa & the General then arrived amid much cheering & excitement.

The sight of the crowds was unforgettable – people had clambered into the trees – and were clinging to the chimney pots. The parade was long & splendid – the Garde Républicaine on horses looked simply lovely. After Papa & the General drove away amid shouts & cheers – we were taken back to the Quai d'Orsay. Unfortunately we were not able to see Papa lay wreaths on Foch's and Clemenceau's tombs.

Papa & the 'boys' were lunching together – so Mummie & I lunched at the Embassy. Diana, Mummie, Mlle Eve Curie, Virginia Cowles, 'Blogs' Baldwin, Victor Rothschild, Cecil Beaton. Scrumptious lunch. Victor – to whom I am truly devoted – then whisked me off in a car to try and get some scent for Mummie – we didn't get the scent – but it was delightful driving around. He dropped me at the Quai d'Orsay & I then braced up my courage & rang up Madame de Ganay – who sounded charming & said I might visit her. Mummie & I walked to their house – & I then left Mummie & feeling very nervous called on Mme de Ganay. I was charmed by her & her three other sons – dear, dear Jean-Louis – you have a most delightful family. I now long to have five huge sons to comfort my old age.*

Once back at the Quai I rushed out again to Victor's flat & drank tea & cognac. His cousin Guy de Rothschild arrived plus a little later his 'date', an American girl. Also there was Tess Rothschild† who helped Victor in his contre-sabotage.

We dined at General de Gaulle's house in the Bois de Boulogne. M & P, the Duff Coopers, the Massiglis, M Bidault & M Palewski‡ (between whom I sat), Capt de Lévis-Mirepoix, Elisabeth & M Guy. It was most enjoyable. Diana Cooper was I thought <u>awful</u> after dinner – she attacked the seating arrangement at the parade in the morning – hot making – <u>very</u>. She is a donkey.

---

* A wish partially granted with three sons – and two daughters
† Tess Mayor, Victor Rothschild's second wife
‡ Gaston Palewiski, 1901–1984, born in Poland. A lifelong believer in Gaullism and supporter of General de Gaulle in his adopted France, Palewiski was also a relentless womaniser, most famously enjoy a long relationship with Nancy Mitford that only ended with her death in 1972. He is now remembered for his lightly disguised appearance as Fabrice de Sauveterre in Mitford's novel, *The Pursuit of Love*

Sunday 12 November

After church we drove a little round the Jardins des Tuileries.
Before lunch Papa & Anthony, M & Beatrice went and
visited Beatrice's club. Lunch was at the Quai d'Orsay,
given by M Bidault [. . .] After lunch I whisked off to see
Victor for a few minutes. Rushed back just in time to go to
the reception at the Hôtel de Ville. This was the centre of
Parisian resistance & played a tremendous part in the
Liberation. All the officials were wearing splendiferous
sashes of scarlet & royal blue. The 'girls' all arrived first &
we were installed in large fauteuils. We walked up stairs &
along corridors lined with la Garde Républicaine – and the
sight of them in the huge hall where the chandeliers were
reflected as pools of light on the parquet floor – is something I shall never forget.

Papa arrived & was welcomed by the Préfet de Police –
M Luizet and the President of the Parisian Council of
Liberation M Tollet. The room, on whose walls were depicted
the most bloody & 'resisting' events of French history – was
full of members of the resistance movement, headed by that
dream – M D'ASTIER*. It was very moving. Papa made a
great & remarkable speech in French, and I think they all
liked it. Then he was presented with the swastika hauled
down from the Hôtel de Ville & a dagger. Then we retired &
drank champagne.

---

* Emmanuel d'Astier de La Vigerie, 1900–1969, was a French poet,
journalist, politician and leading member of the French Resistance.
In 1943 he met General de Gaulle and joined his Free French Forces
government-in-exile as a Commissioner to the Interior. While in London
in 1943, he wrote the lyrics for the song 'The Partisan', which was later
recorded by Leonard Cohen

On the way back the streets were still lined with people although it was after dark & they could have no reasonable hope of seeing anything. Papa & Mummie dined with Duff & Diana – and Eric [Duncannon] gave a dinner party for me.

We had to go early because of the train – Mummie stayed on in Paris. My wagon-lit was bursting with white gladioli and tiger lilies – simply <u>lovely</u> – but rather overcrowded.

I left the boys rather quickly – & went to bed to gather strength for tomorrow's excursions.

Monday 13 November

We trundled across France from West to East & when we woke up it was to find SNOW – with a white heavy sky threatening more to come. I lost control at breakfast & guzzled an omelette au jambon! We arrived at Besançon at 10. Here General de Lattre de Tassigny plus his staff etc met us. After a guard of honour & bands we bundled into a long caravan of cars. I found myself with General Valny (Gen de Lattre's chief of staff – I think) and a French colonel whose name I never got and also Commandant Bullitt – *ci-devant* American ambassador to France & now in the French army. They were all <u>charming</u> to me – and I couldn't have had a gayer journey. It was indeed très *gai* for as we climbed & climbed the snow thickened & it got colder & colder – then a tyre burst on Papa's car – after that there were continually halts to unditch various cars which got stuck firmly in the snow. I decided to trade on my sex rather than my rank – & therefore sat in great comfort while various generals, colonels & brigadiers heaved & pushed the car about.

We eventually arrived at Maîche. Eight kilometres only from the enemy & the battle was explained to Papa & the

General in Gen de Lattre's HQ in a most attractive & dimin-
utive chateau. I sat on General de Gaulle's right and next to
Gen Juin. It was rather nervous work <u>at first</u> – but I hope it
was all right. At the end of lunch Papa made a short & very
moving speech proposing conjointly the health of the First
French army, its commander – 'ce général ruse . . .' Gen de
Lattre de Tassigny & Gen de Gaulle. Gen de Gaulle replied
shortly & well & said Papa was 'le Clemenceau de cette
guerre' (or was it Gen de Lattre who said it?), anyway then
Gen de Lattre made a speech & then our own CIGS – in
perfect & graceful French. I was so proud to be at this occasion in this snowbound village and to be able to drink with my
whole heart to resurgent France. May God speed & prosper
their forthcoming attack.

We then – considerably warmed by cognac & emotion –
bundled into the cars & now fortified with champagne dashed
back along the ways we'd so painfully climbed.

We arrived at Valdelion as twilight was falling. It was still
snowing & bitterly cold. Papa and the General drove in a
Jeep right down the assembled parade. After a quick goûter
in the equivalent to NAAFI – there was a march past. Most
of the troops were maquis & FFI* just completing their
training. I thought they looked splendid. Small, tough &
ferocious, and animated with one desire – to confront the
enemy. There was also a battalion of the Foreign Legion
who marched by impressively to their own 'March
Consulane'. Then in the gathering gloom about 100 tanks
rumbled past.

It was such a sombre setting. Snow, wind, barracks &
twilight, and it will remain in my memory forever. I think all
of us there, who loved France, must have prayed for this small

---

* Free French Forces of the Interior

but infinitely determined army – the new army – recruited from the Maquis & the FFI with the best of the old la Légion Etrangère. '. . . *le jour de gloire est arrivé*'. We all got icy cold, but thank God Papa was all right.

At dinner on the train I again sat between Gen [de] Gaulle & Gen Juin, and it was our last meeting for the present. Dinner was passed in the most genial and friendly spirit. I do truly trust & think a real rapprochement has resulted from these last few days – Long may it last. When we all parted it was to say 'Goodbye'. General de Gaulle sent one of his aides Lt Guy along with a little Croix de Lorraine for my uniform – I am so proud of it.

Tuesday 14 November

We arrived at Rheims and spent the morning with Gen Eisenhower. I went for a walk, while Papa worked, with the dreariest possible WAC – who has been to so many warfronts that this bedraggled & impoverished little French village – Gueux – was not very exciting to her. To me every step seemed significant – I can not get over being in France again.

In the afternoon we flew away over the spacious Champagne country – dotted with war cemeteries and made so lovely by the soft wet lights and the different shades of the 'Cultures'. I wish I could begin to describe its rather sad beauty. 'Lord, thy glory fills the heavens; Earth is with its fullness stored . . .'

And then we arrived back and Papa's visit to France was over.

Saturday 9 December

I've got very behind with 'My Day' – it's now the 9th of December. After the Paris visit there was the very personal excitement of the new job. Then rumours began wafting around – then we were told cautiously to begin to prepare – & finally General Tremlett told the assembled ATS of 137 that we have been chosen for service in N W Europe. <u>Wild</u> excitement and enthusiasm. And lots of work – preparing for the move to Weybridge – where we 'concentrate'.

But before we had to leave London, there was Papa's seventieth birthday – it was a great family occasion.

St Andrew's Day, Thursday 30 November

Rushed home earlyish to say 'Happy Birthday' & to present the usual buttonholes (which he wore <u>all</u> day) and his present – some Gilbert & Sullivan recordings. Then wild shoppings for kit etc. Then back for lunch at No. 10. The Cranbornes and Dr & Mrs Fisher. Very agreeable lunch. Sat between Betty C [Lady Cranborne] & the Bishop [of London]. Dr Fish [dentist] – ugh – Dashed back to site for pay – Nana came & collected me and I went home for dinner.

Mummie had made the sitting room ablaze with flowers. The guests were Cousin Venetia, Brendan & Max besides the family – the 3 girls – Aunt Nellie, Uncle Jack & Nana. When we were all assembled – the candles were lit on the cake, 70 of them. Papa looked so pleased & well. At dinner Diana & Sarah sat on either side of Papa – & I sat between Nana & Duncan. Dinner was delicious & ended with peaches, birthday cake & real cream (a present!). All Papa's presents were loaded on a table and there was a magnificent 'bottle-scape'. Max proposed Papa's health – not <u>very</u> well – but Papa's reply made me weep. He said we were 'the dearest there are' – he said he had been comforted and supported by our love. It was short – but I couldn't see the faces at the end & then very slowly – almost solemnly he clinked glasses with each one of us.

Judy came in for coffee – Papa sang 'Poultry' – & 'Half a Woman & Half a Tree' & 'It Makes Me Wild When I Go Out, There's Nowhere to Go But Back'. After dinner a great pile of telegrams was brought in & Papa read them to us.

Thursday 14 December

On Saturday December the 2nd 481 left Hyde Park. We were all so excited at the prospect before us – service in N W Europe, that I don't think many of us could stop to feel nostalgic or regretful. What do the next few months hold – will we ever really get there – how – why – so many questions – and a sphinx-like silence is maintained by those who (we presume) know.

We have moved to Weybridge. I am writing this in the middle of my 'EMBARKATION LEAVE' – on the way to Chequers. The life at Weybridge is hectic & muddling – but I love it – although I find I get rattled rather more easily than I should – & the work is worrying and I keep on getting 'scares' about this, that and the other. I came on leave on the 9th – today is the 14th. I am only now really beginning to enjoy myself – and the days are slipping remorselessly away.

Last weekend & the first part of this week were spoilt by 2 rows – (1) a SPAM row – unleashed stupidly and emotionally by me, which has caused repercussions with every member of the family. (2) Slight *froissement* with Mama over me & Victor [Rothschild] (who is here – and being kind & delightful to me). Mama has been tired & strained – Greece, Papa and family upheavals being too much all at once.

I have seen *Uncle Harry* and *Henry V* – this last, I thought, was enchantment from start to finish. I have shopped in a rather desultory way – I have felt utterly depressed & miserable. Now it is better – and I – I hope – am a little wiser. I dined last night with Victor. I like him so very, very much. I ran into Judy & we gossiped about life in the vastnesses of the Ritz. I went with M & P on their being presented with lovely gifts by the Committee of Conservative members of the House. Mummie's speech was a gem and memorable for its grace & distinction. Mummie has given me a copy of a Cézanne for Christmas. We went & chose it together. It is lovely.

I have been thinking a lot about Jean-Louis and his offer – and I have been wishing, suddenly and unavailingly, how much, how very much I would like to have a baby. I have been feeling not-so-young-in-heart.

Sunday 17 December

Drove down with Nana to Chequers. Mummie and I went to lunch with Victor at Tring ... I ate myself silly & then admired his Cézannes. Peggy Ashcroft & a sweet & very good small daughter arrived. Mummie & I walked a long part of the way home. The lights in the sky were lovely & dramatic. I played G & S records to Papa for about an hour – And he was so very sweet to me. The first part of this leave was <u>so</u> bloody – But now it suddenly has come right.

Christmas Day, Monday 25–Tuesday 26 December

Got up & helped cook the men's breakfast. Nick & I & the Major all walked to church. Lovely service. Preparations for lunch – lunch – preparations for dance – dance. Managed to go to evening service. Felt tired & longed for bed. Eventually tumbled into it – cold & dirty & slept like a log till 10. Got up in a rush – ate an egg & drove off to Chequers.

Hard white frost & the beauty of the countryside when we emerged from the fog of the Thames Valley was quite indescribably beautiful. Arrived at Chequers to find – ah what a blow & a shock – Papa flown off on Christmas Eve to Athens. Mama terribly anxious. So are we all & champing for news.

Diana & Duncan there with the children – Clarissa who has regained her glamorous looks – but I find her so heavy & dreary – Uncle Jack – Mr Winant – Prof. In the afternoon a children's party – with films & ice cream & slight squabbles! Sarah & I are sharing a room – & it's such heaven gossiping away … Richard Stanley & the other 'young gentlemen' from the camp came to tea & dinner.

1945

Liberation

'The war is over – I can't quite grasp it.'

Maundy Thursday   29-3-45

The news continues to be quite
extraordinary

Everyone is saying 'its over' –
oh God, grant it may be so

Went with the Bingo et famille
to Bach's Cantatas at le Palais
des Beaux Arts

I found them quite, quite
lovely – they transported me.
Full of form and grace &
purity.

Mary's battery departs for Belgium on 25 January and takes up a position in the countryside outside Brussels, before moving in mid-April to Antwerp. Events move quickly and she is well placed to observe the final phase of the war in Europe, recording the Allied crossing of the Rhine and the deaths of President Roosevelt and Hitler. The mood of the diary lifts and the social engagements proliferate as the peace approaches. She is awarded the MBE (Military).

On VE Day (Victory in Europe) in May, Mary's celebrations in Brussels are followed by an urgent request to join her father in London, Clementine being away in the Soviet Union because of her work chairing the Red Cross Aid to Russia Fund. She accompanies her father to some of the celebrations but records his worry and weariness in the moment of victory. Thereafter, there are lively visits to Paris and Brussels but her battery moves into Germany, just outside Hamburg, from where she visits the former concentration camp at Belsen. Her diary contains nothing on the horrors of that visit or the sufferings of the German people but she writes about them in letters to her mother.

Worries begin to surface about the results of the pending 1945 general election. Mary loyally exercises her vote for her father's Conservative Party on 2 July, but the fact that she thinks the Labour candidate would make the better MP for her local constituency ominously foreshadows the result (which is delayed until 26 July due to the difficulty in retrieving and counting the large service vote from overseas).

Churchill decides to take a brief holiday in the south of France prior to the Potsdam Conference and the election results. Mary is summoned to accompany her parents and enjoys an interlude of sea and sunshine at Château Bordaberry, near Saint-Jean-de-Luz on the Bay of Biscay. Her father swims and paints but does not entirely escape from worries about the election.

After the holiday, Mary accompanies her father to Germany and to the Potsdam Conference. This is the last big wartime Allied summit, held on the outskirts of Berlin, and attended by President Truman and Joseph Stalin. However, she does not seem to have kept a diary and our account again relies on her descriptive letters to Clementine.

The Churchill party returns to London halfway through the conference for the result of the general election. Mary is in Downing Street to observe the end of her father's premiership and records its impact upon him and his inner circle. Afterwards, she returns to Germany but is quickly transferred back to Whitehall so that she can be nearer her parents. Her war is over.

Sunday 7 January

Today is the 7th January – so clearly I am a very bad 'journal-iste'. During the last fortnight the battle has waxed & waned & now rages again. We are all prepared & longing to get going. Battery life – battery problems and battery gossip is super-imposed on everything. I went to a wonderful New Year's eve party – dining first with John & Richard Stanley, then dancing at Lady Queensberry's house. It was gay & glamorous. I loved it. Nearly everyone was wearing long – except me –!

Through all the fun & gaiety I felt the power of absent friends – living and dead. But especially J-L – '49' have me & him all lined up for the B[rompton] Oratory . . . I enjoyed myself more & more as the night wore on. It is so exhilarating to feel oneself admired and liked. I stayed till the band stopped – Alex drove me home in brilliant moonlight.

A perfectly bloody New Year's day ensued – full of riot acts & raspberries – from me to ATS offi[cer]s & everyone – O HELL. And bed at last was all I longed for!

All these last few days I am thinking constantly of Jean-Louis – & his sweetness & his offer – and I try to imagine what a life with him would be like. I am so frightened of letting all the worldly part of it weigh subconsciously with me.

Last Wednesday   I forget the date [3 January] I went up to lunch with Mummie & Papa – but again I missed him – an hour before he'd flown off to visit Monty & IKE. He left me a letter, written in his own handwriting – I was overcome with love & gratitude – he needn't – he is so so busy & preoccu-pied. He thanked me for the G/S operas – he'd liked them. If he only knew how happy & glorious I feel that they have made him happy. It will join the other letter he wrote me – the week I joined up. To me they are a sort of 'Talisman'.

Churchill to Mary, 2 January:

Darling Mary, Last night we played through 2 of yr records, 'Pirates of Penzance' & 'Patience'. I read and brooded on the flowing music. On the whole one of the happiest hours I have had in these hard days! How sweet of you to have the impulse! How clever to have turned it into action & Fact! Your ever loving Father, W

Saturday 13 January

Wednesday the 10th was a day I want to remember. I caught the 8.46. It was a cold, snowy morning. I walked from Waterloo to the annexe, with snowflakes blowing about. I love that walk across the bridge – today it was cold, the sky a white mistiness – roofs & towers covered with this cracked snow – the barges moored in great islands snow caked – accentuated the leaden look of the river – that was today. But crossing the bridge at night with the lights winking here and there and long gleams of wavering reflections in the river – and how the air seems to freshen as you cross the crest of the bridge – and you are isolated and all alone – shapes loom up & are gone – people passing quickly – the trains – ghostly and rather threatening rumble by – the mass of the Houses of Parliament rising on the left, and always I have that feeling of expectancy and confidence – because I am going home, and for a little while I shall be my own mistress – belong to the people I love.

When I got home – Mama was resting at Chequers – Papa was in bed with a bad cold. I found Mr Oswald Birley* waiting to see Papa – I introduced myself & we talked till Papa

---

* The artist Oswald Birley, 1880–1952, painted several famous portraits of Churchill

was ready. Mr B was very agreeable & looked at all the pictures. He said he admired the William Nicholsons. I invaded darling Mummie's room, telephoned – steamed in a delicious bath – weighed myself – joy, oh joy, I'm down a pound! And finally about 12 I set out shopping – dressed up to the nines and feeling elegant & happy!

I lunched alone with Papa. A rare and precious occasion for me. He sat up in bed, resplendent in his bed jacket – I sat near his bed & we had a delicious lunch on trays. Crab – beef mince pies – with Liebfraumilch to drink. At first Papa read the *Manchester Guardian* & *Yorkshire Post* & then talked to me – Greece – Monty – the battle – the House. He was so kind and I did so love being alone with him. Only I'm always afraid of boring him – so I was careful not to stay too long & went away at half past two – that hour having flown.

Shopped all afternoon. Had tea with Diana – Aubrey Moody there. Alex Cullen came for a drink, bringing an exquisite jacquard scarf to tie round my head. I pressed him to a drink – no, no 'I came to see you' . . . Which sort of remark made casually and unstrainedly gives great pleasure – and greatly oils the wheels of existence. He went away, promising to return at 10.30 & take me out. He brought letters from J-L, who it appears is miserable and desolate beyond all words – no letters reaching him yet. Poor sweet.

I dined alone with Papa at half past eight. His cold was better since lunch time & he was in a gay & tender mood. He was sweet to me – unaffected, affectionate and showing an interest in my humble affairs (of the heart & of the barrack square) which moves me beyond all words.

Sunday 14 January

My wisdom tooth is starting to hurt. So far however I'm ignoring it.

Tuesday 16 January

After persuasion from Mama (telephonically) I rushed up for visit to Dr Fish.* Oh bliss – I had lunch alone with Papa – who is in bed & still contending with a cold which now threatens his vocal chords [sic]. He read me part of his speech.† Nana turned up – hooray. Went to Dr Fish, who has saved the situation. I had gas – and retreated to bed, where I was cossetted & petted by Mama and everyone. Sucked boiling water & penicillin tablets & read *Laura*. Papa visited me after dinner – WOW & RE-WOW – so did Mummie. Goodnight.

Saturday 20 January

Another day of enforced idleness. Oh <u>how</u> I wish we could get off. Letter from J-L – who I think of more & more as the anchor – and harbour of my heart.

Wednesday 24 January

The day's gone slowly enough. It's hard, crisp snow & very cold.

Caught warmish berth just in time. A Mr O'Brien from the publicity dept has arrived – which is truly rather trying – <u>However.</u> And now I'm ready for bed & feeling very excited

---

* The dentist
† Speech to the House of Commons on the war situation, 18 January

and on the verge of an adventure. I think I'd better say some pretty urgent prayers – for courage – for endurance, for good sense and to me the most difficult – SELF-abandonment. Oh with my whole heart I hope we none of us will fail. I could not wish to set out with any other companions – and how I hope they'll win golden opinions for themselves and for the battery. I must go to bed now – I wouldn't have missed this.

Thursday 25 January

Woke up with that warm, expectant feeling. Breakfast – fried egg, bacon, toast & raspberry jam. Finished packing & tidying up. Kit is very heavy & tiring to carry.

We set off at 08.45 – marching through snowy icy roads to the station. Singing – 'Tipperary' – 'Pack Up Your Troubles'. 3 hour icy train journey to Tilbury. Passed W9 – wouldn't be them for anything. Changed money. Girls had tea & sandwiches & then were hustled on board to make way for incoming prisoners of war. I could not resist as I passed giving them a look of what I intended them to interpret as triumphant loathing – But I fear – & how just – it probably made me look a discontented, served up fat ATS officer – comparing on the whole unfavourably with Hitler's Rhine Maidens.

Once on board ATS thronged onto the decks. They looked – smart – excited – gay and smiling. I could not help feeling proud to be there with them – and as we moved away from the quayside we sang 'Auld Lang Syne'. Red caps – naval officers – WRENS waved us off. Conditions on board are not too bad, & as good as they can be. Everything is very much under control and well organised. There was a small dance in the evening. After the girls were in bed I went up on the bridge & the 1st Lt & officer of the watch treated me to tea & naval chit chat. Rather chilly night.

Friday 26 January

And this morning – Friday – we are still here off Southend, fogbound. But thank God it is calm – so far. Paraded on deck – PT – hectic & all very vertical owing to confined space. It's so wonderful to be on our way at last. I always find it difficult to believe things really will happen when one has to wait & I try to imagine what it'll be like & then suddenly it all happens quickly & calmly – and another chapter begins.

Spent afternoon in a torpor. Had dinner in Captain's cabin – which was a little dreary – more so as my right neighbour talked 'racing' about which I am dumb and my left hand neighbour didn't talk at all. The Capt was very pleasant. Spent rest of the evening talking with a good-looking 'desert rat' frontwards bound after a month's home leave. There are a number of them on board. What a record the Royal Scots Greys have had – '38 Palestine, then Syria, then the Desert – backwards & forwards – then Italy – & now Holland. I don't think they were looking forward very much to going back. My acquaintance I thought looked a little strained – I longed to say 'Why should you want to go back to squalor & cold & mud & fear & death & pain' – I longed to say something even half adequate about all they've done & endured – I longed to say 'For God's sake don't pretend to me that you're indifferent' – but of course I didn't say any of these things – it would have been an emotional indecency.

But I realised how <u>little</u> it is we have to face – I realised what I so easily forget, the controlled everyday courage men have. 'Pitifully behold the sorrows of our hearts.'

We sailed at about 01.30 **Saturday 27 January**

We docked in Ostend at 11.30. Very cold – icy & snowy with a sun struggling through the frosty atmosphere. We slithered through the streets to the ATS staging camp – & thankfully – how thankfully laid down our heavy kit. The town is full of British troops – and hordes of pale ragged children – 'Cigarette pour Papa.' The girls spent the afternoon washing & tidying – and in the evening went to parties given in their honour at the NAAFI. We had 'nightcaps' with the Signals officers from the mess next door. Tomorrow's arrangements had to be tied up – I felt exhausted & very dirty. On my way to bed I pinched a large jug of hot water & washed. Felt much better.

Sunday 28 January

A snow blizzard in progress. Thank God the arrangements worked smoothly & all the girls <u>&</u> kit were loaded in the trucks. We drove through Bruges – over a snowy countryside – flat as a pancake – frozen canals & pale shafts of sunlight illuminating distant roofs & spires. We met crowds of people going to Mass – they all smiled & waved. At Ghent we stopped for 1½ [hrs] & had buns & tea in the large NAAFI there. Then we clambered aboard again and continued our cold trek across to Brussels & finally as twilight was falling we arrived in Huldenberg and the trucks struggled up the tortuous narrow road up onto the hill under which the village nestles. For miles as far as we could see was undulating snowy countryside.

Joan & the advance party had a hot meal ready in both sites – & fires burning in the huts. The girls tired out by their travels tumbled into bed & slept the sleep of the excited & exhausted. BHQ returned to the chilly fastness of 'le chateau

Franchomme' which is an elegant summer 'bagatelle' & mostly glass & large open doorways.

Bed at last was heaven. I could hardly believe that at last we have arrived.

Monday 29 January

Settling in – in ever deepening freezing snow. Priorities: Food, water, heat.

Every expedition in transport is an adventure – quite 50% of one's time is spent pushing, pulling, coaxing & undigging cars. When the sun comes out it is beautiful. The snow is untrammelled for miles & miles.

Thursday 1 February

Drifts of snow have given place to quagmires of mud & slush. The roads if possible are worse than ever. The SUBS & site staff generally are working very hard. I poodle around & feel rather ineffectual & underworked & overfed! The girls are really being wonderful & working hard. But it's a struggle to stop them wearing fancy dress.

Sunday 4 February

Busyish. Visited the church at St Agatha Rode for the evening service. 15 rather desolate British graves in the churchyard.

Letter from Montgomery to Mary, 11 February:

My dear Mary, I had lunch in London last week with your Father & Mother and heard of your arrival in 21 Army Group. I am sending Noel Chavasse, one of my ADCs, to visit you and make certain all is well. I am also sending by him a present for your Battery of a case of Bovril and 10,000 cigarettes. Let me know if there is anything I can do for you.

I hope your Battery is shooting down the flying bombs. Yrs sincerely, B L Montgomery

Tuesday 13 February

American Signals Corps dance at Namur. Took 30 girls. We all had a wonderful time . . . candy cake & champagne! I also have an invitation to go boar hunting in the Ardennes.

Saturday 17 February

Collected canteen stores. Johnnie collected me at 7. Went to Medical Section dance at Namur – it was a WOW. I had a wonderful time – lots of good-looking young men – not too many girls and lovely champagne. Was thoroughly spoilt – flirted outrageously with anyone I fancied & generally had a memorable evening.

Sunday 18 February

Went to Mass at Huldenberg with Joan & floundered my way through the Mass. Long heart to heart talk with Joan as to whether I ought to become RC if I marry Jean-Louis – If I marry J-L.

Tuesday 20 February

A wasted day. An interminable and uncomfortable journey to Antwerp to visit 569. Lunched at their BHQ and returned. But the day was really a dead loss from the point of view of work. Tonight I'm manning at B Troop.

I am feeling greatly depressed and discouraged . . . I feel I'm not doing all I should as a Junior Commander – and yet I cannot lay my finger on the trouble.

Friday 23 February

Battery dance. More successful than last. The 'boys' were in tremendous form. The Major found a café with delicious Curacao.

All day I felt very headachy & terribly tired. By the time I'd been to a Regimental conference and collected canteen money I was exhausted – I sat gloomily in the office surrounded by mountains of uncounted cash. Suddenly 2 letters from Mummie arrived – how strange one is & what silly things fatigue does to one – one of the letters spoke of Sarah and Gil Winant – perhaps it will happen – they are so suited. I love Sarah – I would love it to happen – and yet there & then I just burst into floods of tears. Jimmy appeared – evidently took in the situation at a glance, & with a promptness (which shows his sweetness of character) started to count the money. Jock helped too – I sniffed but counted – Then struggled with SD & went to the dance – where my spirits revived. The Major, Sam, Jimmy & Jock – what a delightful crowd to be with.

Jimmy & I went for a walk in the square to cool off after an eightsome. It was delicious – with fine cool rain on my forehead – & the noises from the café and the dance reaching us faintly. 'Were you crying this evening?' he asked. 'Yes' – and I explained it all as homesickness, but mostly weariness.

Bed at last was very, very welcome.

Sunday 25 February

Slept at A Troop.

05.00 Called

05.30 Fried egg, toast, & tea

05.45 Ed* arrived in a jeep.

06.45 Namur & breakfast. Grapefruit juice – hot cakes – syrup, bacon & coffee.

07.30 Left Namur and made for Marche. Met M Charlier et compagnie on the way, who had broken down. Roadside conference. Gave Chef de Police & huge suitcase a lift through Marche and past country where the 'bulge' was turned.† Rusting carcasses of tanks lay upturned here & there – the fields bore the marks of giant tracks. But otherwise a pale sun gleamed on a peaceful Sunday countryside. We crossed a wide plain – and gazed back across it to the ridge we'd just left.

Rochefort – devastated – and then the Ardennes. Wooded hills and valleys stretching as far as the eye can see. 'Les chasseurs' assembled on the roadside at Le Bestin. M Hye – le propriétaire (in an elegant shooting ensemble in bottle green) – a burgomaster – a lawyer – some farmers – a crowd of beaters and a motley pack of dogs. Also M l'Inspecteur des Eaux et des Forêts – in a shooting garb reminiscent of a Drury Lane production of *Babes in the Wood*.

I was given a carbine by Ed, who lent a note of originality to the scene by appearing garbed as if for an airborne invasion, and bristling with lethal weapons. M Charlier *et cie*

---

* Ed Chandler, 'a charming American officer' according to Mary's memoir, *A Daughter's Tale*

† 'The Battle of the Bulge was an unsuccessful German counter-offensive that had been recently fought out in the Ardennes, December 1944–January 1945

arrived later – triumphant over events & his truck. From 9 till 5 we 'chassed' – Long, long periods of silent waiting. The air was like iced white wine – the wind sighed through the pine branches – fir cones lay at my feet. Never, never, I thought, do I want to live in a city. 3 boars were shot. I saw a beautiful fox – I'm glad to say Ed missed it – and watched a huge boar break cover and gallop across a clearing.

I adopted (how unwisely I see in the light of subsequent experience) a baby boar captured by one of the beaters. At 5 we adjourned to M Hye's hunting lodge, where a Mme Davis (the corporal driver told me she lives there & is sans doute M H's mistress) fed the hungry hunters with luscious cakes. Then the long drive back – Ed & I both kept dropping off to sleep. The poor Chef de Police held the boar until he piteously exclaimed '*Ah – il fait pi-pi*' – when I took it. After stopping at Namur for supper we drove back to camp.

. . . A long & lovely day ended in tears of fatigue & despair as to what to do with a baby wild boar – who showed every sign of intractability & violent disposition. I spent a slightly disturbed night with it rampaging in its box in my room – I must say I felt relieved when Atherton appeared in the morning & removed it to the gamekeeper's cottage.

Wednesday 28 February

Expedition to Malines for more furniture. Took a short cut – with disastrous results on our travelling time! A letter from Mummie to say she is coming on Sunday. Oh frabjous day, callooh, callay!

The Burgomaster collected myself & the Major at 18.30. We went to Brussels and had drinks with the '*cousin* germain' of the Burgo & his wife (who I'd met last time I'd dined at the Chateau) – Guillaume de Limburg Stirum & Elisabeth is his wife. He worked as a secret agent – she helped airmen to escape & was in prison for 5 months. Various people there for drinks – Jean Greig came too for dinner. I did not recall her being so pretty – & as the Burgo said '*elle est gaie comme un pinson.**' We went to La Savoie for dinner and then to La Habanera – a most luxurious looking night club.

As the days go by I find Jean-Louis more & more in my thoughts – I wish I knew if I loved him. I feel I know him so little – he isn't the type I imagined I should fall for. But from half across the world his image entangles my heart – even against my will. I flirt – but that's only skin deep – when I dance I think of him and our evenings in London. When I think of the future it is him I see. And yet this is so foolish – we are almost strangers – he will be away perhaps for years – he may have changed his mind, and most dangerous of all perhaps during his absence I am building him into a personality to suit my own dreams & wishes. And if I married him – I must live away from England – what about religion?

Oh it's all too complicated & in addition am I being swayed by worldly considerations? 'O God unto whom all hearts be open, all desires known, and from whom no secrets are hid . . .'

Friday 2 March

10.00 Harry Llewellyn collected me & took me to Embassy.

11.45 Left for airfield with Sir Arthur Coningham.

12.30 Papa and Mummie arrived, plus CIGS, Pug, Tommy, John Peck. We lunched with Sir Arthur and there was also Sir Francis de Guingand etc. Papa left for the front after lunch. M & I went for a brief visit to the battery.

---

* Literally cheerful as a chaffinch, i.e. happy as a lark

We stayed at the cocktail party [at the Embassy]. Quiet supper in M's room.

Sunday 4 March

Went with Jock to early service. Sir Hughe* & Lady K-H, Mummie & I lunched at Laeken with the Queen. At lunch also were Prince Bernhard [of the Netherlands] and the entourage. In pouring rain M flew away home.

Sir Hughe & Lady K-H took me to dinner with the Spaaks. Various ministers there, also the Prince Regent's secretary, who conducted Sir H & Lady K-H, myself & the 2 jeunes Spaaks to the Palace where after some rather halting conversation we all started to play ping pong till midnight, which was the greatest fun.

Monday 19 March

Sir Arthur Coningham & party – great fun. Spent all the evening practically talking to Prince Bernhard.

Sunday 25 March

PALM SUNDAY.
Communion service. General Tremlett† and cortege visited 54 in the afternoon. It was very nice to see him

---

* Sir Hughe Knatchbull-Hugessen, 1886–1971, British ambassador to Belgium
† Major General Erroll Tremlett, 1893-1982. One of the most experienced commanders of anti-aircraft formations. He commanded the brigades responsible for countering the threat caused by V1 and V2 flying bombs

again – and I think the troops were themselves genuinely pleased.

But what a dolt I am – in writing my diary retrospectively I've omitted Saturday 24 March.

We knew by Friday evening that today was D-Day* – Sam, Major M & I watched the weather anxiously all day. On Saturday – thank God – it was perfect. Sam read out Monty's Order of the Day. About 20 minutes later the airborne armada swept across the sky. We all rushed out to watch – and wave them on their way. It was an unforgettable sight.

I went to Brussels as usual for canteen supplies – collecting a road accident casualty on the way.

The Germans announced the landing – news in the evening was long & exciting – Papa is at TAC HQ. The day went well – thank God – Oh thank God.

Dance at B Troop. Late to bed – with nothing but thoughts of the battle raging not so far away.

Monday 26 March

During the last two days I've had some lovely long letters from Mummie written in her gayest and most entertaining style. My flowers reached her in time and she writes that they are beautiful, 'I love them not only because of their beauty but because they represent your dear love for me which warms and enriches my whole life.' Darling, darling Mummie, I can never tell you, how much your love and tenderness, with Papa's, have made my life overflow with happiness. Nor how the thought of it sustains me, even when I am away

---

* Operation Varsity, the last great airborne operation of the war, to secure the Rhine crossings

from home. And, spoilt child that I am, I confess I dread the next 8 weeks when M's letters will not be a thing to look forward to with eager impatience, when I shall not know from one day to another where she is – and I suppose Papa will be on the hop too. I wouldn't <u>of course</u> have it otherwise. But <u>how</u> I miss them.

Maundy Thursday 29 March

The news continues to be quite extraordinary. Everyone is saying 'it's over' – oh God, grant it may be so.

Easter Sunday 1 April, Brussels

Went to early service at Garrison Church at 8. Met the K-Hs going in – they very kindly took me into their pew – otherwise I should have had to stand, the church was packed to the doors. Lovely service.

Sam and I walked to the Chateau for lunch. Blustering, warm wind, the may is coming out. Easter lunch en famille was delightful. It banished much homesickness. The table was gaily decorated with goose-eggshells painted with flowers on them. After lunch I was bunched by the Comtesse – a basket full of exquisite spring flowers – the Burgo gave me a flapjack and some luscious sweets. An extraordinary-looking Dutch man with his wife (quite normal looking) arrived – I was riveted by his wig! Then we went for a tour of *les serves** – the rabbitry and *le jardin potager*, the swimming pool. I demanded *renseignements* about arum lilies & the age at which rabbits may be wrenched from their mothers' bosoms.

Memories of similar post-prandial walks at Chartwell

---

* The working areas

came back to me – only then I was a child and I remembered thinking how infinitely tedious the grownups were in their conversation – 'well of course we can never manage polyanthus at Waterings . . . – But I always find Mr Sproot far the best person for magnolias . . .' and so and so on. Today I found I'd crossed the great gulf fix'd, and was passionately interested to find out how to grow arums and when to start watering cyclamen stalks again. I now long for a greenhouse with arums – '*c'est tout ce qu'il y a de plus facile*' the Comtesse assures me – but I think she has 'green fingers' – arums, polyanthus, geraniums, cyclamen & so on. Farewell at last – but what a lovely Easter lunch – they really are so very, very kind.

Thursday 12 April

Just after midnight. Sam, the Major & I have just heard that the President is dead. God rest his soul. What an incalculable loss. What a triumphant life.

The Major & I spent the whole day with Reg touring American AAOR/guns etc. etc. Beautiful day for motoring & did we! We went miles & miles & miles. We crossed the Dutch frontier. Thrill for the ingenuous child. At a Brigade HQ I met Paul Hodder-Williams[*] again – which was delightful.

Friday 13 April

Busy day. Problems & parades . . . About 11 a despatch rider appeared with a letter from Papa telling me I'd got the MBE. Surprise made me almost hysterical. The Major, Sam & CSM

---

[*] Major Paul Hodder-Williams, 1910–2007, Mary's battery commander when she was at Enfield and later Chairman of Hodder & Stoughton publishing house

toasted me in champagne there & then – & were sweet beyond all words.

I have just written to Papa & Sarah* – I am knocked endways & can't find anything to say – nothing at all. I simply cannot believe it – I think I must go to bed – what lame expressions I use. But I think I shall be sick or cry with excitement & gratitude if I don't just go to sleep.

Sunday 15 April

The inspection lived up to all my highest expectations of its intense drearisomeness. The Brig was sweet about my medal. The Col has got the OBE – hooray.

Monday 16 April

Rumours of impending move confirmed. GHQ AA troop's dance – lovely flowers – luscious food but rather dreary – had curse & felt rather illish. We move on Wed.

Tuesday 17 April

Packing, planning & preparation. Affectionate farewells to la famille Ourers & then in the evening 'au revoir' to the Limburg-Stiriums.† Their kindness I will always remember most gratefully.

As I packed from 12 to 2 on Wed morning the nightingale

---

* Clementine was in Russia at this time, on a tour for her Red Cross Aid to Russia Fund

† The local Burgomaster and his family, who had been particularly kind to Mary, and the green-fingered Comte and Comtesse Limburg-Stirium, with whom she spent Easter Sunday

was singing almost without rest to the new moon. I love moving on (saved again from the very jaws of the AEC & the PT authorities!) and yet it was with real regret I said 'goodbye' to our little chateau & river & this pleasant valley which the spring is making so lovely. For my last night there my room was full of arum lilies from the Comtesse L-S and lilies of the valley.

Wednesday 18 April

Move was successful. We are on an airfield in Antwerp. Nobody seems to have told the RAF etc that they 'don't live there anymore' – several aircraft have touched down unpleasantly close to our encampment. I arrived later in the evening having stayed to settle up the 100 ATS who were left behind for good. Telegram delivered by RAF officer from M about my MBE – dearest Mummie.

Tuesday 24 April

I find it difficult to believe we've been here nearly a week – I've lost all sense & count of time. The first 2 days were hot & lovely & we all said 'What <u>fun</u> camping is' – & we went all shades of brown, pink & red. The last 2 days have been squally, with downpours of rain & glacial winds racing across the blasted airfield. Poor little ATS trotted about in denims & groundsheets trying to cook on outdoor ranges – trying to wash up in showers of rain – & we all said '. . . and when you think people used to camp for pleasure!' And through it all ran their good humour & perseverance.

The camp has taken shape – amenities & gadgets & order are slowly but surely being established. (Largely owing to Joan's success with a mobile Major – who produces working parties & grease traps instead of orchids). I've been out once to the Officers' Club for dinner – as gooseberry to Joan (but had gt fun). Once a mobile major whisked me out to lunch in a rain sodden windswept condition & gave me champagne, & tonight I've been to a concert at a nearby gun site ('Bicky' Bickerstaff – shades of Arborfield – invited me). I've had many charming & kind letters about my MBE – I shall keep them all to warm the cockles of my heart when I am old.

Saturday 28 April

Wetter & colder. Germany has offered to capitulate to England & US only – what a nerve.

Letter from Papa asking me to go to Picture Exhibition for him in Paris. Oh how wonderful to have a chance to do something for him.

Monday 30 April

Spent all day in anticipation of my date with Harry – which was as much fun as I had thought it would be. It's so <u>very</u> gratifying to be liked & admired by someone I find attractive, intelligent & charming. But why – oh why do I always fall for the people who are married? Is it a malignant fate? Anyway – here we go for just another very beautiful friendship. Sarah once told me when I was very dewy-eyed – 'You can flirt – provided you know <u>&</u> abide by the rules . . .'. So with my 'Nice Girls' Guide to Beautiful Friendships' – I embark once more for a fairly well known voyage. *Plus ça change*. But & however it all improves the complexion & raises my morale.

Wednesday 2 May

Hitler '*on dit*' is dead – so what? But the German armies in Italy have surrendered – thank God. Really the crescendo of news is breathtaking. In contrast to the general tenor of world events I spent the afternoon searching for hair ribbon (because H admired the bow in my coiffure – so a bigger & better one is being introduced!), an invisible mender & a watch shop. I found all three – so heigh ho for glamour (I hope) – slender, silken legs (I HOPE) – & at least I shall know <u>how</u> late I am for everything.

Thursday 3 May

I've spent today feeling slightly desperate, & yet longing for tomorrow night – O hell. It's too idiotic for words – and is doing me no good.

> I said to Heart: 'how goes it?'
> Heart replied:
> 'Bright as a ribstone pippin.'
> – But he lied.

I thought maybe I was through with these adolescent crushes – with that feeling that only the dentist and 'lurve' can give one. Luckily – it can't & won't last.

Monday 7 May

Lovely day. Every news bulletin told us the announcement of victory would come at any minute. At about half past six it was announced that Germany had surrendered unconditionally to the Allies early this morning.

It is such a beautifully calm evening after the winds & rains of the last week. I am feeling quite stunned. The war is over – I can't quite grasp it.

Tuesday 8 May

VICTORY IN EUROPE DAY

Left Deurne [Antwerp] in a cloudburst – which had cleared by the time we had got to Brussels. The whole city is bedecked with flags. Saw Selection Officer. Went to a thanksgiving service & met Christian de Sausmarez there who finding I had no plans invited me to lunch. Lunched with the de Sausmarezes in their charming *appartement* on the *rond point de la Cinquantaine*.

As the morning passed by the streets became fuller of people. By the afternoon there were vast crowds walking all over the place – every car & jeep was overloaded with children & grownups too clinging to the roof & sides. They were quiet crowds on the whole – with a sort of dazed, happy look.

Having arrived on 48 [hours leave] with no plans & no companion, I was feeling that it was enough to be here on 48 hours on VE Day – and now suddenly plans – delightful ones – began to take shape. Had tea with Caroline.* Managed to contact Jacques van den Branden, who took me out to dine chez Bernard . . . Some kind person organised a wireless & reminded us of the King. I stood in an open window looking out on a little, narrow side street – we were in M Bernard's appartement. On the windowsill was a trough with pansies & bachelor's buttons & three little paper flags – down below in the street a young Belgian mother with a sweet inert baby balanced herself to & fro & gossiped to some friends – the

---

* Mary's cousin Lady Caroline Spencer-Churchill, 1923–92

noise of the crowds reached us from the Porte de Namur. The King's voice came over calm and clear – he spoke of God's guidance – of the dead – of victory – of the future.

I stood quite still – and tried to make my stubborn, dulled consciousness accept & realise that the war is over – that the day we have schooled ourselves not to dwell upon – lest in gazing ahead we should falter in our path – that the day of deliverance had come.

Then we trooped back to the restaurant & finished a luscious dinner – I wrote a note to Papa for some kind friend who is going to London to take. As I left – Monsieur B pressed some lovely pink roses into my hand. We walked through the crowded streets to the Grande Place – what a sight – flood-lighting, music, bells, but above all, people. Thousands of them – friendly, jostling, thankful crowds. Some were dancing – others, mostly the children, were leading wild farandoles around the square. Occasionally moving pyramids of people would make their way through the throng – somewhere at the bottom of the pyramid was a car or a jeep.

We went & watched & joined the festivities from M et Mme Bracht's flat overlooking the Place. There were a lot of people there, the Comte de Changy & his sister – he is a sgt in the RAF – sgt, pilot – & others, whose names I did not grasp. I did not feel conversational – I just stood & gazed on the amazing sight. Later Sir Arthur and Lady Coningham came in – she – beautiful & sad & thinking of her beloved son – with such courageous & proud devotion.

About half past twelve we took our leave & walked back to the Splendide – once inside I found Col Galloway there with a message to say I am to go to London tomorrow. At first I was enraged & shocked – at the unwisdom & unsuitability of such a thing & then the Col said 'Don't be so selfish' – & then my heart's desire & the thought of Papa having remembered me – having wanted me – left me only with the longing to be at his side & to hell with everything else.

Went to bed at 2.30 – feeling 'tomorrow' will never come soon enough.

Wednesday 9 May

<u>VE +1</u>

The Col collected me at 11.20. At the airport was Brig Barrow who was sweet. Flew off in Dakota – Sir Robert Frank (Sir Arthur's nephew) also in plane. Flew home to England & gazed with love & happiness once again   first on the white cliffs gleaming across that unbelievably narrow channel & then on the well-known countryside & then Croydon & at last the annexe & Papa in his dressing gown with open arms. He had waited lunch for me. He had his on a tray in bed. I, at his feet. I just had time to titivate before Papa set out with me in tow to pay diplomatic calls at the Embassies.

How can I ever describe the crowds – or their welcome to Papa as he made his way through London. Escorted only by 4 mounted police to clear a pathway through the streets and a few despatch riders. It has all been told – I shall never forget it – nor can I express my pride & joy at the sight of Papa being so received. How wonderful he has been – how wonderful he is now. For it is he who is striking the note of just restraint. 'Retribution & justice <u>must</u> be done – but in the words of Edmund Burke "I cannot . . . frame an indictment against a whole people".' This he talked about to me at lunch and at the American Embassy & used it in his short speech to the staff. At the Russian Embassy there were toasts & caviare & I felt uncomfortable. At the French Embassy M Massigli entertained Papa on a sofa in a rather lovely drawing room – Mme M appeared in a stunning hat looking handsome with glittering tears in her hard eyes – of emotion etc. And so – home.

Diana & Duncan came to dinner. We listened to a wonderful radio programme about Papa. Then Tommy came to say there was a large crowd in Whitehall. So Duncan, Diana & I bolted ahead & got a good place in the crowd – & we & everyone else bellowed happily when dear Papa appeared. He was charming – tender & gay. Then he finally recited a verse from 'Rule Britannia' & we all responded with gusto that Britons <u>never</u> – <u>never</u> – <u>never</u> shall be slaves. Then D & D went off to shout for the K & Q & I waited for Sarah who appeared in the end about 12.15, when I'd nearly given up all hope – with John Winant. We dashed to the Palace & were not too late – the King & Queen – she resplendent in white & a diamond tiara appeared – & we all yelled with happiness & pride. The flood lighting is too lovely – the city is transfigured. The crowds are vast, happy and unbelievably controlled.

Papa in the midst of national victories & personal triumphs suddenly looks old & deflated with emotion, fatigue & a heartbreaking realisation of the struggles yet to come. He is working too late – his broadcast is weighing heavily upon him.[*]

(After shouting for the K & Q we went to the American Embassy & were fed on eggs & bacon cooked by John G [Winant] Jnr. Mr W was there – as sweet & kind as ever).

Thursday 10 May

Felt entirely flattened. Nana came up – & we spent an enjoyable, quiet day together. In the afternoon we rushed out & caught a glimpse of 'Toute la Boutique' as they passed by on their tour through the East End . . . Went & saw half of *Tree*

---

[*] BBC broadcast of 13 May, 'Forward, till the whole task is done'

Grows in Brooklyn – which I thought beautifully done. Sarah & I dined alone with Papa in the sitting room of the annexe.

Max came in after dinner. Much talk & wrangle about the General Election. Max says 'Now' – Papa broods. This is the fifth anniversary of Papa as Prime Minister.

Friday 11 May

James Stuart & John Martin & Sarah to lunch. Mama is to arrive tomorrow at 9, which changed our plans – after almost as much perplexity as that caused by the question of the General Election, we stayed in London for the night instead of going to Chequers. Papa took me to visit dear Uncle Jack, who is very ill. On our return, it being a warm, still evening we had dinner together in the garden at No. 10. The dusk deepened around us. We listened to the news – & then to some romantic waltzes. The floodlighting came on at about half past ten. Papa was wearing his mauve and black quilted dressing gown over his siren suit & a soft black hat. We walked a little on the parade to look at the lights. Nelson gazed down upon Papa.

Smoky the cat slid silently across the lawn to be remotely & coldly polite to Papa. Papa showed me the lovely set of china he has bought from Clare Sheridan*. It belonged to Napoleon III. It appears before the Tuileries were burnt – much of the furniture & china etc were brought out on to the lawns & sold. Great-Grandmama Clara Hall Jerome was in Paris at the time & bought this set then & there. Papa at about 11 went upstairs to lay his golden egg.† I went to bed – knowing I had spent an evening which with so many other memories of Papa will live vividly in my mind & heart until I die.

---

* Writer and sculptor, and first cousin of Winston Churchill, 1885–1970
† i.e. to work on his broadcast

Saturday 12 May

My beloved Mummie arrived home safely – after wildly successful, interesting & I hope fruitful wanderings. She is decorated & looks a <u>wow</u> in uniform. We sped to Chequers. Papa came to meet M at Northolt. Arriving a little late, *ça va sans dire* – but he was there all the same. So was Sarah. Diana & Duncan & Sarah arrived at lunch. Aunt Nelly & Giles (just released from 5 years captivity)[*] for tea. And Randolph. And if a man say 'I love God' but hateth his brother – he is a liar. The evening however passed better than might have been expected.

Letter from Mary to Judy, 27 May[†]:

Darling Toodles
<u>The travels of a Donkey</u>
Brussels   VE Day
London   VE +1
Antwerp   VE +6
Paris   VE +8
Antwerp   VE +11
and since then 2 battery moves – to nowhere very exciting – but at such short intervals that the poor Donkey is in a slightly dazed condition – and jitters with fright when it contemplates the prospect before it   of which I tell you later . . .
    As you know Papa sent for me – & I went, throwing discretion to

---

[*] The journalist Giles Romilly, 1916–67, Clementine Churchill's nephew, had been captured in Norway in 1940, and held at Colditz before escaping in April 1945

[†] Mary stopped writing her diary after 12 May while she went to Brussels and Paris, and wrote this letter several days later

the winds. When I arrived I found Papa and Smoky the cat celebrating Victory a little sadly – Mama in Russia – Diana with her family – Sarah wafting in and out as often as she could. Poor Papa – so tired & triumphant and terribly depressed about the future. But chiefly moved beyond everything by the demonstrations in London. I can't tell you how I felt to see him so received. You will understand – I sat & watched & listened & could find no words to tell him or anyone else. I thought back across these long years – thought of 1940 – thought of the darknesses & hours he had worked through with such unrelenting courage and perception.

Oh God – no wonder one loves him. I feel one will always be different because we knew and loved him. And when he goes, I cannot think of anyone or anything that will take his place in life.

And now the General Election – I'm in such a muddle I can't think clearly – only feel a macedoine of emotions. I wish I could talk to you for hours & hours & hours of cabbages, kings, drainage & state control!

Saturday 19 May

I am writing in bed. I have just arrived back from Paris. Fatigue and my reflections combine to make me feel somewhat cast down. During my visit Raimund von Hofmannsthal (who was staying at the Embassy) was very very kind to me in two ways. (1) He thought of arranging interesting things to do & took me to do them (2) He showed an interest in one – I was surprised & so greatly pleased – for he was so helpful & sensible & firm about that problem which has on & off weighed more than usually on my rather untaught and embarrassed consciousness – LIFE in neon lights & capital letters. I found R[aimund] so mature & balanced – so 'adult'. Then too I have been in the company of three women much older than myself – & they have had a great effect on me.

Diana [Cooper], Venetia and Louise de Vilmorin.* They are cultured, elegant, with graceful easy civilised manners. They contribute to conversation – much more – they add to life. I cannot quite explain it – but they made a profound & rather disturbing impression on me.

I am back in my tent feeling humbled – rightly so – before their attainments and graces. I realise what I hadn't realised <u>clearly</u> before, that I am a great deal more UNCIVILISED, UNEDUCATED and UNORIGINAL than I had permitted myself to believe. Now – I feel more comfortable that I've got it off my chest.

Today is Sunday the 20 May. Yesterday's cafard – no that is the wrong word – yesterday's spiritual discontent remains. As I am no longer fatigued I am sure it <u>is</u> spiritual discontent and not my glands or whatever. R made me realise all I have missed – not in the sense of 'dreary debbing' – but of conversation – music – pictures – travelling. I must say – although I have known I should have liked these things I've always felt the experiences army life and the war have brought me, have more than compensated for the loss of those other things – I will not say loss – postponement only I do hope. But I think R lays (for me) so much stress on individualism. I am egocentric enough.

And God knows one's own personal development (which has for me a frightening power of self-absorption) doesn't amount to a hill of beans. But even were such an opportunity to appear – I must first grapple with a great disability

---

* Louise de Vilmorin, 1902–1969, was a novelist, poet and heir to the Vilmorin seedmaking fortune. First married to a Hungarian count, her lovers included Antoine de Saint-Exupery, Orson Welles and André Malraux, but it was Duff Cooper who was the love of her life

– intellectual sloth. Since I possess no accomplishments – nor am I talented in any specific way – I must, must, must exert myself to some reasonable standard of educated intelligence. R suggests a two-year-plan. I feel I would relish it beyond everything – but two is too short.

And now, enough of intro-spection. The relation of the momentous implications of my life is thereby interrupted and rendered more tedious.

Thursday 17 May

Flew from Brussels to Paris.

At lunch were Raimund, Maj Ward, Penelope L T* & I sitting between Eric & Koffy, which made me want to giggle. Every time I am confronted with Eric I am overwhelmed by a feeling of relief at my happy escape. I think he is too. He is quite charming to me – and really completely impossible. He recounted to me how he prepared the Hotel Bristol for the arrival of his mother – by tips all round (which was thought-ful & sensible) but added 'and then I told them she was a vice-reine and this was the first time she'd ever come abroad with-out her maid . . .'. Poor sweet – how he will hate the Beveridgising and Bevinising of life.

After lunch Koffy drove me to Versailles. It was a hot, bril-liant afternoon. We visited his brother who has his office in the Petite Ecurie. Buddy took us then in his jeep for a short drive round part of the palace gardens. I was as deeply impressed with the splendours and more conscious of the miseries of Versailles than upon my first visit when I was 16. We went to the Trianons – which I had never seen before. If I were a modern monarch's mistress I should be much

---

* Penelope Lloyd Thomas, Diana Cooper's social secretary

depressed by the spectacle of Madame de Maintenon's pink and white palace – and would return to my flat in Westminster Gdns to find in my mink and Cartier diamonds indifferent consolations for elegance and terms of the past.

Koffy bores me & is beginning to irritate me. Venetia remarked that next to having no young man the most tedious thing was having one.

Friday 18 May

Woke with a headache and nerves realising I must make a speech. Which with united sympathy & Aid to Mary[*] I did. Felt more nervous than I can remember ever feeling before. However all went well.

Saturday 19 May

Visited Madame de Ganay. Charles & Paul were there & on the mantelpiece handsome photographs of Jean-Louis & André. We were talking of Jean-Louis – his absence – his job. His mother wept. I could find no words – nothing. But O God please let him come back.

How selfish & hard I am. Almost I sincerely wished I could have suffered in some dreadful way. I do not understand – O hell & damnation I can't even make sense in writing.

After lunch I flew back to Brussels. Very tired.

Monday 21 May

The horrors of peace are upon us – once more the radio drones for hours all on the subject of football & cricket & the

---

[*] Mary's way of saying that she got some help

weather. From the ridiculous to the deathly serious – the news is most disquieting – God only knows what lies ahead in the next few months. It is too awful to believe the peace our total hard-won victory has made possible is already being jeopardised.

Wednesday 23 May

Papa resigned. Papa is asked to form a new govt.* Unnatural cloudburst.

Thursday 24 May

Hectic day preparing for move. Hamburg looms ahead.†

Friday I June

Rev[eille] 0330
   Breakfast 0430
   Parade 0500
   Emplaned 0730
   Arrived Luneburg 1100 hrs & to my great astonishment & joy found Olly waiting there to meet me. Caught a glimpse of Monty. Glared at some German generals & fell asleep on & off in the truck during the 2 hour drive to Wenzendorf – from sheer fatigue. We are encamped on a Blohm & Voss airfield.

---

* From 23 May, when the wartime national coalition broke up, until the final result of the general election on 26 July, Churchill led a short-term caretaker government
† 481 Battery was re-formed into an all-ATS unit and moved to a new site at Wenzendorf airfield, near Hamburg

Letter from Mary to Clementine, 7 June:

*. . . It is so strange driving through this beautiful, smiling country
– where 'every prospect pleases and only man is vile' . . . On the
whole one gets blank or sullen looks; the boys of 15 or 16 even look a
bit ferocious at times, and many of them wear peaked military caps.
But sometimes one meets a great eagerness to help or be commanded.*

*I drove through Hamburg a few days ago. Words are inadequate to
describe the devastation. The streets are full – full of crowds of people
who presumably have nowhere else to go and little else to do. Long,
apparently aimless queues – lots of families trundling their possessions
in prams and barrows. I suppose at night they crawl into the cellars
beneath the ruins of their city. On the outskirts of Hamburg there are
many pre-fabricated houses – very small and fragile – built to receive
some of the refugees. People trek to and from the city daily to pick over
the piles of rubble – trying to salvage something from the wreckage.
Houses – apparently completely unfit for human habitation, are lived in
by several families. It is so difficult to describe events and scenes accurately or comprehensively – and these are only my first impressions –
most of them fortified by what people who've been here a longish time
have told me.*

*But I did notice a great difference between the people in Hamburg
and those out in the country. On so many of their faces is a sort of
blank, aimless look.*

*The sight of the terrible revenge has shocked me. Not into any feeling
of weak pity, or a conviction that it was wrong or too horrible. But my
mind had not grasped the exact extent of the devastation – and with
every day that passes I wonder more and more at the toughness of the
fibre of human life. Did you feel the same when you saw the destroyed
cities of Russia?*

What an experience this is. I wouldn't have missed it for anything.

Tuesday 12 June

A party from this regiment visited Belsen. Brig Glyn Hughes took us round. It was a memorable day.

Letter from Mary to Clementine, 15 June:

. . . Brigadier Glyn Hughes is a very grand and distinguished doctor, and commands the medical arrangements for the 2nd Army. He has the CBE, 3 DSOs and an MC. He organised the relief of Belsen and was there from the moment of its liberation until the relief system was working smoothly. I met him on several occasions and he arranged for several of our officers and about two ATS NCOs to pay a visit to the site of Belsen.

The actual horror camp has been burnt to the ground – it is a gloomy sight – twisted, burnt and charred remains of huts and structures cover a few acres – here and there symmetrical mounds of smooth earth appear, with a little white notice: 'Grave No. 12 – 2,000 bodies' – and then the date of the burial.

The Brigadier reconstructed the ghastly scene for us. On all sides a beautiful pinewood presses in on the camp, and the air is full of skylarks singing. We all walked dumbly from the camp, and were taken to the hospital. 16,000 internees are left – of these 7,000 are bed patients. The death rate is down from 500 a day to 10 a day. But there are some very, very ill people there; and an enormously high percentage of TB cases. The typhus epidemic is now under control and almost at an end. But the results of starvation are not attractive to look upon. We walked through many wards. The nurses are mostly British with quite a number of Germans and a large number of Belgian medical students to help the doctors, and a small party of serene-faced Nuns from the Vatican.

In one women's ward a Polish Jew sat up in bed and welcomed us in broken French: 'We are so happy to receive here today' she said 'the daughter of the great man who made our deliverance possible.' I nearly wept. I've never seen so much human suffering. And then we went to the small Maternity block where a few wrinkled, shrivelled little babies make their way into a strange world from half-starved Mothers – who have little or no milk to feed their children. The doctor in charge is a Rumanian Jewess. Until 1935 she was in a large Berlin hospital – but then, being a Jewess, she was sent to one concentration camp after another. Wherever she went she tried to care for the other prisoners. At Aus[ch]witz [they] say pregnant women were automatically sent to the gas chamber; as it was a mixed camp many women became pregnant. This Doctor aborted them in secret by night, and strapped the poor creatures up tightly to conceal the operation. Thus she saved countless women. When she came to Belsen she started a maternity ward – no instruments – no water; but she struggled on until liberation. She is 36 and looks 58. She has a passion for her work – for the pathetic mothers she delivers and the thin delicate babies she cares for. I have never seen such an ardour for life – such a victorious manifestation of the human spirit.

Then we went to the Sergeants Mess where a party was being given to about 100 pale-faced, solemn children. About the first party they've ever had. They were quiet and dazed and I hope just beginning to be a little happy. Then we got into our trucks and drove home.

. . . I watch with passionate interest the progress of the Election. I think of Papa so much. I know it must be a strain on him and a grief to have to mawl and be mawled. About the girls – I haven't asked many of them for obvious reasons – but I think they will vote Labour or Liberal. The Officers' Mess – RA – will I think go Labour – ATS Conservative. Papa's first election address was not received very well I'm afraid. If I collect any more information or tit-bits I will let you know. I think you will find the Army votes will largely go to Labour. You must remember the Daily Mirror is <u>widely</u> read by all Ranks and especially the Other Ranks. But it is very difficult to tell. I do feel gloomy about it – I must confess – gloomy and uncertain.

I find too, that I'm not yet re-acclimatised to the slings and arrows of party dissension – which perhaps makes one more shocked and sensitive to the really violent attacks upon Papa. I know one should try to feel impersonal about these things and take the detached view – but I can't, I can't, I hate these scathing, unjust, untrue attacks on Papa. Wow – oh wow – I <u>wish</u> I could talk to you about it. Miserable kitten with electionitis.

Wednesday 27 June

I never thought that yesterday would come. I planned & looked forward to it all Sunday & Monday, but always with a feeling that <u>something</u> would happen to stop it – or the weather would be bad – or – or. And yet it did come – and it was hot & sunny, and it was a <u>perfect day</u>.

'Should old acquaintance be forgot' – I found it enchanting to spend a whole afternoon and evening with someone I respect & admire & like* – someone I've met before – with whom I don't have to start all over again right from the start. Someone adult – amusing – calm and kind to me beyond everything.

I had lunch at 99th RHQ – & then played tennis – then tea – then sunbathed & swam. Then a long, luxurious pansying up – including weighing myself. And then out to the Offrs Club for dinner – where Ross brought Joan. Long, conversational dinner – and then home in the dusk and bed – feeling happy & content and somehow 'better' – after the tearful worries & scenes with Sam in the early morning about how suddenly I realise Major M is irritated by – with & for me. But last night was the end of a perfect day.

----

* A happy day with Mary's old friend and commander Paul Hodder-Williams

(Still) Wednesday 27 June

Took girls to a REME dance. Thursday & Friday – no dates – spent lazy evenings deep in reading – sewing & gossiping & early nights.

The accounts of Papa's election tour are too wonderful – Oh how much I hope he is returned to carry out some at least of his plans. God grant him strength & wisdom and courage – and keep him safe.

Saturday 30 June

Went to last night of our concert given at REs at Fischbeck. Afterwards there was an agreeable supper party in the Mess. I become more and more conscious of the fact that conversation is an art, involving application of one's brain and heart. It is a besetting temptation to natter, chatter and dissipate thoughts (notions is a better word) and squander words. I grieve to think of the many tedious tête à têtes I have endured which I might have enjoyed had I only taken the trouble to either listen agreeably – or talk with intelligence. I am ashamed to remember the many occasions when I must have been an arch-bore for (I hope!) no other reason than that I didn't take pains to be otherwise.

I am starting a self-improvement campaign – intellectually and spiritually for I am convinced that through mental laziness I am wasting any attributes of mind or character God may have given me. And it all has its origin in egotism. Enough of the Idiot Moralist!

Sunday 1 July

The Idiot Moralist continues: I see that 75% conversation is attentive, sympathetic listening. A weakness of mine.

Monday 2 July

A day of downpours. I await Wednesday and the weekend with great pleasure and excitement. I used my first vote today. Col Ponsonby (Con. – TA Retd) was happy recipient of my X. But oh how dreary & I'm sure Mr Pudney [the Labour candidate for Sevenoaks] would make a <u>much</u> better MP.

<u>The Diary of Mary Churchill, started in the Skymaster flying to Bordeaux with my beloved Papa & Mama, 7 July</u>*
Yesterday started so <u>un</u> specially. The CO and Sen Cmdr inspected – I was thinking more of Trotting Races & Paul on Saturday & feeling a little frail after a wild naval party the previous night & THEN
  SUDDENLY
  I am told I must report to an airfield – which meant leaving at 2. I had about ½ hr to pack & get ready. Then we went to the wrong airfield. But finally at 1800 hrs I took off in a Mosquito perched up in front on a wooden stool. I felt in an utter whirl – home? – O God how wonderful. The flight was lovely & most interesting – flying low over the Dortmund-Ems Canal – Walcheren – & so home. Nana met me.
  At home – Mummie & Papa having dinner. Sarah came in looking beautiful & pleading passionately with Papa about something to do with Medmenham. Sorted out my clothes – talked – feverishly & finally bed – still in a whirl.

---

* Mary has added that polling day was 5 July

Sunday 8 July*

This morning Nana sweetly packed for me – I rushed round shopping & so forth.

Papa went to Windsor to see the King – & then we all left from Northolt. Now I'm sitting replete after a huge lunch – our holiday has started. The party is –

Papa
Mummie
Me
Jock (hooray)
Tommy
Lord Moran

Papa is reading a life of Frederick the Great – for which M & I are queueing. I'm dazed with excitement & happiness to be with him. I pray God he may be given a week's respite – sun – peace – a little painting. He is much worn & battered by the election. He feels the attacks so deeply – so intensely. We all await the results with impatience & anxiety. I hope he will be returned – though it will be a bitter journey's end. So much can go wrong. He is sitting now transported to the age of Frederick the Great – occasionally breaking away to tell Mummie something about the book. Meanwhile we forge through blue skies & white heaped clouds towards Bordeaux and I feel ecstatic & speechless, & for the moment 'Life like a dome of many colour'd glass Stains the white radiance of eternity.'

---

* Mary's dating gets a little confused here, so this may actually be Saturday 7 July

Monday 9 July

We arrived at Chateau Bordaberry on Saturday evening (7th) after a four hour car drive. It is an ugly white comfortable house gazing over the Bay of Biscay. Solitary & peaceful.

Here the weather is perfect, the food delicious & fattening! Yesterday in the afternoon Papa (feeling low & tired) went to visit the Nairns at St Jean de Luz – & O joy – started to paint. He has laid his first picture. We are all delighted. Mummie & I spent the morning bathing at Hendaye – with Mr & Mrs Nairn & Judy – & the afternoon being rolled & tossed by breakers at St Jean de Luz – while halfway up the hill Papa in sombrero & beneath a mushroom umbrella puffed & painted. Jock & I were nearly arrested for walking along the front without peignoirs.

After tea, we drank champagne & then trundled back to Bordaberry. We all feel knocked out & happy, Papa from his painting & Mama & I from the ozone, food & sun!

I feel idle. I am being idle. I am happy.

On Monday itself
Poor Mama has bruised & cracked her toe – ouch. But she has been plastered up carefully & can move quite freely.

Papa is beginning to feel the benefit of this complete rest. Occasional depressions *au sujet des élections* come over him. But between times he is happy & conversational.

Thursday 12 July

Beachcombed all morning. Lovely hot sun. Papa came down & bathed for the first time. We had a tent pitched à la Sultan halfway down the beach – from which Papa emerged in shapeless drawers, smoking & with his ten gallon hat on

– Sawyers uncrowned & uncigared him as he took to the waves. I was <u>so</u> happy to see Papa – floating peacefully like a charming porpoise washed by lucent waves. We are all enjoying ourselves so very much.

In the afternoon there was a Basque fête – arranged specially in honour of Papa by the General. The police prinked themselves up – & wore their royal blue pants & immaculate white cotton gloves. Mummie & I both put our best feet forwards and put on our crepe de chines & I dripped with my aquamarines – put a rose in my bosom and enjoyed myself inordinately. Les boys struggled into white suits & collars & ties. Papa was not in his most amenable mood, which was a pity – but he wanted to paint – also it was violently hot.

After it was all over Papa made a little speech in French. Then we all bathed again with thunderstorms careering over the Spanish border & some menacing shafts of lightning. Later that night there was a violent storm.

Dinner was agreeable. I sat between George & Jock. With the latter I indulged in a session of indiscreet intimate gossip – constituting what the Americans have aptly named a 'bitch session'.

Friday 13 July

Bathing parade 1130. Although the sky was overcast Papa bathed & loved it. The sun came out later. During the swim a determined 'pounce' was made by a woman called la Comtesse de Beaumont, who so reliable '*on dit*' goes was an enthusiastic and passionate collaborator, and is in danger of being lynched by the people here! The pounce was made & parried at & by M & I who floated away on the clearest wave fixing our eyes on Spain.

. . . After dinner we repaired to the Casino at Hendaye – where the Mayor received Papa & M on the steps – a large crowd had assembled – and the scene was lit by arc lamps and great gleams of summer lightning.

Then a fandango was danced & then they let loose a 'toro fuego', a feature of the Basque pays. It is a splendid model bull, borne aloft, & it is riddled with squibs & the most lovely catherine wheels & rockets. It 'charges' the crowd who scream & run, as it makes its crackling blazing way among them. It was the first time for four years that a toro fuego had been organised. It was all so moving & spontaneous – Papa loved it – & the crowds waved & cheered & laughed. And despite the horrors & terrors, the difficulties & dangers of the newly born soi-disant peace, one did feel that a little gaiety was returning at last for France.*

Letters from Mary to Clementine from Berlin, 16–24 July:

My darling Mummie, Our air journey was, I thought, horribly bumpy – and I felt definitely sick. We arrived in blazing sunshine at 5 o'clock. A band, troops of all three services, and a posse of generals, marshals and so on were assembled to greet Papa, headed by Monty, Sir Sholto Douglas and of course American and Russian opposites. Identification was difficult because it was all so quick, but I did see Pug and Archie Clark-Kerr† and Monsieur Gusev.

. . . This morning Papa paid his first visit to President Truman, who is installed in a monstrously ugly house about 400 yds down the

---

* After the holiday, Mary accompanies her father to Germany and to the Potsdam Conference. This is the last big wartime Allied summit, held on the outskirts of Berlin, and attended by President Truman and Marshal Stalin. Sadly, Mary does not seem to have kept a diary

† Archie Clark-Kerr, British ambassador to Russia, later 1st Lord Inverchapel

road. While Papa talked to the President, I, Tommy and John Peck were entertained by the 'court' – only Admiral Leahy remains from the previous establishment. Papa remained closeted for about two hours – during which time Anthony [Eden] joined them, and <u>our</u> circle was enlarged by Sir Alexander Cadogan – as dry as ever – but I like him.

When Papa at length emerged we decided to walk home. He told us he liked the President immensely – they talk the same language. He says he is sure he can work with him. I nearly wept for joy and thankfulness, it seemed like divine providence. Perhaps it is FDR's legacy. I can see Papa is relieved and confident . . . I spent a 'domestic' afternoon snooping in the kitchen . . . I am trying to beat my sword into a feather duster!

<u>Late this evening</u>: At four this afternoon in sweltering heat, Papa, Anthony, Archie C-K, Sir Alexander, Sawyers and all tootled off to visit the ruins of Berlin. They are quite extensive. The utter squalor and dilapidation of the place – the stunned look on the faces of the people are not easily forgotten. We gazed on the ruins of the Chancellery – saw the disordered air raid shelters where Hitler is said to have died. The sun beat down on dust and devastation – the Press rushed round madly photographing – and Sir Alexander complained how badly the tour was organised – which it was. But it was worth it.

General Marshall* has been to dinner, and has just left. Papa is reading the evening papers and making plans for tomorrow – which I am accepting with a good deal of scepticism (silent) as I'm sure they'll all be changed in the morning. Papa is sorry you will not come out – and means to have another try!

19 July:
Yesterday President Truman lunched with Papa. I spent the morning flapping around the chef, Mr Pinfield and the soldier-gardener . . . I

---

* General George C. Marshall, US Chief of Staff

*was very nervous that Papa would be late. However, in the end every-
thing worked out beautifully. Papa was actually down at the garden
gate five minutes before the President arrived.*

*. . . We all had delicious iced cocktails on the terrace in the sun, and
then Papa took the President to the study, where they lunched à deux.
His two aides lunched with all of us in the dining room . . . At three
the President left to go and visit Uncle Jo[e], and when they arrived
<u>there</u> they found another enormous lunch awaiting them. So they must
have felt pretty full by the time the Conference began!*

24 July:
*. . . Papa entertained the Chiefs of Staff to luncheon. As soon as they'd
finished . . . a horde of furniture movers and myself descended like a
swarm of locusts on the rooms and a scene of disorder and scramble
ensued, which I can leave to your imagination.*

*I had undertaken (very nervously) to arrange the flowers – and for
most of the afternoon I sat amid a heap of rather sodden wind blown
sickly-pink hydrangeas, and wondered what I could possibly make of
them. However I eventually worked something out. Then I rushed like a
whirlwind through the reception room, casting out furniture – banishing
statues, and trying to remember what you always say about chairs 'talking' to each other.*

*When Papa returned from the conference he inspected the arrange-
ments and was very much pleased, and was sweet about the flowers,
and I felt greatly relieved. Then Papa said 'Have you got a pretty
dress here?' and I said 'Yes I have'. 'Go and put it on' said Papa. So,
I wore my printed crepe de chine, and clanked with your lovely aquamarines. At last the guests started to arrive, all our chiefs of staff and
Field Marshals and of course American and Russian opposite
numbers – then a fleet of cars swooped up and out skipped Uncle Joe
attended by a cloud of minions (the house had already been
surrounded and laid siege to an hour earlier by what appeared to be
half the Red Army).*

Uncle J wore the most fetching white cloth mess jacket blazing with insignia. Close on his heels the President arrived, having walked from his house. When they all went in to dinner I went off and dined at the mess with the private office. Afterwards we returned through cordons of G men and Ogpu, and I slipped into the dining room (on Papa's instructions) and sat on a stool behind his chair, and this was lovely because I heard many of the toasts, and was able to watch the proceedings from a very good vantage point. The party appeared to be a wild success – and presently Uncle Joe leapt up and went round the room autograph hunting! The evening broke up at about midnight, in a general atmosphere of whoopee and goodwill.

Tomorrow I shall be home. I long to see you darling Mummie.

Friday 27 July

I am writing in the sitting room of the annexe – it is just before dinner. Mummie is with Papa.

There is an atmosphere of finality throughout the flat – the Private Office dark and untenanted – an unusual feeling of unhaste and quiet – for after all there is no hurry now – no decisions, no meetings, no minutes, no telegrams.

I will try to recount accurately and calmly the crashing events of the last 2 days. I will try, if only as a mental exercise, to keep my recital of these hours, which to Papa and those who love him, have brought a bitter and overwhelming defeat, I will try and keep this account beyond the sway of my emotions, and free from any trace of the tears, which seem to spring unbidden from my eyes.

On Wednesday 25 July Papa conferred in the morning & we all met at the airfield at one o'clock. We had an uneventful flight home. I think we were all feeling soberly confident that Papa would return on the 27th having a workable majority. This view was supported & indeed chiefly derived from the reliable estimates of both big parties. Our farewells at Potsdam were therefore lighthearted and of a very 'au revoir' nature. Little did we then guess what lay within the sealed ballot boxes.

Mummie was at the airfield. Papa on his return proceeded straight to work. R[andolph] came to dinner & then caught the night train to Preston. He was <u>very</u> confident. Duncan & Diana came in after dinner – they were both gloomy. D was certain he was 'out'. Robin M whisked me off to Michael Parish's house – friends there v confident.

Thursday 26 July

Felt v excited when I woke up. At breakfast M told me Papa was suddenly feeling low about the results, & feared a stalemate perhaps . . . M & I drove down to the constituency & were admitted to the count. Here the first inkling of a setback occurred – Mr Hancock – a crackpot & non-representative polled 10,000 & early reports from London showed 44 Labour gains to 1 Con. gain.

We drove home rather silently & went to the Map Room, where all had been prepared to record & tabulate the results – on our way we met Jock, with black looks – 'It is a complete debacle,' he said, 'like 1906 . . .' We went in – Papa, David Margesson, Brendan, & the results rolling in . . . Labour gain, Labour gain, Labour gain.

It was now one o'clock & already it was quite certain we were defeated. I watched Papa taking it in – grasping defeat . . . savouring the humiliation. Every minute brought news of more friends out & Randolph – Bob – Brendan – out. Anthony in . . . Fitzroy in . . . Leo Amery out – Ralph Assheton – out.

Duncan out . . .

Hot tears came & had to be hidden. Everyone looked grave and dazed. We lunched in Stygian gloom – David Margesson – Brendan – Uncle Jack. Max had been invited but – O strange to relate – evidently had a subsequent engagement. Sarah arrived, looked beautiful & distressed – we both choked our way through lunch. M maintained an inflexible morale. Papa – what can I say? Papa struggled to accept this terrible blow – this unforeseen landslide. Brendan & David looked unhappy. But not for one moment in this awful day did Papa flinch or waver. 'It is the will of the people' – robust – controlled.

The day wore very slowly on – with more resounding defeats. All the Staff and all our other friends looked stunned & miserable. Papa spent the afternoon watching the results – M went to rest. I wandered from the sitting room to the Private Office – from the kitchen (where Mrs Landemare moved unhappily among her saucepans) to the Map Room & then back again. Finally I could endure it no longer & went for a long purposeless walk. It was a relief to feel the sun on my face & the wind in my hair, to walk rapidly through the streets.

Back in the annexe Robin rang me up. Dinner – Uncle Jack (so thin & ill-looking), Venetia (battered by her illness but such a kind & supporting friend), Duncan, Diana, Sarah looking aggressively beautiful – Brendan & Anthony. Papa was in courageous spirits – Mummie riding the storm with unflinching demeanour – Sarah only a little less brave – Diana pale but philosophic. I am ashamed to say I think I of them all, was the least composed. But I struggled – truly I did. But I could not gaze at Papa or talk to his devoted friends without feeling overwhelmed with sadness.

After all but Brendan & Duncan had gone away – Robin came to see me, bringing with him Michael Parish. When Papa came from the dining room he sat down & talked to them. His stature seems to grow with every hour of this bitter personal calamity. He talked to us of the new government . . . 'give them a chance . . . let's see what they can do . . . Only this – let them try to tamper with the constitution & we will be at their throats. But now is <u>your</u> chance (to Robin & Michael) keep in touch – keep alert – you are our hope.' Sombre, noble words – & witty ones, too.

Papa – '. . . I've thrown the reins on the horse's neck.'

Michael – '. . . But you won the race.'

Papa – 'And in consequence I've been warned off the turf.'

And then the future – his future – painting, writing. He looked at the picture he did at Hendaye. And presently he went off to discuss with Brendan. Of course – at 7 he'd been to the Palace & laid down his burden taken up in darker days.

God, what a long, long day. I felt stunned, numbed, incapable of thought or action – dried up even of prayers.

Friday 27 July

In many ways Friday was worse than Thursday. Cares & anxieties & the tedium of moving descended in their full force on M. Papa woke up to no boxes – no cabinet. Letters began pouring in – sweet, consoling friendly letters. Expressing love & indignation & loyalty. Randolph arrived from Preston & is even now on the search for a seat.

M for the first time looks tired & shattered. But she set to work with Hambone. Judy & I spent afternoon together. Saw Hugh Fraser – he is IN. Met Ronnie & swept him off to give us tea at Gunter's. It was rather a relief to giggle feebly.

Dined alone with M & P. A sad dinner on the whole. Papa said 'Yesterday seems years ago.' I thought so too – the days seem endless. After dinner Robin & the Hillyards* came & I

---

* Jane Forbes and Toby and Miles Hillyard

went off to Jane's flat. We sat in the cool darkness of the garden. But conversation was only an inquest. My resolve for complete calm & dignity was broken once or twice – home too late, too tired & too sad.

Saturday 28 July

Mummie & Miss J beetled off to an Aid to Russia tennis match. I remained with Papa. He talked to Jock – and then we went over to the garden at No. 10, Papa read the papers in the friendly quiet of the cabinet room, and then we sat in the sunshine in the garden, looking at the lovely herbaceous border and watching white butterflies flirting with the flowers.

While Papa perused the evening papers I sat & thought of the times we'd lunched or dined en famille in the garden – thought of the old Admiralty House days, and then our move – and scenes & people drifted through my mind. This morning Mummie had Leslie & then John [Peck]* in for sherry and to say adieu – for they were both off to Potsdam with the Prime Minister. It was for us both a painful farewell – very little was said, but I know Mummie was deeply moved & I think they are sorry too.

Papa & I went about half past four to see the house at Hyde Park Gate.† It is charming & he has fallen for it. We paddled round & I felt he was visualising his life there – & even finding it agreeable. Back at the annexe – & then to tea with Diana. She & Duncan are lending their flat to M & P

---

* Churchill's 'official' private secretaries were civil servants, working for the Government rather than for him personally, so were assigned to his successor Clement Attlee as soon as Churchill ceased to be Prime Minister
† At this time the Churchills bought 28 Hyde Park Gate, which remained their London home until Winston's death in 1965

until such time as a house is ready. M returned from Wimbledon and we all repaired to Chequers – for the last weekend.

The party is: Uncle Jack, Tommy, Jock. Papa seemed fairly cheerful all through dinner. M went to bed. We all saw news reels of the beginning of the conference – & Ike's documentary film *The True Glory*. As we came downstairs I noticed Papa looked very gloomy – he said to me 'This is where I miss the news – no work – nothing to do . . .' It was an agonising spectacle to watch this giant among men – equipped with every faculty of mind & spirit wound to the highest pitch – walking unhappily round & round unable to employ his great energy or boundless gifts – nursing in his heart a grief and disillusion I can only guess at.

This was the worst moment so far – unavailingly we played Gilbert & Sullivan – but finally French & American marches struck a helpful note. 'Run Rabbit Run' raised great attention & *The Wizard of Oz* was a request number. Finally at 2 he was soothed enough to feel sleepy & want his bed. We all escorted him upstairs. Dear Sgt Davies (Inspector Hughes & Sgt Green left him sorrowfully this morning) had waited up. O darling Papa – I love you so, so much & it breaks my heart to be able to do so little. I went to bed feeling very tired & dead inside me.

Sunday 29 July

It has been a peaceful evening – Randolph was pleasant & quiet & has twirled Sarah & me round waltzing. Gil is sweet & sympathetic. Jock is sense & loyalty – intelligent and good company personified. We've all signed on one page – in that memorable 'visitors' book where you can follow the plots & stratagems of the war from the names there. Papa has signed at the bottom of the page and beneath his name has written 'Finis'.

Friday 10 August, Wenzendorf

I am sitting in my tent in a fury of resentment and depression. I cannot bear these attempts appearing in the press to patronise Papa. How dare they – how have they the heart? – and from where the stature? I should laugh – but angry tears are in my eyes as I write. Kick him out – all right – you can't fight elections on gratitude – criticise him – say he is a man of war and not a builder of peace – but for Christ's sake don't give him the benefit of your kind & lofty patronage.

This sort of smartiness rankles so deeply. 'Freeze, freeze thou wintry sky, Thou dost not bite so nigh as benefits forgot.' O darling Papa – does this hurt very deeply? I never dared ask you? Charles Moran writes of him '. . . and in my heart I have come to think of him as invincible.'

Wireless & papers have one subject – the atomic bomb – since it burst on this already much battered world. I fear much – and I can find very little hope in my heart that this discovery will really be controlled. I hope (& yet do not believe) it will be used to bless and not blast humanity. It strengthens in my mind the conviction that one should expect & hope & pray for very little – except courage. Courage to face & accept & wrestle with life however black & evil. What's happened to my golden hopes & beliefs? Just now I feel dead at heart.

Thursday 6 September

Today is the 6th September – a long gap since I last wrote up my diary. Now I am in a train trundling home across North West Europe. To become a 'Whitehall warrior' . . . The last few weeks at Wenzendorf have been very lazy & quiet. The regiment breaking up each week, as far as the ATS were concerned. I was to go to 8 Corps as a general duties company commander – then I got [a] letter from Mummie. I nearly behaved with heartless selfishness – it is a long story – nearly but for Padre Thomas – but for – Anyway I'm going home – gladly & proudly – because it's so wonderful to think Mummie feels I can help. God grant I may – I will try. As far as the ATS is concerned I feel a bit depressed – & I hope no one will think I'm 'ratting'. But I think now there is the greater duty at home.

I am made confident in my decision because Joan, Paul, the Major, the Padre, Controller Mackenzie – all of whose opinions I respect & trust – have all said 'You should go.' Another chapter is closing – oh how glad I am I came over. It's been all & more than I hoped or expected.

Letter from Churchill to Mary from Lake Como, 10 September:

My darling Mary, 'Many Happy Returns of the Day!' This shd reach you on yr Birthday the 15th: but if it comes earlier or later it carries with it the fondest love of yr Father. I have watched with admiration & respect the career of distinction & duty wh. you have made for yourself during the hard years of the war. I look forward in the days that may be left me to see you happy & glorious in peace. You are a gt joy to yr mother & me & we are hoping that vy soon you will be living w. us at Chartwell and in our new house in London. It will be lovely having you w. us.

Epilogue

In the immediate aftermath of her return to London, Mary's time centred around her parents, who were finding life difficult after leaving 10 Downing Street – the Post Power Blues. She also had a job at the WOHU (Whitehall Holding Unit) and an increasingly frenetic social life. Her work as a 'Whitehall warrior' was never going to last but she was not thinking of looking outside the Army for a career. It seems extraordinary now that my highly competent 23-year-old mother, and thousands like her, never considered a career, but in 1945 the thoughts of single young women were focussed on finding a husband, and Mary was no exception

She did however have much to distract her from this mission: most memorably and importantly, the trips she made with her father to the countries of Western Europe whose people wished so much to thank him for their salvation from Nazi occupation and to put a face to the voice that had sustained them during the dark days of the Forties. In November 1945 father and daughter travelled together to Brussels and Antwerp where Winston was greeted by wildly enthusiastic crowds and much municipal rejoicing. After their return Mary wrote, 'Never, never could I forget those cheering crowds – the beauty of the sunlit, frosty, festive city. The ceremonies – so beautifully arranged & conducted – full of dignity & colour – emotion & charm. And then the

realisation of how much Belgium does love & respect & vener-
ate Papa & England – the two are inextricable.'*

Mary accompanied her father on a similar trip to Holland in
May 1946. Among other delights organised by their hostess
Queen Wilhelmina and the Dutch government was a lunch in
the Hague at the seventeenth century Treves Zaal, where all the
china and glass used for the lunch came from the local museum
– and had to be washed up afterwards by the curators. Everywhere
they went, governments and municipalities metaphorically got
out their best china to honour Churchill. Just after her 24th
birthday, Mary and her father made yet another journey to
Switzerland where he was cheered to the rafters in Geneva and
Bern before going on to Zurich. Here, addressing the students of
the University of Zurich, Winston made the renowned speech
'Europe Arise', which still echoes down the years.

Back at home Mary was having some difficulty slipping back
into normal life. Active service was the great divider among her
contemporaries at the end of the War. At a glamorous party
given for her cousin Sunny Blandford by his parents the Duke
and Duchess of Marlborough, Mary found that she didn't know
many of the young men there, and the ones she did meet she
found lacking – mostly in this key experience of having seen
action. She found herself miserably sitting on the dowagers'
bench, before leaving the Ball early, alone and in tears.

During all this time there was a mild flirtation going on
between Prince Charles of Belgium† and Mary, which was

---

* Mary's diary, 19 November 1945
† Prince Charles, Count of Flanders 1903–1983. He became Regent of
Belgium in 1944 when his elder brother King Leopold III was obliged to
stand down from the throne while under investigation for his role in the
surrender of Belgium in 1940. He remained single until in 1977 when, aged
74, he married Jacqueline Peyrebrune

being watched with interest by the Prince's mother Queen Elisabeth of Belgium who, according to Mary's diary, asked to see her on a trip to London in 1946. This would suggest that the relationship was being encouraged by the Belgian Royal Family and Mary evidently felt pressured; she wanted to get married and 'do the right thing' but Prince Charles was very much not the right thing for her emotionally. Without naming him, Mary writes of her heartache at this time, 'I feel so uncertain about my own feelings – even about my true duty. I feel all my life I'll let things happen to me and never take a determined decision. Never have I felt less that "I am the Master of my fate" – I am the Captain of my soul'.* In late September 1946 Mary returned to Belgium with her father on a painting expedition. On their last day in Brussels both English and Belgian newspapers were speculating that Prince Charles and Mary were about to become engaged. This caused confusion and considerable embarrassment on both sides. Of the farewell lunch where she sat next to Prince Charles Mary wrote, 'all ease had vanished. I felt suffocated and wretched'.

Instead of returning directly to London from Belgium, Mary and her father flew to Paris so that Winston could meet with the US Secretary of State. Just two days after her unfortunate farewell to the Prince Regent in Brussels, Mary met Christopher Soames, the junior Military Attaché, at the British Embassy in Paris. It was but a fleeting introduction and one that Mary didn't dwell upon, but a few weeks later Christopher declared a wish to see Mary again. He impetuously jumped on a train Mary was taking to Rome in order to see her sister Sarah, who was ill and confined to bed. By the time they arrived in Rome Christopher had proposed and

---

* Mary's diary, 21 May 1946

been turned down. On the second time of asking — on the steps of St Peter's Basilica — Mary accepted.

In that very first week of their still unofficial and whirlwind engagement, Mary's sister Sarah saw a lot of the couple, and formed a high opinion of Christopher. And so, on 27 October, Sarah felt able to write a reassuring letter to their parents.

Darling Mummie and Papa

. . . I feel an enormous responsibility that it should have happened while she was with me, and far from home – and yet at the same time a great joy to have seen it grow and bloom into the sort of relationship I believe you would want it to be.

. . . Of this I'm sure, though I know less about him than you, that he loves her the way we love her, and for the truly lovable and unique qualities we know her to possess.

. . . I like him enormously and increasingly, and I'm sure he truly loves our Mary.

No doubt encouraged by Sarah's enthusiasm and reassured by their own subsequent meetings with Christopher, the engagement was announced in early November 1946.

Mary was well aware of how leaving home, even if for the happiest of reasons, was going to interfere with how much she would be able to support her parents – particularly her mother. In some distress, she wrote to her mother on Christmas Eve 1946 from Blenheim:

Mummie darling,

As I write to you so many memories of Christmases spent together come to my mind. Here, at Blenheim, at Admiralty House. Then those unforgettable, exhausting homesick Christmas Days in the army – and now this last one together again.

I am so certain – so happy and confident in my beloved Christopher's love for me – I feel I am setting out on a great adventure. But I have a good companion. And I have too the sure support and assurance of yours and Papa's love. I have the strength of all the right and wise and true things you have taught me. I have my faith.

But although I ardently long for my wedding day – I find it hard to leave you both – and today especially the threads of childhood memories and my life's association tug very hard upon my heart.

I shall seek with every capability within me to help to found a home worthy of the one I am leaving. To build it on foundations that will not shift. Yours will be a cherished, reverenced name and influence in our family life.

. . . I do truly grieve to grieve you – and wish my joy and the fulfilment of my life did not leave you rather alone. I look ahead already to the fun we shall have again together. How I long to welcome you in our home wherever it will be. And how often and often we shall meet and do things together.

Tender, loving, grateful thoughts from your Mary

Two months later, during the coldest winter in living memory, Mary married Christopher Soames in a freezing but packed-out St Margaret's Westminster almost entirely lit by candlelight. Then, with most fortuitous timing, the farmhouse in the valley below Chartwell came up for sale. The Churchills bought it and offered it to Christopher and Mary as their first home. This happy solution allowed Mary to continue to see and support her parents as she so dearly wished to do, whilst building a family of her own. In these rather idyllic circumstances four of us five children were born at Chartwell Farm.

One part of an already eventful life was over, and another, that of her early married life and motherhood, was just beginning but further chapters – of which there were so many – had yet to be written. They still lay in the stars.

A glossary of military terms

AA: Anti Aircraft

ABCA: Army Bureau of Current Affairs

ADC: Aide de camp

AEC: Army Education Corps

BHQ: Battalion Headquarters

CAS: Chief of Air Staff (Sir Charles Portal, Oct 1940–Jan 1946)

CIGS: Chief of Imperial General Staff (General Sir
   Edmund Ironside, Sept 1939–May 1940; Field Marshal
   Sir John Dill, May 1940–Dec 1941; Field Marshal Sir Alan
   Brooke, Dec 1941–Jun 1946)

CO: Commanding Officer

CP: Command Post

CSM: Company Sergeant Major

CWAC: Canadian Women's Army Corps

FANY: First Aid Nursing Yeomanry

G/L: either Gun Laying or Gun Light (radio direction
   finding)

G man: US government agent

GOC in C: General Officer Commanding-in-Chief

Guns: sleeve badge for gunnery

HG: Home Guard

MO/MD: Medical Officer/Doctor of Medicine

MTB: Motor torpedo boat

NAAFI: Navy, Army and Air Force Institute

NCO: Non-commissioned officer

OC: Officer Commanding
OCTU: Officer Cadet Training Unit
OGPU: Soviet secret police
O/Sgt: Orderly Sergeant
RA: Royal Artillery
RAMC: Royal Army Medical Corps
REME: Royal Electrical and Mechanical Engineers
RHQ: Regimental Headquarters
WAC: US Women's Army Corps
WREN: Women's Royal Naval Service
WVS: Women's Voluntary Services

Acknowledgements

Mary Churchill's wartime diaries would not have come this far without the contribution, the unstinting support, and sound historical advice of my co-editors at the Churchill Archive Centre, Cambridge where my mother's papers reside. The Archives Director Allen Packwood has kept the project on track and provided invaluable historical context. I have benefitted from all the above, as well as his patience and kindness. Katharine Thomson, Archivist of laser eye initially catalogued my mother's papers. For this project she has transcribed the greatest number of the fifteen diaries, assisted by her colleague Amanda Jones. Katharine's forensic knowledge of the period and of Mary's letters and diaries has been indispensable in shaping the diaries into a manageable narrative. I am grateful to all the staff at the Churchill Archive Centre. I also formally thank and acknowledge the Master, Fellows and Scholars of Churchill College who are the owners of the diaries.

Our publishers Two Roads have been a revelation. We could not have wished for a better editor than Kate Craigie who has made the whole process a delight. I am also grateful to Lisa Highton, Two Roads publisher, to Jacqui Lewis for her copy edit, Mandi Jones in the Production department, Janette Revill for text and inset design and Sarah Christie for cover design. Indeed I am grateful to everyone at Two Roads who helped set this ship on the seas. I would particularly like to thank Katherine Stroud who has done so much to get *Mary Churchill's War* to a wide audience.

Gordon Wise and Curtis Brown have been cheerleaders for the diaries from Day One and have been a source of excellent advice and encouragement. I warmly thank him and all at Curtis Brown.

I thank John Byrne, literary scholar and friend who proof read the manuscript, which is much improved by his eye for detail and encyclopaedic knowledge. I am grateful to Erik Larsen for his support. I am thankful to my kinswoman Anna Mathias for her hospitality and her generosity in sharing her mother's (Judy Montagu's) letters with me. I would also like to thank Harriet Bowes-Lyon and Rupert Colville for permission to quote from Jock Colville's *Fringes of Power*.

I would like to thank all my family for their enthusiasm and support, particularly Jeremy and Susanna Soames whose excitement about the diaries on a visit to the Archive Centre in Cambridge proved to be the first foot on the long and winding road to publication.

Above all I must record my gratitude to my mother. It has been a great privilege to come close to her in her youth and to understand where her defining attributes of loyalty, patriotism and faith were forged while her diaries' very existence bear witness to her resilience and determination.

About the authors

Mary Churchill, Lady (Mary) Soames, LG, DBE, FRSL (1922–2014), was the youngest daughter and last surviving child of Sir Winston and Baroness (Clementine) Spencer-Churchill.

In 1941, Mary joined the Auxiliary Territorial Service, the women's branch of the British Army, and subsequently served as an officer commanding mixed anti-aircraft batteries in England and Europe, for which she was awarded the MBE (Military). She saw action and witnessed both the defence of Britain and the liberation of Europe.

After the Second World War, Mary continued to assist her father and to travel with him. She married Christopher Soames (later Lord Soames). This led to further political and diplomatic adventures. In 1968 Soames was appointed HM Ambassador to France, with an unwritten brief to mend relations with the United Kingdom. In 1979 he became the last Governor of Rhodesia, with the tricky brief of implementing the Lancaster House Agreement. Mary accompanied him.

Mary was also the author of several books, including a biography of her mother, an edited edition of her parents correspondence and a memoir of her early life. She acted as Chair of the National Theatre Board, and was patron of Churchill organisations and charities around the world. She died on 31 May 2014. In 2005 she was made Lady Companion of the Order of the Garter.

Emma Soames is a writer, broadcaster and columnist who has been editor of the *Literary Review, Tatler, ES Magazine, the Telegraph magazine* and *Saga.* She is the second child of Mary and Christopher Soames and is her mother's Literary Executor, and is a granddaughter of Winston and Clementine Churchill.

The Churchill Archives Centre is located in the grounds of Churchill College, Cambridge. It was purpose-built in 1973 to house Sir Winston Churchill's Papers, and is now home to the papers of almost 700 important political, military and scientific figures from the Churchill era and after. The papers and diaries of Mary Churchill sit alongside many of her contemporaries, as well as major political, military and scientific figures such as Margaret Thatcher, Ernest Bevin, John Major, Neil Kinnock, Admiral Ramsay, Field Marshal Slim, Frank Whittle and Rosalind Franklin. Situated within the grounds of Churchill College, itself the national and Commonwealth memorial to Sir Winston, the Archives Centre's mission is to preserve and make available to the public the unique materials in its care

Illustration credits

Every reasonable effort has been made to trace the copyright holders of photos reproduced in this book. Any copyright holders not credited, are invited to be in touch with the publishers.

Section 1

1939 diary: The Papers of Lady Soames, MCHL 1/1/1; Bertram Mills circus: The Broadwater Collection, BRDW V 3/3/44, reproduced with permission of Curtis Brown Ltd., London on behalf of the Broadwater Collection; 1939 diary: MCHL 1/1/1; Randolph wedding: The Papers of Baroness Spencer-Churchill, Churchill Archives Centre, CSCT 5/2/68; Mary and Patsy: CSCT 5/2/81; Mary's debut: CSCT 5/4/90; Antony Beauchamp photo: CSCT 5/2/75; Photo for *Vogue*: CSCT 5/4/60; Sukie photo: CSCT 5/4/20; HMS *Gurkha*: MCHL 6/1/3; Westerham photo: CSCT 5/4/10; Mary and Judy: CSCT 5/4/65; Mary polishing shoes: CSCT 5/4/71; Mary scrubbing doorstep: CSCT 5/4/70; Mary, Clementine and Nana: CSCT 5/5/20; 1942 diary: MCHL 1/1/7; Battle drill: AP/ Shutterstock; Freedom of the City: CSCT 5/5/74; Queen's visit: CSCT 5/5/90.

Section 2

Waving from Quebec City Hall: © Imperial War Museum A 18823; Niagara: BRDW 1/1/203; Mary and the AWACs: CSCT 5/5/147; Mary and Clementine at Williamsburg: CSCT 5/6/69; Birthday cake: MCHL 6/2/3; 1943 diary: MCHL 1/1/11; Waving from HMS Renown: © Imperial War Museum A 19210; Watching flying bomb: BRDW 1/1/180, reproduced with permission of Curtis Brown Ltd., London on behalf of the Broadwater Collection; Mary, WSC and Clementine with fingers in ears watching guns: BRDW 1/1/177, reproduced with permission of Curtis Brown Ltd., London on behalf of the Broadwater Collection; Mary with Hollywood actors: © Imperial War Museum FRE 4823; Euston Station: ANL/Shutterstock; Paris, Armistice Day: MCHL 5/7/21; Embarking for Belgium: CSCT 5/5/131; ATS baggage: CSCT 5/5/133; 1945 diary: MCHL 1/1/14; With WSC on VE Day: CSCT 5/6/81; WSC and Mary at Potsdam: BRDW 1/1/248, reproduced with permission of Curtis Brown Ltd., London on behalf of the Broadwater Collection; Potsdam seating plan: The Churchill Papers, CHUR 1/104/133; Chancellery steps, Berlin: MCHL 5/7/20; Southern Belle: Fred Ramage/Keystone/Getty Images.

Index

In subheadings, CC refers to Clementine, MC refers to Mary, and WSC refers to Winston.